The criminal justice system has become a du
This book's in-depth and timely considerat
extends understanding of a crucial participatoi
helps offer practical routes out. A must-read t
those on the receiving end of criminal justice.

CW01336901

—*Peter Beresford, Professor of Citizen Participation,*
University of Essex and Co-Chair, Shaping Our Lives, the
national service user-led organization

Peer mentoring in criminal justice has a long history, but a remarkably thin
theoretical and research base, considering the rich potential of this work
to transform our ideas about criminality and the justice process. Buck's
comprehensive treatment of the subject is exactly what is needed, therefore –
a genuine breakthrough that will become a sort of 'bible' for future research
in this area.

—*Shadd Maruna, Professor of Criminology,*
Queen's University Belfast

Gill Buck's important new book takes our understanding of mentoring to
an entirely new level, exploring not just its relationship with desistance
from crime but also its complex, contested and emergent role in criminal
justice and its reform. In revealing how mentoring interacts with questions
of identity, agency, values, change and power, this book will intrigue,
inspire and challenge students, practitioners and scholars of criminal and
social justice alike.

—*Fergus NcNeill, Professor of Criminology &*
Social Work, University of Glasgow

This book takes us beyond aspirational and fashionable approaches to desistance
by making a compelling case – both critically and in practice – for participatory
self-determination on the part of those with experience of criminal punishment.
In *Peer Mentoring in Criminal Justice,* Gillian Buck retrieves traditions of radical
pedagogy and self-help movements to present a contemporary way forward for
sustainable recovery from criminalisation.

—*Mary Corcoran, Senior Lecturer in Criminology and*
Director of programmes in Criminology, Keele University

Peer Mentoring in Criminal Justice

Peer mentoring is an increasingly popular criminal justice intervention in custodial and community settings. Peer mentors are community members, often with lived experiences of criminal justice, who work or volunteer to help people in rehabilitative settings. Despite the growth of peer mentoring internationally, remarkably little research has been done in this field. This book offers the first in-depth analysis of peer mentoring in criminal justice. Drawing upon a rigorous ethnographic study of multiple community organisations in England, it identifies key features of criminal justice peer mentoring. Findings result from interviews with people delivering and using services and observations of practice.

Peer Mentoring in Criminal Justice reveals a diverse practice, which can involve one-to-one sessions, group work or more informal leisure activities. Despite diversity, five dominant themes are uncovered. These include *Identity*, which is deployed to inspire change and elevate knowledge based on lived experiences; *Agency*, or a sense of self-direction, which emerges through dialogue between peers; *Values* or core conditions, including caring, listening and taking small steps; *Change*, which can be a terrifying and difficult struggle, yet can be mediated by mentors and *Power*, which is at play within mentoring relationships and within the organisations, contexts and ideologies that surround peer mentoring. Peer mentoring offers mentors a practical opportunity to develop confidence, skills and hope for the future, whilst offering inspiration, care, empathy and practical support to others.

Written in a clear and direct style this book will appeal to students and scholars in criminology, sociology, cultural studies, social theory and those interested in learning about the social effects of peer mentoring.

Gillian Buck is Senior Lecturer in Social Work at the University of Chester. Her research interests include peer-led services, criminal justice, youth justice and the voluntary sector. Before working in research and teaching, Gill spent eight years as a Social Worker in a youth offending team.

The *International Series on Desistance and Rehabilitation* aims to provide a forum for critical debate and discussion surrounding the topics of why people stop offending and how they can be more effectively reintegrated into the communities and societies from which they came. The books published in the series will be international in outlook, but tightly focused on the unique, specific contexts and processes associated with desistance, rehabilitation and reform. Each book in the series will stand as an attempt to advance knowledge or theorising about the topics at hand, rather than being merely an extended report of a specific research project. As such, it is anticipated that some of the books included in the series will be primarily theoretical, whilst others will be more tightly focused on the sorts of initiatives which could be employed to encourage desistance. It is not our intention that books published in the series be limited to the contemporary period, as good studies of desistance, rehabilitation and reform undertaken by historians of crime are also welcome. In terms of authorship, we would welcome excellent PhD work, as well as contributions from more established academics and research teams. Most books are expected to be monographs, but edited collections are also encouraged.

For more information about this series, please visit: https://www.routledge.com/criminology/series/ISODR

Peer Mentoring in Criminal Justice

Gillian Buck

Routledge
Taylor & Francis Group

LONDON AND NEW YORK

First published 2020 by Routledge

2 Park Square, Milton Park, Abingdon, Oxon OX14 4RN
605 Third Avenue, New York, NY 10017

Routledge is an imprint of the Taylor & Francis Group, an informa business

First issued in paperback 2022

Publisher's Note

The publisher has gone to great lengths to ensure the quality of this reprint but points out that some imperfections in the original copies may be apparent.

British Library Cataloguing-in-Publication Data
A catalogue record for this book is available from the British Library

Library of Congress Cataloging-in-Publication Data
A catalog record has been requested for this book

ISBN: 978-0-367-22874-3 (hbk)
ISBN: 978-1-03-233679-4 (pbk)
DOI: 10.4324/9780429277337

Typeset in Bembo
by codeMantra

In loving memory of Lily Brown

Contents

Preface

The *International Series on Desistance and Rehabilitation* aims to provide a forum for critical debate and discussion surrounding the topics of why people stop offending and how they can be more effectively reintegrated into the communities and societies from which they came. The books published in the series will be international in outlook, but tightly focused on the unique, specific contexts and processes associated with desistance, rehabilitation and reform. Each book in the series will stand as an attempt to advance knowledge or theorising about the topics at hand, rather than being merely an extended report of a specific research project. As such, it is anticipated that some of the books included in the series will be primarily theoretical, whilst others will be more tightly focused on the sorts of initiatives which could be employed to encourage desistance. It is not our intention that books published in the series be limited to the contemporary period, as good studies of desistance, rehabilitation and reform undertaken by historians of crime are also welcome. In terms of authorship, we would welcome excellent PhD work, as well as contributions from more established academics and research teams. Most books are expected to be monographs, but edited collections are also encouraged.

This book is another welcome contribution to the growing literature on desistance, especially desistance in a supported or assisted context, as it deals with the matter of peer mentoring. Gillian Buck's book makes a number of key contributions which I am sure will assist many people – academics, policymakers and, perhaps most importantly of all, practitioners – get to grips with what peer mentoring is and how it can be harnessed in order to assist those wishing to desist from crime. It is especially good to see an ethnographic study of desistance, a topic more commonly approached via one-to-one qualitative interviews, or quantitative studies. Finding that peer mentoring offers much of use to both the criminal justice system and those embroiled in it, Buck is able to reflect on what 'needs to happen next' and to offer many sensible suggestions for both future practice and future research. Coming at a time of such profound re-organising of the criminal justice system and the growing desire to embrace 'desistance-related practices globally, Buck's book I am sure will be a compelling read for many. I welcome this book into the expanding collection in this series and look forward to further contributions from both this author and others interested in these topics.

Stephen Farrall,
Sheffield,
November 2019.

Acknowledgements

Sincere thanks to the mentors, mentees and staff who contributed to this research and to Dr Mary Corcoran and Professor Ronnie Lippens who supervised the study. On a personal level I am grateful to Graeme, Seb and Orla Buck, Linda, Edward and Neil Borg-Olivier, Dr Philippa Tomczak and Dr Emma Murray.

Thanks also to Routledge, John Wiley & Sons, Taylor & Francis and Sage for their permission to reproduce previously published materials in this book and to the ESRC, Clinks and Keele University (studentship reference number 1037698) for supporting the study.

Part One

The background

Chapter 1

Introduction

Peer mentoring in criminal justice

This book explores mentoring in criminal justice settings by community members who often have their own lived experiences of the criminal justice system. Across public services, emergent citizen's rights movements have questioned professionals' objective, rational claims to knowledge, as these accounts become *a* truth, rather than *the* truth about service users' lives (Healy, 2014: 91). Governments in countries around the world are emphasising the importance of *service user involvement* in the development and delivery of a range of public services (Weaver, Lightowler & Moodie, 2019), and peer mentoring has become a growth area in criminal justice (Willoughby, Parker & Ali, 2013). Criminalised populations overrepresent intersecting inequities *and* experience the inequities which flow from criminal justice contact (Buck, Harriott, Ryan, Ryan & Tomczak, forthcoming). Yet, criminalised people have been largely absent from the burgeoning literature on rights, involvement and personalisation which has followed other service user movements (Weaver, 2011). This book therefore addresses a significant gap in service user involvement scholarship by examining a key area of participatory criminal justice.

This is the first book to examine criminal justice peer mentoring in depth, offering an important reference point for criminal and social justice scholars and a range of workers supporting individuals with multiple and complex needs. Its original contribution is to offer a theory of the dynamics underpinning this work, supported by an analysis of the rich and multi-layered lived experience of peer mentoring. The relationships forged through peer mentoring have the potential to support personal goals and changes, which can directly and indirectly support desistance from crime. This is important, given the clear social costs of continued offending and that the estimated economic cost of reoffending in the UK is £18.1 billion (Newton, May, Eames & Ahmad, 2019). Whilst there is growing evidence of how people successfully leave crime behind or 'desist' (Healy, 2012; Farrall, Sparks & Maruna, 2011; Shapland & Bottoms, 2011; LeBel, Burnett, Maruna & Bushway, 2008; Farrall & Calverley, 2006; Maruna, 2001), there has been less focus on interrogating or theorising interventions which support *processes* of desisting

(McNeill, 2006). The book also demonstrates how peer mentoring can support forms of solidarity and socio-political action, focused upon social injustices related to and caused by criminalisation. In mapping the ways that mentors and mentees work towards personal and systemic improvements, this text highlights how lived experiences and core humanistic values, such as caring and listening, are central to this work. It additionally uncovers some of the contradictory and contentious elements of peer mentoring, which will be useful for practitioners and scholars to reflect upon. The book is particularly significant given that peer mentoring is an empirically neglected practice, within a woefully under-researched sector of criminal justice – the penal voluntary sector (Tomczak & Buck, 2019a); this sector is crucial given its actors affect the experience of punishment around the world and 'form part of the mass of institutional interactions through which penal coercion and exclusion is (un)contested, (re)produced and (re)justified' (Tomczak & Buck, 2019a: 898). It therefore contributes to analyses of the sector's (often contradictory) functions of social control (Miller, 2014), campaigning (Benson & Hedge, 2009) and life-saving rehabilitative work (Tomczak & Thompson, 2019).

The book draws upon original ethnographic data from multiple community peer mentoring settings in the North of England, including the following: a mentoring project attached to a Probation Service; a charitable mentoring service for women seeking employment; a grant funded mentoring service for young women at risk of 'gang' involvement and a charitable mentoring project for people with a history of state care and criminalisation. It presents data from forty-four interviews with peer mentors, mentees, service coordinators and Probation Officers. Observations of practice were also carried out, including peer-led group work, volunteer recruitment, training, practice and supervision. Fuller (anonymised) details of all sources are given in Chapter 4. Whilst the data were gathered in England, the findings have applicability beyond the UK and beyond criminal justice. Criminalised people play important roles in the development and delivery of criminal justice services and advocacy around the world. Serving prisoners volunteer as prison 'Listeners' across England, Wales, Scotland, Northern Ireland and the Republic of Ireland, providing a crucial front-line service aimed at reducing suicide and self-harm in prisons (Samaritans, 2019; Jaffe, 2012). Peer-to-peer education is also delivered by Red Cross volunteers in all 14 prisons across Ireland and has inspired similar initiatives in Northern Ireland and Wales, offering volunteers opportunities for personal development and generative, pro-social activities (O'Sullivan, Hart & Healy, 2018). In Finland, peer support organisations for ex-prisoners and prisoners' families stepped into the gap left by the discontinuation of the Probation and Aftercare Association (Helminen & Mills, 2019). Peer mentoring itself is an increasingly popular approach in custodial and community correctional settings in several jurisdictions, including the UK, Republic of Ireland, Sweden and the USA, where mentors are also often involved in working for health and social policy reform (Seppings, 2016). Angola maximum-security prison in Louisiana, USA established a scheme where life-sentenced prisoners mentor other prisoners 'teaching job skills and morals' in readiness for release (Kunzelman, 2018). There are also several models of peer support in Canadian penal settings (Quinn, 2019; Pollack, 2004), including peer counsellors who provide crisis intervention related to mental health, along with general support and advocacy. In Tasmania, Australia, the Red Cross, in consultation with Tasmanian Corrections, has developed training for peer supporters to address extraordinarily high levels of self-harm, bullying and attempted suicide in prison, whilst primarily offered within the prison system, efforts are being made to expand to post-release too (Hinde & White, 2019). Australia has also utilised peer mentoring to supplement the scarce post-release support services available to women exiting prison (Brown & Ross, 2010).

These multinational developments have been driven by people with convictions themselves, and policy plans across a number of countries to transfer key roles from the state to community-level actors (Corcoran, 2012). Across a broad range of human services, there is emphasis on *service user engagement*, given the necessity for methods that better suit service users' primary needs (Hughes, 2012) and reduce the divisions between recipients and providers (Beresford, 2016). Participation in service development can be 'consumerist' in nature (concerned with improving welfare 'products' through 'consumer' feedback and consultation) or 'democratic' (concerned with people having more say in organisations which impact on them and more control over their own lives) (Beresford, 2002). Without 'democratizing imperatives', Cowden and Singh (2007: 20) argue there is a risk of incorporation into a system driven by managerial rules, positioning people who have used services as consultants rather than activists. This book pays close attention to how competing ideologies manifest in peer mentoring settings. Given the centrality of lived experiences to this practice, the book holds valuable messages for the growing range of settings and services which employ relational practice based upon lived experience. These include, but are not limited to, addiction (Bucur, Beckett, Perry & Davies, 2019; Agrawal, Capponi, López, Kidd, Ringsted, Wiljer & Soklaridis, 2016; Bassuk, Hanson, Greene, Richard & Laudet, 2016), mental health (Burke, Pyle, Machin & Morrison, 2018; Chapman, Blash, Mayer & Spetz, 2018), homelessness (Barker, Maguire, Bishop & Stopa, 2018), social exclusion and sexual violence (Buck, Lawrence & Ragonese, 2017). The 'grounded, insider perspectives' respondents provide also have the potential to challenge public misconceptions of (ex-) prisoners and contribute to the development of critical penology (Aresti, Darke & Manlow, 2016: 6).

As mentoring work is often organised by voluntary organisations from local to national scales, the nature of the 'voluntary sector' is explored in detail. Indeed, the study of peer mentoring is best conceptualised as part of the growing field of penal voluntary sector studies (Tomczak & Buck, 2019a).

The penal voluntary sector comprises specialist charitable and voluntary agencies working principally with criminalised people, their families and victims in prison, community and policy advocacy programmes (Tomczak, 2017). The sector is diverse in its organising forms, which include statutory volunteers (e.g. Magistrates), quasi statutory volunteers (e.g. independent custody visitors) and voluntary organisations (e.g. *The Prison Reform Trust*) (see Tomczak & Buck, 2019b). Peer mentors typically work in *voluntary organisations,* which have historically offered a test bed for new thinking, a platform for dissent, campaigning and social action (Benson & Hedge, 2009: 35). Yet, recent scholarship has highlighted the potential neutralisation of 'charitable qualities through marketisation and associated closer involvement with the punitive and coercive aspects of criminal justice work' (Tomczak, 2017: 178). This raises the concerning potential for partnerships between the state and voluntary sector to curtail critical/innovative action (Benson & Hedge, 2009), or results in organisational cloning as organisations adapt to the bureaucratic, hierarchical organisational forms of their statutory partners (Corcoran, 2011: 34). Successive UK governments' reforms towards a 'mixed market' of criminal justice were fortified through the *Transforming Rehabilitation* policy agenda (MoJ, 2013), which 'heavily committed to promoting collaborations across civil society, private capital and public prison and probation services' (Corcoran, Maguire & Williams, 2019: 97). Described as 'disrupter par excellence of publicly owned and managed probation' (Corcoran et al., 2019: 109), this policy faced a series of censorious inspections and reports (Corcoran & Carr, 2019: 3), before being abandoned in May 2019. The current model of UK Probation is therefore still in development but will see each National Probation Service region having 'a dedicated, private or voluntary sector "Innovation Partner"' (HMPPS, 2019). Whilst neoliberal criminal justice service delivery has received a blow in England and Wales, clear commitments to cross-sector justice 'delivery' and resettlement mentoring remain within the *Probation Reform Programme* (HMPPS, 2019). The book therefore pays attention to the challenges for voluntary sector peer mentoring organisations working alongside a variety of partners in rapidly shifting and marketised contexts.

The book is split into two parts. Part one comprises Chapters 1–4 and provides the background to peer mentoring in criminal justice and to this study. Following this introductory chapter, Chapter 2 reviews the relevant literature and introduces the voluntary sector as the contextual landscape. It interrogates dominant extant claims that peer mentoring *changes people*, is *better than what has gone before* and is *egalitarian.* It then critically considers desistance research and argues that peer mentoring has the potential to promote desistance by offering new social connections along with opportunities to 'do' and 'make' good. It therefore offers a vehicle to facilitate desistance as distinct from the claimed goal to cause it explicitly. Chapter 3 introduces several social theorists (Freire, 1997; hooks, 1994; Girard, 1987; Bernstein, 1971;

Goffman, 1963), who help to make sense of peer mentoring in new ways. It contends that four precepts underpin peer mentoring in criminal justice: the *identity precept;* the *pedagogical precept;* the *fraternity or sorority precept* and the *politicisation precept.* These precepts constitute a framework to ground the subsequent findings chapters and are used to shine new light on the intricacies of peer mentoring practice. Chapter 4 details the research methods and explores ethical dilemmas related to research in this area.

Part two of the book comprises Chapters 5–10 and explores the findings of this study. Chapter 5 explores the importance of *identity* to peer mentoring. The 'ex-offender' identity is constructed as a useful resource, which can inspire self-improvement and facilitate new forms of communication. Peer-to-peer relationships are presented as horizontal, rather than hierarchical, delivered by workers who attempt to level power dynamics and engage as equal partners in mentoring relationships. Paradoxically, however, the chapter highlights several barriers faced by mentors as they attempt to employ identity in these ways, not least because mentees are not the equals of their mentors but are expected to become more like them. Both mentors and mentees must also continually negotiate the power of criminal stigma, which can diminish their legitimacy. Chapter 6 examines the importance of *agency* within peer mentoring. Participants do not necessarily have a clear sense of self-direction or motivation at the outset of the work, but agency often emerges falteringly from exchanges with others and interactions in social environments. Chapter 7 details the *core conditions* of peer mentoring in these settings as advanced by peer mentors themselves. These conditions include individualised practice, caring, listening and encouraging small steps. These values illustrate what peer mentoring work often means to those involved and highlights elements commonly missing from existing hierarchical rehabilitative approaches. Chapter 8 focuses upon concepts of *change* in peer mentoring, illustrating that personal transformation can be inspired by others. However, mentors *and* mentees also recount vivid fears, difficulties and conflicts which problematise the notion that role modelling alone can change people. Respondents outline how peer mentoring often requires a broader focus than individual change, calling for changes to services and wider social attitudes. Chapter 9 seeks to make explicit some of the implicit transactions of *power* in peer mentoring settings. In doing so, it reveals the rich and multi-layered nature of authority in mentoring transactions. Chapter 10 summarises how this book advances knowledge in this field; it also discusses the limitations of the study and implications for future research.

Peer mentoring is an increasingly popular approach within criminal justice, yet the research base to underpin this practice is lacking. This book demonstrates how mentoring can indeed support important desistance processes, such as realising personal strengths and imagining a new identity. It also illustrates that there is more to this practice than we currently recognise, as it enables criminalised people, who have often had their voices excluded or submerged by dominant empirical and/or professional understandings to find voice. In finding voice, convicted people challenge professionalised understandings of 'offenders' and suggest new approaches. They also begin to assert the centrality of struggle, suffering and social exclusion in their lives, realities which are often missed or immersed in approaches that seek to correct flawed individuals. As new voices emerge, however, so do new forms of governance. 'Ex-offenders' are permitted roles within rehabilitation, but they are often heavily policed and contained. Indeed, mentors and mentees themselves often collude with these forms of governance by replicating punitive and/or functionalist criminal justice practices. The book examines these tensions and illustrates the complexity of peer mentoring relationships. Given the interpersonal and socio-political nature of the book's main themes, it holds valuable messages for those interested in criminal justice, criminology, desistance and the voluntary sector, and also more broadly for Social Work, sociology, social policy, youth work and education. It will also be of value to a range of organisations aiming to develop (peer) mentoring practice and to the growing number of organisations internationally which employ relational approaches based upon lived experience. These include, but are not limited to, voluntary sector organisations, Probation, prisons, policymakers and criminal justice service commissioners, along with the range of social welfare settings utilising 'experts by experience'. This text offers a valuable reference for these readers to consider the theoretical background of peer mentoring; how it is used, delivered and practiced and how it could be developed for future use.

References

Agrawal, S., Capponi, P., López, J., Kidd, S., Ringsted, C., Wiljer, D. & Soklaridis, S., (2016)., 'From surviving to advising: a novel course pairing mental health and addictions service users as advisors to senior psychiatry residents', *Academic Psychiatry*, **40**(3), pp. 475–480.

Aresti, A., Darke, S. & Manlow, D., (2016), 'Bridging the gap: Giving public voice to prisoners and former prisoners through research activism', *Prison Service Journal*, **224**, pp. 3–13.

Barker, S.L., Maguire, N., Bishop, F.L. & Stopa, L., (2018), 'Peer support critical elements and experiences in supporting the homeless: A qualitative study', *Journal of Community & Applied Social Psychology*, **28**(4), pp. 213–229.

Bassuk, E.L., Hanson, J., Greene, R.N., Richard, M. & Laudet, A., (2016), 'Peer-delivered recovery support services for addictions in the United States: A systematic review', *Journal of Substance Abuse Treatment*, **63**, pp. 1–9.

Benson, A. & Hedge, J., (2009), 'Criminal justice and the voluntary sector: A policy that does not compute', *Criminal Justice Matters*, **77**(1), pp. 34–36.

Beresford, P., (2016), *All our welfare: Towards participatory social policy*. Bristol: Policy Press.

Beresford, P., (2002), 'User involvement in research and evaluation: Liberation or regulation?', *Social Policy and Society*, **1**(2), pp. 95–105.

Bernstein, B.B., (1971), *Class, codes and control*. Volume 1 – *Theoretical studies towards a sociology of language*. Reprint, St Albans: Paladin, 1973 edition.

Brown, M. & Ross, S., (2010), 'Mentoring, social capital and desistance: A study of women released from prison', *Australian & New Zealand Journal of Criminology (Australian Academic Press)*, **43**(1), pp. 31–50.

Buck, G., Harriott, P., Ryan, K., Ryan, N. & Tomczak, P., (forthcoming), 'All our justice: People with convictions and 'participatory' criminal justice'. In: McLaughlin, H., Duffy, J., Beresford, P., Casey, H. & Cameron, C., (Eds.), *The Routledge handbook of service user involvement in human services research and education*. Abingdon, Oxon: Routledge.

Buck, G., Lawrence, A. & Ragonese, E., (2017), 'Exploring peer mentoring as a form of innovative practice with young people at risk of child sexual exploitation', *British Journal of Social Work*, **47**(6), pp. 1745–1763.

Bucur, H.M., Beckett, D.S., Perry, G. & Davies, T.H., (2019), 'Peer recovery provides sustainable avenues for addiction treatment, but is not a one-size-fits-all proposition', *Addictive Disorders & Their Treatment*. May 30, 2019 – Volume Publish Ahead of Print. doi: 10.1097/ADT.0000000000000179

Burke, E.M., Pyle, M., Machin, K. & Morrison, A.P., (2018), 'Providing mental health peer support 2: Relationships with empowerment, hope, recovery, quality of life and internalised stigma', *International Journal of Social Psychiatry*, **64**(8), pp. 745–755.

Chapman, S.A., Blash, L.K., Mayer, K. & Spetz, J., (2018), 'Emerging roles for peer providers in mental health and substance use disorders', *American Journal of Preventive Medicine*, **54**(6), pp. S267–S274.

Corcoran, M., (2012), '"Be careful what you ask for": Findings from the seminar series on the "Third sector in criminal justice"', *Prison Service Journal*, **204**, pp. 17–22.

Corcoran, M., (2011), 'Dilemmas of institutionalization in the penal voluntary sector', *Critical Social Policy*, **31**(1), pp. 30–52.

Corcoran, M. & Carr, N., (2019), 'Five years of transforming rehabilitation: Markets, management and values', *Probation Journal*, **66**(1), pp. 3–7.

Corcoran, M.S., Maguire, M. & Williams, K., (2019), 'Alice in wonderland: Voluntary sector organisations' experiences of transforming rehabilitation', *Probation Journal*, **66**(1), pp. 96–112.

Cowden, S. & Singh, G., (2007), 'The "user": friend, foe or fetish? A critical exploration of user involvement in health and social care', *Critical Social Policy*, **27**(1), pp. 5–23.

Farrall, S. & Calverley, A., (2006), *Understanding desistance from crime*. Berkshire: Open University Press.

Farrall, S., Sparks, R. & Maruna, S., (2011), *Escape routes: Contemporary perspectives on life after punishment*. Abingdon, Oxon: Routledge.

Freire, P., (1997), *Mentoring the mentor: A critical dialogue with Paulo Freire*. New York: Peter Lang.

Girard, R., (1987), *Things hidden since the foundation of the world*. London: Continuum.

Goffman, E., (1963), *Stigma: Notes on the management of spoiled identity*. Middlesex: Penguin.

Healy, D., (2012), *The dynamics of desistance: Charting pathways through change*. Oxon: Routledge.

Healy, K., (2014), *Social work theories in context: Creating frameworks for practice*. Basingstoke: Macmillan International Higher Education.

Helminen, M. & Mills, A., (2019), 'Exploring autonomy in the Finnish and New Zealand penal voluntary sectors: The relevance of marketisation and criminal justice policy environments in two penal voluntary sector organisations', *The Howard Journal of Crime and Justice*, **58**(3), pp. 404–429.

Her Majesty's Prison & Probation Service (HMPPS), (2019), *The proposed future model for probation: A draft operating blueprint, probation reform programme*. Available at: https://assets.publishing.service.gov.uk/government/uploads/system/uploads/attachment_data/file/822222/The_Proposed_Future_Model_for_Probation_-_A_Draft_Operating_Blueprint_-_HMPPS_-_19-06-2019_v.2.pdf [Accessed August 2019].

Hinde, K., & White, R. (2019), 'Peer Support, Desistance and the Role of the Third Sector', *The Howard Journal of Crime and Justice*, **58**(3), pp. 329–348.

hooks, b., (1994), *Teaching to transgress: Education as the practice of freedom*. New York and London: Routledge.

Hughes, W., (2012), 'Promoting offender engagement and compliance in sentence planning: Practitioner and service user perspectives in Hertfordshire', *Probation Journal*, **59**(1), pp. 49–65.

Jaffe, M., (2012), *Peer support and seeking help in prison: A study of the listener scheme in four prisons in England*. PhD thesis, Keele University.

Kunzelman, M., (2018), *Murderers are mentors in prison once notorious for violence*. Marin Independent Journal. Available at: www.marinij.com/2016/04/13/murderers-are-mentors-in-prison-once-notorious-for-violence/ [Accessed October 2019].

LeBel, T.P., Burnett, R., Maruna, S. & Bushway, S., (2008), 'The "chicken and egg" of subjective and social factors in desistance from crime', *European Journal of Criminology*, **5**(2), pp. 131–159.

Maruna, S., (2001), *Making good; how ex-convicts reform and rebuild their lives*. Washington, DC: American Psychological Association.

McNeill, F., (2006), 'A desistance paradigm for offender management', *Criminology and Criminal Justice*, **6**(1), pp. 39–62.

Miller, R. J. (2014), 'Devolving the Carceral State: Race, Prisoner Reentry, and the MicroPolitics of Urban Poverty Management', *Punishment and Society*, **16**, pp. 305–35.

Ministry of Justice (MoJ), (2019), *Justice Secretary announces new model for probation*. May 2019. London: Ministry of Justice. Available at: www.gov.uk/government/news/justice-secretary-announces-new-model-for-probation [Accessed August 2019].

Ministry of Justice (MoJ), (2013), *Transforming rehabilitation: A strategy for reform*. Response to consultation, May 2013. London: Ministry of Justice.

Newton, A., May, X., Eames, S. & Ahmad, M., (2019), *Economic and social costs of reoffending. Ministry of justice*. Available at: https://assets.publishing.service.gov.uk/government/uploads/system/uploads/attachment_data/file/814650/economic-social-costs-reoffending.pdf [Accessed August 2019].

O'Sullivan, R., Hart, W. & Healy, D., (2018), 'Transformative rehabilitation: Exploring prisoners' experiences of the community based health and first aid programme in Ireland', *European Journal on Criminal Policy and Research*, 1–19. Published online 31 August, doi: 10.1007/s10610-018-9396-z.

Pollack, S., (2004), 'Anti-oppressive social work practice with women in Prison: Discursive reconstructions and alternative practice', *British Journal of Social Work*, **34**(5), pp. 693–707.

Samaritans (2019), *The listener scheme*. Available at: www.samaritans.org/how-we-can-help/prisons/listener-scheme/ [Accessed October 2019].

Seppings, C., (2016), *To study the rehabilitative role of ex-prisoners/ offenders as peer mentors in reintegration models – in the UK, Republic of Ireland, Sweden and USA*. Available at: www.churchilltrust.com.au/media/fellows/Seppings_C_2015_Rehabilitative_role_of_ex-prisoners__offenders_as_peer_mentors.pdf [Accessed August 2019].

Shapland, J. & Bottoms, A., (2011), 'Reflections on social values, offending and desistance among young adult recidivists', *Punishment & Society*, **13**(3), pp. 256–282.

Tomczak, P., (2017), *The penal voluntary sector*. Abingdon, Oxon: Routledge.

Tomczak, P. & Buck, G., (2019a), 'The penal voluntary sector: A hybrid sociology', *The British Journal of Criminology*, **59**(4), pp. 898–918.

Tomczak, P. & Buck, G., (2019b), 'The criminal justice voluntary sector: Concepts and an agenda for an emerging field', *Howard Journal of Crime and Justice*, **58**(3), pp. 276–297.

Tomczak, P. & Thompson, D., (2019), 'Inclusionary control? Theorizing the effects of penal voluntary organizations' work', *Theoretical Criminology*, **23**(1), pp. 4–24.

Quinn, K., (2019), 'Inside the penal voluntary sector: Divided discourses of "helping" criminalized women', *Punishment & Society*, Online First. doi: 1462474519863461.

Weaver, B., (2011), 'Co-producing community justice: The transformative potential of personalisation for penal sanctions', *British Journal of Social Work*, **41**(6), pp. 1038–1057.

Weaver, B., Lightowler, C. & Moodie, K., (2019), *Inclusive justice-co-producing change: A practical guide to service user involvement in community justice*. Available at: https://strathprints.strath.ac.uk/68901/ [Accessed August 2019].

Willoughby, M., Parker, A. & Ali, R., (2013), *Mentoring for offenders: Mapping services for adult offenders in England and Wales*. London: Sova.

Chapter 2

The penal voluntary sector, peer mentoring and desistance from crime

Peer mentoring in criminal justice has been most evident and clearly rationalised within the penal voluntary sector (e.g. *St Giles Trust*, 2019; *User Voice*, 2018; *Princes Trust*, 2008), as such it is often supplementary to state managed carceral and community justice. This is also the case in other jurisdictions, such as Canada, where people with lived experiences are invited in to support the work of criminal justice charities (Quinn, 2019) and the USA, where peer interventions predominantly take the form of targeted prevention work (Sullivan & Jolliffe, 2012). The voluntary sector itself is not peripheral, however, indeed the *penal* voluntary sector is an overlooked giant of criminal justice, both in the UK and internationally (Tomczak & Buck, 2019a). It is made up of voluntary (non-profit) agencies working principally with prisoners, (ex-) offenders, their families and victims and affects the experience of punishment and penal policy around the world, including at least the UK, Nordic countries, France, USA, Canada, Australia and New Zealand (Tomczak, 2017). In the UK, 'The voluntary sector working in criminal justice [has] a workforce larger than that of the prison and probation services combined' (Mullen, 2018). In the USA it is the primary provider of prisoner re-entry programming (Kaufman, 2015) in the jurisdiction that is the world leader in incarceration (Wildeman & Wang, 2017), and in Japan there are nearly fifty times more Volunteer Probation Officers 'hogo-shi', than Professional Probation Officers 'hogo kansatsu kan' (Watson, 2019). Despite its size, scope and potential to influence criminal justice policy and practice (internationally), there has been a lack of commensurate research by scholars of punishment (Tomczak & Buck, 2019a, 2019b). Furthermore, the principles underpinning a growing penal voluntary sector are not always complementary or consistent:

> In recent decades several countries have transferred some welfare and penal roles from the state to community-level actors including for-profit and third sector interests. This handover is premised on a blend of ne-oliberal political rationalities for restructuring state welfare systems as

'mixed service markets' in late capitalist societies and communitarian aspirations to liberate the untapped social capital of the community and voluntary sectors.

(Corcoran, 2012: 17)

The sector is a space where competing ideologies converge and collide. It is often idealised as 'a platform for dissent, campaigning and social action... [wherein] holding to account state agencies and interests is crucial' (Benson & Hedge, 2009: 35) and a place of ideological conviction, where people can be socially productive within an alternative, noncapitalist framework (Wolch, 1990). Simultaneously the sector been critiqued as a space where 'Victorian England buried their guilt in good works and headed off potential revolution by smoothing the jagged edges of capitalism's flotsam' (Gill & Mawby, 1990: 5). Voluntarism itself has been said to shift 'the burden of guilt from men in power to men on the street' circumventing analyses which consider social structure (Abdennur, 1987: 94).

There are not only concerns that the sector may excuse and compensate for the more negative consequences of modern capitalist societies, but also that it has become too closely tied to state agendas, given voluntary organisations have increasingly been contracted as 'providers' of welfare state services (Seddon, 2007). Such concerns were crystallised in the Coalition Government's *Transforming Rehabilitation* agenda (MoJ, 2013), which aimed to open the 'market' of offender rehabilitation to a 'diverse range of providers' (Home Office, 2013). The resulting *Community Rehabilitation Companies (CRCs)* were primarily led by the private sector; with two multinational companies winning eleven out of the twenty-one contracts (MoJ, 2014). These prime contractors then handed out subcontracts according to their own commercial priorities, positioning existing voluntary sector providers as clients (Corcoran, Maguire & Williams, 2019). The penal voluntary sector is not just a place of dissent and campaign (Benson and Hedge, 2009) or ideological conviction (Wolch, 1990), therefore, but many organisations have been *subcontracted* to undertake the work of the state and the global private sector. Whilst it remains to be seen how voluntary sector organisations will fare as 'innovation partners' for the (new) National Probation Service, it is clear that voluntary engagement in criminal justice is an extremely 'complex arena of social activity' (Corcoran, 2012: 22). Few have analysed how this shifting, encompassing landscape impacts upon those delivering and using peer-to-peer services. This book therefore pays attention to the broader voluntary sector context within which peer mentors and mentees undertake their practice. Chapters 5, 7, 8 and 9, for example, examine how volunteers negotiate mixed competitive markets and encounter roles and contexts which can (often simultaneously) be experienced as restrictive *and* empowering.

Peer mentoring

Peer mentoring in criminal justice involves formerly criminalised people and community members with an (often personal) interest in criminal justice working in helping relationships with people who are still subject to criminal justice interventions. 'Peer' mentors employ their experiences of criminalisation, their efforts at leaving crime behind and other shared life experiences to inspire, motivate and support their mentees. This approach has a long history. Davidson, Bellamy, Guy and Miller (2012) trace an unacknowledged history of peer support in the context of severe mental illness, dating back at least to 1793, when patients were noted by one hospital governor to be 'better suited to this demanding work because they are usually more gentle, honest, and humane' (p. 123). In a criminal justice arena, Cressey noted as far back as 1955 the 'retroflexive' reforming benefits of criminalised people helping others to change. In 1965, Riessman documented the "helper therapy principle", calling attention to benefits the "helper receives from being in the helper role" (both cited in LeBel, Richie & Maruna, 2015: 32). In recent years, peer mentoring in criminal justice has grown in popularity (South, Bagnall & Woodall, 2017) and peer-to-peer support is utilised as a criminal justice 'intervention' in, at least, Ireland, Northern Ireland and Wales (O'Sullivan, Hart & Healy, 2018; Barr & Montgomery, 2016); North America (Reingle Gonzalez, Rana, Jetelina & Roberts, 2019); Australia (Brown & Ross, 2010); Finland, Canada & South Africa (Fair & Jacobson, 2017) and Sweden (Seppings, 2016). In some parts of England, it is estimated that peer mentors constitute as many as 92% of offender mentors (Willoughby, Parker & Ali, 2013: 7). In the UK, the recruitment of criminalised people as mentors has been accompanied by an idealist discourse which frames peer mentors benevolently as 'wise friends' or 'old lags' helping offenders onto the straight and narrow (Grayling, 2012), yet the concept of peer mentoring remains under researched and variously defined. Most available research focuses on mentoring generally or on peer support in other settings (such as education or health). Indeed, Lebel et al. (2015: 188) note that the lack of research on mentoring 'among prisoners and formerly incarcerated persons is startling considering how much research is funded each year to examine the impact of interventions to reduce recidivism'. Those studies which have been done have also struggled to define mentoring with clarity 'it is widely acknowledged that no one single definition or model of mentoring exists; rather there are a number of different models providing support to young people in a range of settings' (Parsons, Maras, Knowles, Bradshaw, Hollingworth & Monteiro, 2008: 5). Bozeman and Feeney's 'table of mentoring definitions' (2007) included no fewer than thirteen descriptions of mentoring based just on academic articles written between 1984 and 2005. 'The "peer" element of the intervention is [also] open to interpretation' (Finnegan, Whitehurst & Denton, 2010: 6), with little clarity about what constitutes a 'peer' in these settings. Schinkel and Whyte (2012: 361) argue that:

> In the context of human service, a peer is generally taken to mean a person who has shared experiences in common with the client and uses these to provide support with a view to exchanging practical and emotional help, generally in ways that are outside the realms of a professional relationship.

Yet in practice there is ambiguity, indeed during my own fieldwork, *peer-hood* was variously constructed to mean shared past experiences (e.g. an offending history), shared demographics (e.g. gender or age) and sometimes very few shared characteristics at all – as some organisations included enthusiastic 'community members' or university students looking for experience of working with offenders. This study does not explore the pros and cons of what 'peers' from different backgrounds have to offer specifically, highlighting an opportunity for further research, which will be discussed further in conclusion. What it does do, however, is identify several recurrent themes, or truth claims about peer mentoring, which run through the literature. These are as follows: that it changes you, that it constitutes an approach which is better than what has gone before and that it is egalitarian. This chapter will explore each of these claims, before considering them in the context of growing academic interest in how people come to desist from crime.

Peer mentoring changes you

A consistent claim made about peer mentoring is that it has the potential to change and improve participants. Unsurprisingly, in terms of criminal justice, the claimed *change* often evidenced is a reduction in re-offending. Evaluations commissioned by *St Giles Trust* claim that peer-supported clients re-offending rate is 40% lower than the national re-offending rate' (Frontier Economics, 2009: 15) and 'the reconviction rate for WIRE [female ex-offender led service] participants was 42%, against 51% for the national average for women offenders' (The Social Innovation Partnership, 2012: 5). In both cases 'reoffending' was measured in binary terms after a period of twelve months. Summarising the evidence on mentoring more broadly, Jolliffe and Farrington (2007: 3) concluded that mentoring 'reduced subsequent offending by 4 to 11%'. However, they noted that the 'best studies, designed to provide the most accurate assessment of the impact of mentoring, did not suggest that mentoring *caused* a statistically significant reduction in re-offending' (Jolliffe & Farrington, 2007: 3, emphasis added). Rather, 'mentoring was only successful in reducing re-offending when it was one of a number of interventions given' (Jolliffe & Farrington, 2007: 3). They also found that, 'only studies in which mentoring was still being given during the follow-up period led to a statistically significant reduction in re-offending' (Jolliffe & Farrington, 2007: 3). Mentoring may have the capacity to support change in recorded offending patterns, therefore, but perhaps only within a wider system of support and potentially only whilst the intervention continues. Of the eighteen studies assessed by Jolliffe and Farrington, only two were based in the UK and both focused on young people.

Mentoring is, however, claimed to have a 'modest positive effect' in other areas, including 'delinquency, aggression, drug use, and achievement' (Tolan, Henry, Schoeny & Bass, 2008: 3) and interestingly, noted effects were stronger when emotional support featured, and when professional development was a motive of the mentors (Tolan et al., 2008: 3). It is potentially not just mentoring that changes people then, but the type of mentoring and the individual motivations (and no doubt skills) of mentors. A caveat that should be added here is that the above studies all considered mentoring *generally*; this is because 'peer'-specific evidence is scarce (Finnegan et al., 2010: 9). Most evidence of the effects of peer mentoring, other than the small-scale evaluations of *St Giles Trust* work cited above, comes from North America. The three-year Buddy System study conducted in 1979, for example, concluded that the 'peer network effect' in some cases helped reduce recidivism among offenders (cited in Clayton, 2009: 6). Young people participating in peer mentoring in the USA were found to be less likely to use drugs and alcohol, less likely to be violent or support violence and to have improved school attendance and performance, improved relationships with their parents and peers and increased self-esteem (Parsons et al., 2008). Formally incarcerated citizens experienced significant improvements in subjective factors, including self-esteem, levels of hope and self-identity (self-knowledge, self-awareness and self-reflection, self-care) (Lopez-Humphreys & Teater, 2019). Zimmerman and colleagues (2002), whilst not looking at 'peer mentors' specifically, explored the role of 'natural mentors' or non-parental adults such as teachers, extended family or neighbours in a North American city. They found that 'those with natural mentors were less likely to smoke marijuana or be involved in nonviolent delinquency and had more positive attitudes toward school' (Zimmerman, Bingenheimer & Notaro, 2002: 221). An evaluation of a female prisoners' peer-led programme in Canada, 'found that both the peer counsellors and recipients of the service said the programme decreased feelings of isolation and increased feelings of self-worth and autonomy' (Pollack, 2004: 702). Similarly, Mok's (2005) study of self-help groups in Hong Kong documents increased self-confidence and self-efficacy. These findings are significant for criminal justice given that the success of people to maintain desistance from crime is often linked to their sense of self-control or agency (Zdun, 2011; Maruna, 2001).

Another arena where peers play an important, influential role is recovery from addiction. Peer education has been found to improve attitudes and behaviour relating to substance misuse (Parkin & McKeganey, 2000: 302). In 'Alcoholics Anonymous' (AA) peer recovery groups, it is argued that members 'enter, or rather are recruited to, a new figured world, a new frame of understanding' (Holland, Skinner, Lachicotte & Cain, 1998: 66). For Holland et al. (1998: 66), it is not just the peer element of AA that factors this shift, but the *personal stories*, which constitute: 'a transformation of their identities, from drinking non-alcoholics to non-drinking alcoholics'. The personal story, which becomes the narrative of these relationships is therefore 'a cultural vehicle for identity formation' (Holland et al., 1998: 71). For Asencio and Burke (2011), however, the *peer identity* itself holds power. They explored how 'reflected appraisals' (the expressions of others, which feedback how one's identity is coming across in the situation) were internalised among prisoners:

> Results suggest that the internalization of reflected appraisals is dependent upon the identity at issue and the source of the reflected appraisal. We showed that the strength of the criminal identity and the drug user identity (both deviant identities) were influenced by the reflected appraisals of *significant others and peers* (though not the guards).
>
> (Asencio & Burke, 2011: 177, emphasis added)

These findings suggest that peers in mentoring roles may have more influence than figures of authority over how identity messages are internalised. However, it is not the authority or profession itself that the authors interpret as influencing appraisal internalisation here:

> Since the guards at the jail are not likely to interact with participants on a regular basis due to the rotation schedule, it is likely that participants do not consider what the guards think of them to be relevant to how they see themselves. These results are consistent with the idea that others who are not close to the self have less influence on the self-view.
>
> (Asencio & Burke, 2011: 179)

Therefore, interaction levels and 'closeness' are potentially important in terms of how far identity reflections or labels are internalised. This interpretation is significant for peer mentoring given the practice often involves 'relatively high levels of contact time between mentors and mentees' (Brown & Ross, 2010: 32). Moreover, ex-offender mentors are claimed to have personal insight into prison life, which makes it easier for [mentees] to bond with the volunteers (Hunter & Kirby, 2011: 1).

Peer mentoring is better than what has gone before

Another message from the literature is that peer mentoring brings something new to criminal justice in terms of the *actors* involved and the *knowledges* they bring: 'Ex-offender mentors' personal insight into prison life makes it easier for the young people to bond with the volunteers and provides the all-important initial hook with which to engage them in the project' (Hunter & Kirby, 2011: 1). Peers are therefore claimed to have a credibility that 'professional' rehabilitation workers may not. Glasgow-based 'Routes out of Prison' project uses trained 'ex-offenders to mentor released prisoners, precisely because they have the credibility that [workers from] statutory agencies don't often have' (Nellis & McNeill, 2008: xi). Moreover, peers are claimed to have 'specific knowledge about risk behaviour occurring both inside and outside the prison and have an understanding of realistic strategies to reduce the risk' (Devilly, Sorbello, Eccleston & Ward, 2005: 223). Peers have a claimed advantage over Probation Officers and related professionals because they have experienced first-hand many of the problems faced by their 'clients' and can relate to the challenges of life after prison (Boyce, Hunter & Hough, 2009: viii). Peer mentors are not just imagined to offer something better than what has gone before because they can bond with mentees and relate to their experiences, but also because they provide 'inspiration and hope... proof that it was possible to move on and sort your life out' (Boyce et al., 2009: 20). Whilst this philosophy is relatively new to correctional work, it has been dominant in the field of addictions:

> It is only through recovery forums and peer-led services that people in recovery can become visible. Once these people become visible recovery champions, they can help people to believe that recovery is not only possible but desirable.
>
> (Kidd, 2011: 174)

In a closely related activity to peer mentoring, 'peer navigators' employed to assist formerly incarcerated individuals in Washington DC were positioned as *role models* as they exemplified the successful navigation of re-entry from correctional institutions (Portillo, Goldberg & Taxman, 2017: 335). The theory that people will feel inspired by the visibility of others to affect their own change will be developed further in Chapter 3, and indeed, throughout the book. The point here is that we can trace within the literature a belief in shared experience as an inspirational factor. Peer mentoring is not only imagined to be *better* because of what it offers potential mentees, but also what it offers to mentors and the services they work within. In practical terms, it offers a valuable opportunity to people who often find it difficult to obtain work otherwise due to having a criminal record (Clinks & MBF, 2012; Corcoran, 2012). This opportunity to gain constructive employment is important given that desistance requires access to opportunities alongside individual will (Boyce et al., 2009: 27). An additional benefit for rehabilitation services is the (potential) cost-effectiveness of peer support groups compared with professional interventions (Pistrang, Barker & Humphreys, 2008):

> Offender mentoring... gives fiscally stretched non-government organisations the capacity to leverage the services of community volunteers as

a way of providing a greater range of services... they involve relatively high levels of contact time between mentors and mentees. In contrast, the contacts between professional support workers and their clients are likely to be brief and episodic.

(Brown & Ross, 2010: 32)

A report by two national charities in the UK similarly described peer mentoring as a support which 'goes beyond that offered via statutory contracts as well as the mobility aspect of mentoring support as opposed to office based statutory workers who are unable to take clients anywhere' (Clinks & MBF, 2012: 9). These features may be particularly important for women leaving prison, 'offering access to a prosocial source of support, independent from the insecure networks that may be available within the social environments of women offenders' (Rumgay, 2004: 415). Women leaving prison in Norway unanimously 'emphasized the importance to coping well of having some close relationships providing emotional and practical social support' (Servan & Mittelmark, 2012: 254). In the UK, it has also been recommended that women have a supportive 'mentor to whom they can turn when they have completed any offending-related programmes, since personal support is likely to be as important as any direct input addressing offending behaviour' (Gelsthorpe, Sharpe & Roberts, 2007: 8). Whilst there are pragmatic gains to be made from using volunteers to offer emotional and social support and indeed to fill gaps in existing services, there is an equally 'strong consensus that volunteer labour should not substitute for paid professional jobs' (Corcoran, 2012: 20). Indeed, health unions have expressed concern 'that volunteers might be used to replace lower grade paid staff, or to fill gaps in the event of industrial action' (Neuberger, 2008: 18). In addition to offering high contact levels and a sustainable support network, there is some evidence that peer mentors may be *better* at improving compliance with other services. For example, mentoring schemes were found to be particularly successful 'in reintegrating the targeted young people into education, training and the community' (Finnegan et al., 2010: 10). Similarly, Portillo et al. (2017: 328–329), found that peer navigators' adopted roles included acting as 'legitimizer' (increasing clients' trust in organisations and staff members), and as 'resource broker' (connecting clients with other service providers).

However, the existing literature does not wholly endorse peer-led services as an *improvement* on what has gone before. One issue is that it can be difficult 'to isolate the direct effects of mentoring, as a number of studies have considered the effectiveness of mentoring within a package of interventions' (Finnegan et al., 2010: 9). Indeed, mentoring theory itself remains underdeveloped and difficult to sort from adjacent concepts such as training, coaching, socialisation, and even friendship (Bozeman & Feeney, 2007: 735). There are also potential pitfalls to be considered, including the following: mismatches of mentor and mentee in terms of expectations, gender, culture or race; a reluctant or over-zealous mentor/mentee; emotional involvement;

broken confidentiality; conflicting roles of manager, assessor, mentor or obstructions from/conflicts-of others and parameters/boundaries not agreed in advance (McKimm, Jollie & Hatter, 2007: 13–14). Other apprehensions relate to the charged contexts in which criminal justice mentors operate. Boyce et al. (2009), for example, highlight:

> The potential for the Peer Advisors to be subject to bullying or pressure to traffic items such as drugs or mobile phones through the system [although they acknowledge that this] was a concern about the possible opportunity rather than a worry about the number of such incidents.
>
> (Boyce et al., 2009: 11)

Nonetheless this concern was also raised by Devilly et al. (2005), who argued in their review of prison-based peer education schemes that 'clarification of the many ethical issues… needs to be addressed' (Devilly et al., 2005: 233), issues such as professional conduct, boundaries, abuse of the system and [particular to the prison setting] 'the passing of information and or/drugs' (Devilly et al., 2005: 233). Problems have also been highlighted in terms of volunteering specifically, given 'funding tends to be short-term… limiting the time for projects to become established and effective' (Boyce et al., 2009: 22). Indeed, in a sector survey the 'most frequently expressed challenge was related to future funding and sustainability' (Clinks & MBF, 2012: 7). In personnel terms there have been problems with 'access to good quality volunteer managers… and the resource intensive and time-consuming duties of managing mentors' activity and supporting them' (Clinks & MBF, 2012: 9), along with difficulties in relation to 'recruitment, selection and retention with some specific problems outlined around the [criminal records] clearance process leading to loss of motivation for the volunteer whilst waiting' (Clinks & MBF, 2012: 11). A 2016 inspection of the UK government's flagship 'Through the Gate' prison resettlement policy highlighted serious shortfalls in the promise to provide a mentor to every person leaving prison:

> None of the prisoners had been helped into employment…and we did not see examples of handover to specialist education or training resources in the community. The low number of mentors available did not match the early promise of CRC [community rehabilitation company] contract bids, or the numbers of prisoners who might have benefited from this type of support on release.
>
> (HMIP, 2016: 8)

This signals that the number of suitably motivated and skilled mentors available (in the UK) may be insufficient. Finally, but not insignificantly, there are warnings that volunteering, particularly in prison settings, can take a high personal toll with harms including burnout, post-traumatic stress, injury or even death (see Corcoran, 2012: 22). Peer mentoring is claimed to be better than what has gone before because mentors draw upon lived experiences, which enable them to bond with, relate to and inspire mentees in a personal way. Peer mentors are also able to offer high levels of support and, therefore, fill gaps in existing services. Despite these claims of virtue, however, there are concerns about the efficacy and security of the practice, the lack of mentoring theory and workforce, and the personal demands upon mentors.

Peer mentoring is egalitarian

Not only is peer mentoring claimed to change people and offer something better than the professionally dominated approach to offender management that precedes it, but it is also declared to be more egalitarian than other forms of practice. This is not an intervention delivered by an expert 'other', but a peer, purportedly allowing people to engage in a less hierarchical rehabilitation relationship. In this sense, it is a form of mutual aid. The *St Giles Trust* peer advice project, for example, tests out 'the concept that prisoners themselves can be an important resource in the rehabilitation and resettlement processes' and as such is said to serve 'as a counterbalance to the widespread belief that programmes are something that are "done" to offenders by specialists' (Boyce et al., 2009: vi). This repositioning of 'offenders' as intervening agents – as opposed to intervened upon subjects – potentially offers something quite different to existing criminal justice approaches, which have been strongly reliant upon assumptions of deficit in 'offenders' cognitive skills (Rex, 2011: 68). Pollack (2004: 694), for example, points out that:

> Cognitive behavioural programming considered to be 'what works' to reduce recidivism... [is] based on the premise that criminal offending is a result of the offender's inability to think logically, reason appropriately and to make rational decisions.

These dominant psychological approaches pathologise criminal behaviour, 'delineating between "us" (law abiding citizens) and "them" (offenders)' (Pollack, 2004: 695). When (ex) 'offenders' become the intervenors, however, this constructed divide is destabilised. The reimagining of providers and users of services is itself part of a broader movement of 'levelling' the field of human services. Hughes (2012: 50) argues that this levelling is encapsulated in the 'user engagement' discourse, which places emphasis on service user engagement in the interventions to which they are subject. This is important because expert-led 'what works' defined programmes 'run the risk of pissing [offenders] off... since our methods seem not to match what they see as their primary needs (and most pressing goals)' (Porporino, 2010, cited in Hughes, 2012: 50). Hughes (2012: 52) contends that *offender engagement* exists on a scale, from 'motivating individuals to participate and attend for interventions determined by a Probation Officer' to 'securing the full participation of individuals, fostering a sense of ownership, and encouraging them to take the lead on decisions regarding their goals and objectives'. Whatever its form, it is argued that 'a greater voice needs to be given to service users in the design and implementation of approaches, to ensure that they are experienced as meaningful and supportive of desistance' (Hughes, 2012: 64). This argument has also been forwarded by McNeill and Weaver (2010: 10) who argue that a more radical desistance supporting approach might be to 'involve current and former service users in co-designing, co-developing, co-implementing and co-evaluating a desistance-supporting intervention process'. They argue that:

> A strong evidence-based case could be made for this; partly on the grounds that desistance research itself is often about learning directly from offenders' and ex-offenders' experiences, partly because of what the desistance research has to say about the importance of and merits of developing agency, generativity and civic participation and partly because services co-designed by their current or former users may well be more likely to be fit for purpose and thus effective.
>
> (McNeill & Weaver, 2010: 10)

'Desistance research' itself will be introduced more fully in the final section of this chapter. Before we get there however, there are clearly several arguments within the literature, which advocate that *listening* to the people who are subject to criminal justice interventions may constitute a less repressive approach than imposing expert knowledge upon them. Founded in 2009 the charity *User Voice* attempts to put this theory into practice by arguing that 'only offenders can stop re-offending' (User Voice Website, 2019), and that there is a need to meaningfully include voices of lived experience in improving the criminal justice system. This approach represents a challenge to the dominant discourse, which holds that offender rehabilitation requires *experts* to 'manage' people and affect changes. Rumgay (2004: 405) termed this dominant discourse 'a cognitive deficit model' and argued that 'within this paradigm, offenders are deficient individuals whose faulty thinking requires correction by professionals with special expertise in cognitive training' (Rumgay, 2004: 405). The claims to knowledge within this discourse are often based on statistical quantifying practices, rather than asking recipients what intervention programmes are most meaningful to them (Spalek, 2008).

In the last decade, it could be argued that there has been a reduction in the *cognitive deficit* discourse, replaced by the scientific framing of 'offenders' in terms of *empathy deficit* (e.g. Winter, Spengler, Bermpohl, Singer & Kanske, 2017), *attention deficit* (e.g. Young et al., 2018) or deficits in their childhood experiences (e.g. Baglivio, Wolff, Piquero & Epps, 2015). The danger of such framings is that practice aims to by predict, pathologise and treat, rather than seek potential, strengths and collaboration. In contrast, the increased inclusion of *user* or *offender* voices and indeed the push for people who have used services to deliver services, challenge the prioritisation of professionalised 'expertise'. These developments call for a more *egalitarian* form of rehabilitation practice, which imagines that expertise may reside as much within people's lived experiences as it does within academic and professional knowledge. In this sense peer mentoring can also be a political act. Little has previously been written about the political action of criminalised people. Where reference is made, it is in the context of broader campaigns of resistance, such as those of political prisoners (Corcoran, 2013), or in terms of 'disturbance', rather than positively organised challenge. Martinson (1972: 3), for example, refers to rioting as an attempt to improve conditions from within, and to 'expressive mutiny [which] aims to communicate the inmates' plight to the public so far as he understands it'. Bosworth and Carrabine (2001) note that terminology, such as 'disturbance, disorder or riot', which frame acts of resistance, has political connotations – 'deployed by the Right to conjure up images of pathological and dangerous individuals', similarly the terms preferred by the Left, such as 'rebellion, protest and resistance' are hardly neutral (p. 506). Their nuanced analysis illustrates that power in prison is constantly contested, and that while subversive actions are structured in part by identity, by the available scripts of gender, ethnicity, class and sexuality, 'prisons may be altered from the inside out by those very individuals who are subject to its control' (p. 513). There are also some implied references to politicisation within the peer mentoring literature, Kavanagh and Borrill (2013: 403), for example, have recognised that mentoring can be 'empowering in both prison and probation settings' in contrast to previous experiences of feeling 'powerless'. Similarly, Pollack (2004) argues that peer support services can be liberatory for women in prison. Peer mentoring here, emerges as a stylistic rebellion to the stigma and exclusion that 'offenders' often experience. It is an activity which politically turns the power of these exclusions on their head. Past experiences of offending are transformed from a limitation into a unique resource. How far this rebellion is critical, or transforms relations, will be explored in Chapters 3, 9 and 10.

Peer mentoring has been conceived as egalitarian in that it includes voices previously excluded from rehabilitation practice. However, there are also claims that mentoring itself aims for a more democratic kind of intervention, one which allows both helper and helped to be afforded a voice within the relationship. Such an egalitarian learning space was theorised by critical pedagogue Paulo Freire:

> The fundamental task of the mentor is a liberatory task. It is not to encourage the mentor's goals and aspirations and dreams to be reproduced in the mentees, the students, but to give rise to the possibility that the

students become the owners of their own history... to assume the ethical posture of a mentor who truly believes in the total autonomy, freedom, and development of those he or she mentors.

(Freire, 1997: 324)

Pollack (2004) examined peer support services as an example of such liberatory practice with women in prison and found the 'fact that the group was co-facilitated by prisoners, rather than by professional staff, greatly enhanced a sense of self-reliance and the autonomy of prisoner participants who have so few opportunities to author their own stories and define their own needs' (Pollack, 2004: 703). This highlights how peer work encourages solidarity alongside egalitarianism. Pollack suggests that peer support 'helps counter the notion that women in prison have few skills, are unable to assume responsibilities, cannot be trusted and are emotionally unstable' (Pollack, 2004: 704). Consequently, it constitutes a move 'away from deficit model to one that emphasises women's strengths and acknowledges their varied and skilful modes of coping' (Pollack, 2004: 704; see also Burnett & Maruna, 2006). An important difference in principle between peer mentoring and other forms of rehabilitation is that both parties are positioned as collaborators in the problem-solving process. A prison-based peer programme in New York State, for example, was found to provide:

> leadership, support, and guidance for female offenders, and not only created a prosocial environment, but fashioned an entire community. This community continued outside of the prison walls, provided women with emotional support, and subsequently resulted in increased levels of institutional and post-release success.

(Collica, 2010: 314)

Such personal connections and links into support networks represent an increase in 'social capital', described by McNeill and Weaver (2010: 20) as 'relationships, networks and reciprocities within families and communities', a key factor in desistance (Farrall, 2011). This approach closely resonates with 'strengths-based' practices, which 'treat offenders as community assets to be utilized rather than merely liabilities to be supervised' (Burnett & Maruna, 2006: 84).

Whilst peer mentoring may offer people with convictions roles which recognises their strengths and skills, there is also a problem with the claim that peer mentoring relationships are more egalitarian than 'expert' interventions, given they essentially maintain a hierarchical relationship structure. This is not a space where 'nobody is a receiver' (Burnett & Maruna, 2006: 84), but rather there are intervenors (mentors) and intervened upon (mentees). Mentees, whilst benefiting in practical and social terms, are still subject to a paternalistic relationship with an *other* who has something to teach them, a way to help them improve. Furthermore, peer mentoring is often voluntary or indeed prison labour without adequate pay (Walby & Cole, 2019: 14). To expect skilled emotional labour for free, sometimes whilst workers are still subject to punishment delivered by paid professionals is arguably the antithesis of egalitarianism.

Desistance from crime

'Desistance' refers to ceasing a pattern of criminal behaviour, or: 'going straight' (Maruna, Porter & Carvalho, 2004b: 221). Desistance studies examine 'not why people *get into crime* but how they *get out* of it and what can be done to assist them in this process' (McNeill, 2012: 95, emphasis in original). Knowledge of how people desist is important to any criminal justice provider because 'desisting from crime is what practitioners in the field of offender programming and treatment have always wanted for their clients' (Maruna, Immarigeon & LeBel, 2011: 10). Interestingly, the study of desistance emerged out of a critique of the professionally driven 'medical model' of corrections. To explore desistance was to 'study those persons who change *without* the assistance of correctional interventions' (Maruna et al., 2011: 11, emphasis in original). Indeed 'almost all of the research suggests that "programmes" have a remarkably minor impact on life outcomes like going to prison' (Maruna & LeBel, 2010: 68). In contrast, desisters' 'own resources and social networks are often more significant factors in resolving their difficulties than professional staff' (McNeill and Maruna, 2007: 229). As a result:

> The desistance paradigm suggests that we might be better off if we allowed offenders to *guide us* instead, listened to what they think might best fit their individual struggles out of crime, rather than continue to insist that our solutions are their salvation.
>
> (Porporino, 2010: 80, emphasis in original)

The implication here is that 'offender management services need to think of themselves less as providers of correctional treatment (that belongs to the expert) and more as supporters of desistance processes (that belong to the desister)' (McNeill, 2006: 46). These arguments partially explain how the notion of peer mentoring has gained ground. It draws upon the perspectives of people who have experienced crime and change *and* invites convicted people to take a central role in their own (and others') change processes. This context makes the concept of desistance worthy of specific consideration.

Most academic studies present desistance as a process, whereby people either grow out of crime, make new decisions based on social ties, or experience an identity shift through new stories, narratives or scripts about their true good self (see McNeill, 2006: 46). Farrall and Calverley (2006) drill down into the more intricate 'factors and processes' associated with desistance, including the routine of work habits, the quality of intimate relationships, leaving the area you have grown up in, feeling shame, having a motivation to avoid offending, experiencing a significant shock; for example, being wounded, growing tired of prison following a period of re-evaluation and experiencing serious physical harm (Farrall & Calverley, 2006: 4–7). Moving away from crime, it appears, is a complex process influenced by a number of social, emotional and subjective factors. Applying a theoretical lens, Maruna (2001) identified three broad perspectives in desistance literature: *maturational reform*, based on the links between age and certain criminal behaviours; *social bonds theory*, suggesting that ties to family, employment or education in early adulthood explain changes across the life course and *narrative theory*, stressing 'the significance of subjective changes in the person's sense of self and identity, reflected in motivations, greater concern for others and more consideration of the future' (cited in McNeill, 2006: 46). Reflecting upon this theoretical shape, McNeill (2006) concludes: 'It is not just the events and changes that matter; it is what these events and changes *mean* to the people involved' (McNeill, 2006: 47, emphasis in original). More recent debates on desistance are therefore particularly concerned with the 'complex interaction between subjective/agency factors and social/environmental factors' (LeBel, Burnett, Maruna & Bushway, 2008: 131); in other words, how individual influences on desisting from crime such as maturation, decision-making and new self-narratives relate to social factors such as employment, housing and pro-social relationships. By highlighting 'possible structural impediments to desistance' and asking 'how far do social structures impede or encourage that process' (Farrall, Bottoms & Shapland, 2010: 549), the focus is shifted from simply problematic individuals to structures which may require change. Desistance from crime then is a complex process, which is linked to maturing, entering positive intimate relationships, experiencing criminal activities negatively and perceiving legitimate opportunities as possible. It also involves a positive concept of self, something which can be enhanced by opportunities to *do good*.

Claims that peer mentoring and desistance may be related

Whilst it remains to be seen whether peer mentoring is related to 'desistance', there is an alluring correspondence between the language of desistance and peer mentoring that has led to claims that they might well be. Considering mentoring in the light of desistance research, Brown and Ross (2010: 37) argue that whilst maturational changes 'lie beyond the scope of mentoring projects' social factors such as 'ties to family, community, employment and the like, seems to lie squarely within the domain of mentoring and concerns the acquisition or maintenance of social capital'. Furthermore, they suggest that 'the narratives offenders construct around themselves, their circumstances and their future goes to the issue of human capital and would also be a reasonable process target for mentoring relationships' (Brown & Ross, 2010: 38). Reflecting upon peer mentoring specifically Maruna (2012a) stated:

> It was shocking how many [voluntary sector] staff and managers were familiar with and motivated by the desistance literature. As several told me, if desistance is the theory, the *St. Giles Trust* [charity] (with its commitment to hiring ex-prisoner resettlement mentors) is very much the practice.
>
> (Maruna, 2012a: 1)

Nixon (2019: 44) argues that prisoner peer relationships 'can prove transformative, contributing to the desistance process' and signalling desistance to others. Peer mentoring is therefore theorised as 'desistance in practice'. It provides a solid opportunity for people with convictions to 'do' and 'make' good (Clinks & MBF, 2012). This is important in a system where 'released, ex-prisoners [are often] prohibited from finding legitimate means of self-support as a result of their involvement with the system meant to "correct" them' (Maruna, 2012b: 75). Peer mentoring also offers a practical opportunity to make amends, realise strengths and skills and to heal. It therefore presents a vehicle for 'allowing individuals to identify themselves credibly as desisters, rather than on trying to "cause" desistance explicitly' (Maruna, 2012b: 75). The following discussion will expand on this hypothesis by suggesting there are three ways that peer mentoring could potentially support desistance processes: first, by offering *scripts* for mentees to work with; second by offering a *readership* for the new stories which emerge and third as a *redemptive* practice.

The potential of peer mentors to co-author desistance scripts

One of the ways which peer mentoring may have the capacity to promote desistance is by offering mentees a co-author to create a new identity story. Stories relating to the self, or 'scripts', run throughout work on desistance, but are conceived of slightly differently by different authors. Maruna (2001), for example, characterises the self-narratives of desisters as 'redemption scripts', which begin by establishing the goodness of the narrator who is believed in by an outside force and is now positioned to 'give something back' (Maruna, 2001: 87). Rumgay (2004), however, suggests that 'certain common identities that present themselves as available (e.g. mother) may also provide a "script" by which to enact a conventional, pro-social social role' (Rumgay, 2004: 405). MacDonald and colleagues (2011) describe the 'critical moments' [of desistance] as insights of *biographical* insight and reflection from which new directions in life are pursued (MacDonald, Webster, Shildrick & Simpson, 2011: 147–148, emphasis added). The *story* is indeed an appropriate motif to accompany work about people changing as the 'personal story is a cultural vehicle for identity formation' (Holland et al., 1998: 71). Crucially, however, the author of desistance stories is not always, solely, the desister. Maruna's work (2001: 96), for example, revealed a 'looking glass recovery' process wherein at first the offender has no belief in themselves, but someone else believes in them and makes them realise that they do have personal value. This could indicate the value of peer mentors – as respected others to have belief in mentees. Indeed, 'if secondary [or sustained] desistance… requires a narrative reconstruction of identity, then it seems obvious why relational aspects of practice are so significant' (McNeill, 2006: 49). In Rumgay's account (2004: 409), common social identities – such as parent, student, worker or partner – 'present themselves' to the potential desister. The desister's role is then to co-author or co-perform these roles should they choose. The first task of a peer mentor may be to positively model such identities. The script presented, however, is only ever a 'skeleton' one, containing 'only a fraction of the situations and interactions in which the role must be performed' (Rumgay, 2004: 409). An additional charge for mentors, then, may be assisting with performing the detail of each role through modelling and offering opportunities for new roles to be practiced. Later chapters will focus on whether and how practices of peer mentoring may encourage new 'self-scripts' or facilitate compliance with established social scripts. The multiplicity of authors who create identity scripts, however, also highlight the complexity of the desister's position. In constructing a new 'text' of the self, authors must 'make use of the dominant discourse and its available discursive subject positions (e.g. client, defendant, complainant, service receiver) [hence becoming] subject to discourse's constitutive effects' (Henry & Milovanovic, 1996: 85). In context the desister is expected, by the demands of modern neoliberal societies, to have full responsibility for her or his story; to author her or his choices, roles and truths, and yet in order to do so s/he is bound by the socially constructed, discursive, powerful social scripts available. The story that then emerges when people are aware that change is expected of them is one that must draw on shared ideals, thus 'the voices of inner speech which seem to be mine, are created from an "orchestration"', that is, the 'balance struck among the socially identified voices that comprise inner speech' (Mageo, 2002: 54). The personal story of change, whilst appearing initially to belong to the desister, is actually a combination of individual agency, shared language and socially available scripts. In other words, desistance does not arise in isolation, but there must be a language and roles that appear to be accessible to people making such changes.

The potential of peer mentors to act as co-readers of desistance scripts

As Maruna (2001) indicates above, it is not just having *a script* to draw upon, which is important for the formation of desisting identities, but also having *a readership* who recognise or authenticate these performances. Peer mentors form a crucial part of the social audience, wherein desisters self-stories are

constituted and recognised in fullness as social truths; 'if the counselor believes in the client's abilities, the client will too' (Maruna, LeBel, Mitchell &
Naples, 2004a: 278). Zdun (2011: 307) found that 'desisters can progress
quickly when agency and motivation are acknowledged by society and when
receiving support'. Indeed, when such recognition is absent LeBel and colleagues (2008) found that desistance is compromised:

> research participants who reported feeling stigmatised and socially
> excluded during a prison-based interview were more likely to be re-
> convicted and reimprisoned in a ten-year follow-up study, even after
> controlling for the number of social problems the individual experienced
> after release.
>
> (Cited in Maruna & LeBel, 2010: 75)

The problem for individuals attempting change is that 'desistance is a social
possibility that takes place within a very specific set of social contexts that
may or may not recognise legitimacy of transformation' (Polizzi, 2011: 150).
Peer mentors may, therefore, offer a buffer to such stigma, exclusion and scepticism, offering a forum for acceptance and inclusion.

The potential of peer mentoring to promote desistance through 'redemption'

A third way in which peer mentoring may assist desistance is by offering an
opportunity for redemptive action. Maruna et al. (2004b: 226) suggest that 'a
lifetime that is deemed a "waste" or a shame can be "put to use" by saving one –
"even just one" – other life from repeating the same mistakes'. In this sense, the
act of giving through mentoring becomes a form of desistance in action:

> [H]elping others, as I was once helped, really helps me turn the moral
> corner on deviance. Behaviours previously declared morally reprehen-
> sible are increasingly understood within a new universe of discourse as
> symptoms of a much larger disease complex.
>
> (Brown, 1991: 222)

Burnett and Maruna (2006) similarly make a strong case for meaningful volunteering by 'offenders', suggesting it is a valid 'strengths-based approach'
to promoting desistance. They point to Uggen and Janikula's (1999) study,
which 'found a robust negative relationship between volunteer work and arrest' (Burnett and Maruna, 2006: 88). This correlation is not just explained in
terms of putting a lifetime of mistakes to good use or turning a moral corner,
but also in terms of practical social inclusion:

> As people change they need new skills and capacities appropriate to their
> new lifestyle, and access to opportunities to use them. Another way of

putting this is that they need to acquire both 'human capital' and 'social capital'.

(Maguire & Raynor, 2006: 25)

LeBel (2007) offers evidence of the benefits of such a 'helper/wounded healer orientation... for formerly incarcerated persons' psychological well-being' (LeBel, 2007: 19). His findings indicate:

[A] basic incompatibility between a helper/ wounded healer orientation and criminal attitudes and behavior. This orientation appears to transform individuals from being part of 'the problem' into part of 'the solution' as they give their time in the service of helping others who are less far along in the recovery and reintegration process.

(LeBel, 2007: 19–20)

Peer mentoring, therefore, potentially provides an opportunity to make practical amends through assisting others. It may also offer the opportunity to gain social capital and skills to sustain changes, changes which in turn are incompatible with continued criminality.

This chapter has introduced the landscape from which peer mentoring is emerging. The penal voluntary sector has provided a space for those with lived experience of criminal justice to introduce a new form of practice; and to challenge the dominance of professional expertise in offender 'management'. However, the sector may be compromised as a critical space due to processes of co-option by the state and private sector. The albeit limited, literature on peer mentoring in criminal justice makes three dominant claims for the practice, that it changes people; it is better than rehabilitation efforts that have gone before; and that it constitutes an egalitarian form of practice. The 'ideal typical' peer mentor who emerges, is a mentor who aims to effect change in their mentees by helping them to move away from crime; a mentor who shares their own life experiences for practical and inspirational ends; and one who does so from a non-authoritarian position. The claimed centrality of the *offender experience* within peer mentoring corresponds with emerging research messages about how people come to desist from crime. Indeed, peer mentoring has been described as a form of desistance in practice. The final part of this chapter examined the ways in which peer mentoring may potentially support desistance processes, theorising that peer mentoring offers co-authors for new desistance scripts, an audience to affirm new desisting identities and a physical space for redemptive practice to be performed. Whilst there is some theoretical correspondence between desistance studies and claims for peer mentoring, however, there is currently little evidence of how mentoring relates to desistance processes. Indeed, desistance in itself does not appear to wholly capture the claims that are being made for peer mentoring. The following chapter will therefore offer a broader theoretical framework with which to read this practice, outlining four precepts, which although not fully articulated, appear to underpin the practice. They are processes of identity work, critical pedagogy, collective action based upon fraternity/sorority and politicisation.

Acknowledgements

This chapter has adapted material from the following works:

Buck, G., (2019), 'Mentoring'. In: Ugwudike, P., Graham, H., McNeill, F., Raynor, P., Taxman, F. & Trotter, C., (Eds.), *Routledge companion to reha-bilitative work in criminal justice*. Abingdon, Oxon: Routledge.
Buck, G., (2019), 'Politicisation or professionalisation? Exploring divergent aims within UK voluntary sector peer mentoring', *The Howard Journal of Crime and Justice*, **58**(3), pp. 349–365.
Buck, G., (2017), '"I wanted to feel the way they did": Mimesis as a situational dynamic of peer mentoring by ex-offenders', *Deviant Behavior*, **38**(9), pp. 1027–1041.

I am thankful to the publishers for their permission.

References

Abdennur, A., (1987), *The conflict resolution syndrome: Volunteerism, violence, and beyond*. Ottawa: Ottawa University Press.
Asencio, E.K. & Burke, P.J., (2011), 'Does incarceration change the criminal identity? A synthesis of labelling and identity theory perspectives on identity change', *Sociological Perspectives*, **54**(2), pp. 163–182.
Baglivio, M.T., Wolff, K.T., Piquero, A.R. & Epps, N., (2015), 'The relationship between adverse childhood experiences (ACE) and juvenile offending trajectories in a juvenile offender sample', *Journal of Criminal Justice*, **43**(3), pp. 229–241.
Barr, N. & Montgomery, G., (2016), 'Service user involvement in service planning in the criminal justice system: Rhetoric or reality?', *Irish Probation Journal*, **13**, pp. 143–155.
Benson, A. & Hedge, J, (2009), 'Criminal justice and the voluntary sector: A policy that does not compute', *Criminal Justice Matters,* **77**(1), pp. 34–36.
Bosworth, M. & Carrabine, E., (2001), 'Reassessing resistance: Race, gender and sexuality in prison', *Punishment & Society*, **3**(4), pp. 501–515.
Boyce, I., Hunter, G. & Hough, M., (2009), *The St Giles trust peer advice project: Summary of an evaluation report*. London: The Institute for Criminal Policy Research, School of Law, King's College. Available at: http://eprints.bbk.ac.uk/3794/ [Accessed August 2019].
Bozeman, B. & Feeney, M.K., (2007), 'Toward a useful theory of mentoring: A conceptual analysis and critique', *Administration and Society,* **39**(6), pp. 719–739.
Brown, D., (1991), 'The professional ex-: An alternative for exiting the deviant career', *The Sociological Quarterly*, **32**(2), pp. 219–230.

Brown, M. & Ross, S., (2010), 'Mentoring, social capital and desistance: A study of women released from prison', *Australian & New Zealand Journal of Criminology (Australian Academic Press)*, **43**(1), pp. 31–50.

Burnett, R. & Maruna, S., (2006), 'The kindness of prisoners: strengths-based resettlement in theory and in action', *Criminology and Criminal Justice*, **6**(1), pp. 83–106.

Clayton, A.N., (2009), *Mentoring for youth involved in Juvenile justice programs: A review of the literature*. Massachusetts: University of Massachusetts. Available at: https://rhyclearing house.acf.hhs.gov/library/2009/mentoring-youth-involved-juvenile-justice-programs-review-literature [Accessed August 2019].

Clinks & MBF, (2012), *Supporting offenders through mentoring and befriending: Clinks and MBF survey findings September 2012*. Available at: www.2ndchancegroup.org/wp-content/uploads/2014/06/Clinks-and-MBF-survey-report-findings-final-version-Sept-2012.pdf [Accessed August 2019].

Collica, K., (2010), 'Surviving incarceration: Two prison-based peer programs build communities of support for female offenders', *Deviant Behavior*, **31**(4), pp. 314–347.

Corcoran, M., (2013), *Out of order*, Cullompton: Willan.

Corcoran, M., (2012), '"Be careful what you ask for": Findings from the seminar series on the "Third sector in criminal justice"', *Prison Service Journal*, **24**, pp. 17–22.

Corcoran, M.S., Maguire, M. & Williams, K., (2019), 'Alice in Wonderland: Voluntary sector organisations' experiences of transforming rehabilitation', *Probation Journal*, **66**(1), pp. 96–112.

Davidson, L., Bellamy, C., Guy, K. & Miller, R., (2012), 'Peer support among persons with severe mental illnesses: A review of evidence and experience', *World Psychiatry*, **11**, pp. 123–128.

Devilly, G.J., Sorbello, L., Eccleston, L. & Ward, T., (2005), 'Prison-based peer-education schemes', *Aggression and Violent Behavior*, **10**, pp. 219–240.

Fair, H. & Jacobson, J., (2017), *Peer relations: Review of learning from the Winston Churchill memorial trust prison reform fellowships–Part IV*. Available at: http://eprints.bbk.ac.uk/18951/1/peer_relations_FINAL.pdf.

Farrall, S., (2011), 'Social capital and offender reintegration: Making probation desistance focused'. In: Maruna, S. & Immarigeon, R., (Eds.), *After crime and punishment: Pathways to offender reintegration*. Abingdon, Oxon: Routledge.

Farrall, S., Bottoms, A. & Shapland, J., (2010), 'Social structures and desistance from crime', *European Journal of Criminology*, **7**(6), pp. 546–570.

Farrall, S. & Calverley, A., (2006), *Understanding desistance from crime*. Berkshire: Open University Press.

Finnegan, L., Whitehurst, D. & Denton, S., (2010), *Models of mentoring for inclusion and employment: Thematic review of existing evidence on mentoring and peer mentoring*. London: Centre for economic and social inclusion.

Freire, P., (1997), *Mentoring the mentor: A critical dialogue with Paulo Freire*. New York: Peter Lang.

Frontier Economics, (2009), *St Giles Trust's through the gates: An analysis of economic impact*. London: Pro Bono Economics.

Gelsthorpe, L., Sharpe, G. & Roberts, J., (2007), *Provision for women offenders in the community*. London: The Fawcett Society.

Gill, M.L. & Mawby, R.I., (1990), *Volunteers in the criminal justice system a comparative study of probation, police and victim support*. Milton Keynes: Open University Press.

Grayling, C., (2012), *Justice Minister's 'Rehabilitation Revolution' speech*, 20th November 2012. Available at: www.justice.gov.uk/news/speeches/chris-grayling/speech-to-the-centre-of-social-justice [Accessed August 2019].

Henry, S. & Milovanovic, D., (1996), *Constitutive criminology beyond postmodernism*. London: Sage.

Her Majesty's Inspectorate of Probation (HMIP) and Her Majesty's Inspectorate of Prisons, (2016), *An inspection of through the gate resettlement services for short-term prisoners*. Manchester: Her Majesty's Inspectorate of Probation. Available at: www.justiceinspectorates.gov.uk/cjji/wp-content/uploads/sites/2/2016/09/Through-the-Gate.pdf [Accessed August 2019].

Holland, D., Skinner, D., Lachicotte, Jr., W. & Cain, C., (1998), *Identity and agency in cultural worlds*. Cambridge, MA; London: Harvard University Press.

Home Office, (2013), *Policy: 'Reducing reoffending and improving rehabilitation'*. Available at: www.gov.uk/government/policies/reducing-reoffending-and-improving-rehabilitation/supporting-pages/transforming-rehabilitation [Accessed August 2019].

Hughes, W., (2012), 'Promoting offender engagement and compliance in sentence planning: Practitioner and service user perspectives in Hertfordshire', *Probation Journal*, **59**(1), pp. 49–65.

Hunter, G. & Kirby, A., (2011), *Evaluation summary: Working one to one with young offenders*. London: Birkbeck College.

Jolliffe, D. & Farrington, D.P., (2007), *A rapid evidence assessment of the impact of mentoring on re-offending: A summary*. London: Home Office.

Kaufman, N., (2015), 'Prisoner incorporation: The work of the state and non-governmental organizations', *Theoretical Criminology*, **19**, pp. 534–553.

Kavanagh, L. & Borrill, J., (2013), 'Exploring the experiences of ex-offender mentors', *Probation Journal*, **60**(4), pp. 400–414.

Kidd, M., (2011), 'A first-hand account of service user groups in the United Kingdom: An evaluation of their purpose, effectiveness, and place within the recovery movement', *Journal of Groups in Addiction & Recovery*, **6**(1–2), pp. 164–175.

LeBel, T.P., (2007), 'Examination of the impact of formerly incarcerated persons helping others', *Journal of Offender Rehabilitation*, **46**(1–2), pp. 1–24.

LeBel, T.P., Burnett, R., Maruna, S. & Bushway, S., (2008), 'The "chicken and egg" of subjective and social factors in desistance from crime', *European Journal of Criminology*, **5**(2), pp. 131–159.

LeBel, T.P., Richie, M. & Maruna, S., (2015), 'Helping others as a response to reconcile a criminal past: The role of the wounded healer in prisoner reentry programs', *Criminal Justice and Behavior*, **42**(1), pp. 108–120.

Lopez-Humphreys, M. & Teater, B., (2019), "It's what's on the inside that counts": A pilot study of the subjective changes among returned citizens participating in a peer-mentor support initiative', *Journal of Social Service Research*, 1–15. Online only at present. doi: 10.1080/01488376.2019.1656699.

MacDonald, R., Webster, C., Shildrick, T. & Simpson, M., (2011), 'Paths of exclusion, inclusion and desistance'. In: Farrall, S., Hough, M., Maruna, S. & Sparks, R., (Eds.), *Escape routes: Contemporary perspectives on life after punishment*. Abingdon, Oxon: Routledge.

Mageo, J.M., (2002), *Power and the self*. Cambridge: Cambridge University Press.

Maguire, M. & Raynor, P., (2006), 'How the resettlement of prisoners promotes desistance from crime: Or does it?' *Criminology and Criminal Justice,* **6**(1), pp. 19–38.

Martinson, R., (1972), 'Collective behavior at Attica', *Federal Probation,* **36**(3), pp. 3–7.

Maruna, S., (2001), *Making good; how ex-convicts reform and rebuild their lives.* Washington, DC: American Psychological Association.

Maruna, S., (2012a), 'Travelling desistance hucksters and the Hawthorne effect' published on line 7.10.12 at the Discovering Desistance knowledge exchange project. Available at: http://blogs.iriss.org.uk/discoveringdesistance/2012/10/07/travelling-desistance-hucksters-and-the-hawthorne-effect/ [Accessed August 2019].

Maruna, S., (2012b), 'Elements of successful desistance signaling', *Criminology & Public Policy,* **11**(1), pp. 73–86.

Maruna, S., Immarigeon, R. & LeBel, T.P., (2011), 'Ex-offender reintegration: theory and practice'. In: Maruna, S. & Immarigeon, R., (Eds.), (2011), *After crime and punishment: Pathways to offender reintegration.* Abingdon, Oxon: Routledge.

Maruna, S. & LeBel, T.P., (2010), 'The desistance paradigm in correctional practice: From programmes to lives'. In: McNeill, F., Raynor, P. & Trotter, C., (Eds.), *Offender supervision: New directions in theory, research and practice.* Abingdon, Oxon: Routledge, pp. 65–87.

Maruna, S., LeBel, T.P., Mitchell, N. & Naples, M., (2004a), 'Pygmalion in the reintegration process: Desistance from crime through the looking glass', *Psychology, Crime & Law,* **10**(3), pp. 271–281.

Maruna, S., Porter, L. & Carvalho, I., (2004b), 'The liverpool desistance study and probation practice: Opening the dialogue', *Probation Journal,* **51**(3), pp. 221–232.

McKimm, J., Jollie, C. & Hatter, M., (2007), *Mentoring theory and practice.* London: Imperial College School of Medicine. Available at: www.faculty.london deanery.ac.uk/e-learning/explore-further/e-learning/feedback/files/Mentoring_Theory_and_Practice.pdf [Accessed August 2019].

McNeill, F., (2006), 'A desistance paradigm for offender management', *Criminology and Criminal Justice,* **6**(1), pp. 39–62.

McNeill, F. (2012). A Copernican Correction for Community Sentences. How. J. Crim. Just., 51, 94.

McNeill, F. & Maruna, S., (2007), 'Giving up and giving back: Desistance, generativity and social work with offenders'. In: McIvor, G. & Raynor, P., (Eds.), *Developments in social work with offenders (Vol. 48).* London: Jessica Kingsley Publishers.

McNeill, F. & Weaver, B., (2010), *Changing lives? Desistance research and offender management, Research report 03/2010,* The Scottish Centre for Crime and Justice Research. Available at: www.sccjr.ac.uk/pubs/Changing-Lives-Desistance-Research-and-Offender-Management/255 [Accessed August 2019].

Ministry of Justice (MoJ), (2014), *The transforming rehabilitation programme: The new owners of the community rehabilitation companies, 18/12/2014.* London: Ministry of Justice. Available at: www.gov.uk/government/uploads/system/uploads/attachment_data/file/389727/table-of-new-owners-of-crcs.pdf [Accessed August 2019].

Ministry of Justice (MoJ), (2013), *'Transforming rehabilitation: A strategy for reform'* Response to consultation, May 2013. London: Ministry of Justice.

Mok, B.H., (2005), 'Organizing self-help groups for empowerment and social change: Findings and insights from an empirical study in Hong Kong', *Journal of Community Practice,* **13**(1), pp. 49–67.

Mullen, J., (2018), *What the future probation reforms mean for charities*. Available at: www.civilsociety.co.uk/voices/jessica-mullen-what-the-future-probation-reforms-mean-for-charities.html [Accessed August 2019].

Nellis, M. & McNeill, F., (2008), Foreword. In: Weaver, A., (Ed.), *So you think you know me?* Hampshire: Waterside Press.

Neuberger, J., (2008), *Volunteering in the public services: Health & Social Care, Baroness Neuberger's review as the governments volunteering champion, March 2008*. London: Cabinet Office.

Nixon, S., (2019), '"I just want to give something back": Peer work in prison', *Prison Service Journal*, no. 245, pp. 44–53.

O'Sullivan, R., Hart, W. & Healy, D., (2018), 'Transformative rehabilitation: Exploring prisoners' experiences of the community based health and first aid programme in Ireland', *European Journal on Criminal Policy and Research*, 1–19. Published online 31 August. doi: 10.1007/s10610-018-9396-z.

Parkin, S. & McKeganey, N., (2000), 'The rise and rise of peer education approaches', *Drugs: Education, Prevention and Policy*, **7**(3), pp. 293–310.

Parsons, C., Maras, P., Knowles, C., Bradshaw, V., Hollingworth, K. & Monteiro, H., (2008), *Formalised peer mentoring pilot evaluation*. Canterbury: Canterbury Christ Church University.

Pistrang, N., Barker, C. & Humphreys, K., (2008), 'Mutual help groups for mental health problems: a review of effectiveness studies', *American Journal of Community Psychology*, **42**, pp. 110–121.

Polizzi, D., (2011), 'Heidegger, restorative justice and desistance: A phenomenological perspective'. In: Hardie-Bick, J. & Lippens, R., (Eds.), *Crime, governance and existential predicaments*. Hampshire: Palgrave Macmillan.

Pollack, S., (2004), 'Anti-oppressive social work practice with women in prison: Discursive reconstructions and alternative practice', *British Journal of Social Work*, **34**(5), pp. 693–707.

Porporino, F.J., (2010), 'Bringing sense and sensitivity to corrections: From programmes to 'fix' offenders to services to support desistance'. In: Brayford, J., Cowe, F.B. & Deering, J., (Eds.), *What else works?: Creative work with offenders*. Devon: Willan.

Portillo, S., Goldberg, V. & Taxman, F.S., (2017), 'Mental health peer navigators: Working with criminal justiceinvolved populations', *The Prison Journal*, **97**(3), pp. 318–341.

Princes Trust, (2008), *Making the case: One-to-one support for young offenders*, 23 June 2008: Princes Trust, Rainer, St Giles Trust, CLINKS.

Quinn, K., (2019), 'Inside the penal voluntary sector: Divided discourses of "helping" criminalized women', *Punishment & Society*, Online only at present. doi: 1462474519863461.

Reingle Gonzalez, J.M., Rana, R.E., Jetelina, K.K. & Roberts, M.H., (2019), 'The value of lived experience with the criminal justice system: a qualitative study of peer re-entry specialists', *International Journal of Offender Therapy and Comparative Criminology*, doi: 10.1177/0306624X19830596.

Rex, S., (2011), 'Beyond cognitive-behaviouralism? Reflections of the effectiveness of the literature'. In: Bottoms, A., Gelsthorpe, L. & Rex, S., (Eds.), *Community penalties*. Abingdon, Oxon: Routledge.

Rumgay, J., (2004), 'Scripts for safer survival: Pathways out of female crime', *The Howard Journal of Criminal Justice,* **43**(4), pp. 405–419.

Schinkel, M. & Whyte, B., (2012), 'Routes out of prison using life coaches to assist resettlement', *The Howard Journal of Criminal Justice,* **51**(4), pp. 359–371.

Seddon, N., (2007), *Who cares? How state funding and political activism change charity.* London: The Institute for the Study of Civil Society.

Seppings, C., (2016), *To study the rehabilitative role of ex-prisoners/offenders as peer mentors in reintegration models – in the UK, Republic of Ireland, Sweden and USA.* Available at: www.churchilltrust.com.au/media/fellows/Seppings_C_2015_Rehabilitative_role_of_ex-prisoners__offenders_as_peer_mentors.pdf [Accessed August 2019].

Servan, A.K. & Mittelmark, M.B., (2012), 'Resources for coping among women ex-offenders', *International Journal of Mental Health Promotion,* **14**(5), pp. 254–263.

South, J., Bagnall, A.M. & Woodall, J., (2017), Developing a typology for peer education and peer support delivered by prisoners. *Journal of Correctional Health Care,* **23**(2), pp. 214–229.

Spalek, B., (2008), *Communities, identities and crime.* Bristol: Policy Press.

St Giles Trust, (2019), *Peer advisor programme.* Available at: www.stgilestrust.org.uk/page/peer-advisor-programme [Accessed August 2019].

Sullivan, C. & Jolliffe, D., (2012), Peer influence, mentoring, and the prevention of crime. In Welsh, B.C. & Farrington, D.P., (Eds.). *The Oxford handbook of crime prevention.* Oxford: Oxford University Press, pp. 207–266.

The Social Innovation Partnership, (2012), *The WIRE (Women's Information and Resettlement for Ex-offenders) evaluation report.* London: The Social Innovation Partnership. Available at: www.stgilestrust.org.uk/misc/Support%20for%20vulnerable%20women%20leaving%20prison%20full%20report.pdf [Accessed August 2019].

Tolan, P., Henry, D., Schoeny, M. & Bass, A., (2008), 'Mentoring interventions to affect juvenile delinquency and associated problems', *Campbell Systematic Reviews,* **4**(1), 1–112.

Tomczak, P., (2017), *The penal voluntary sector.* Abingdon, Oxon: Routledge.

Tomczak, P. & Buck, G., (2019a), 'The penal voluntary sector: A hybrid sociology', *The British Journal of Criminology,* **59**(4), pp. 898–918.

Tomczak, P. & Buck, G., (2019b), 'The criminal justice voluntary sector: concepts and an agenda for an emerging field', *Howard Journal of Crime and Justice,* **58**(3), 276–297.

Uggen, C. & Janikula, J., (1999), 'Volunteerism and arrest in the transition to adulthood', *Social Forces,* **78**(1), pp. 331–362.

User Voice (2018). *User voice founder visits Australia to spread the peer-led word.* Available at: www.uservoice.org/news/user-voice-news-blog/2018/07/mark-johnson-australia-visit/ [Accessed August 2019].

User Voice (2019) Website Available at: www.uservoice.org/ [Accessed January 2020].

Watson, A., (2019), 'Probation and volunteers in Japan', *Advancing Corrections Journal,* Edition no. 7. Available at: www.globcci.org/researchPapers/JapanProbationAC_Journal_2019_7_Article_3.pdf [Accessed October 2019].

Wildeman, C. & Wang, E.A., (2017), 'Mass incarceration, public health, and widening inequality in the USA', *The Lancet,* **389**, pp. 1464–1474.

Willoughby, M., Parker, A. & Ali, R., (2013), *Mentoring for offenders: Mapping services for adult offenders in England and Wales.* London: Sova.

Winter, K., Spengler, S., Bermpohl, F., Singer, T. & Kanske, P., (2017), 'Social cognition in aggressive offenders: Impaired empathy, but intact theory of mind', *Scientific Reports*, **7**(1), p. 670.

Wolch, J.R., (1990), *The shadow state: Government and voluntary sector in transition*. New York: Foundation Center.

Young, S., Gudjonsson, G., Chitsabesan, P., Colley, B., Farrag, E., Forrester, A., Hollingdale, J., Kim, K., Lewis, A., Maginn, S., Mason, P., Ryan, S., Smith, J., Woodhouse, E. & Asherson, P., (2018), 'Identification and treatment of offenders with attention-deficit/hyperactivity disorder in the prison population: A practical approach based upon expert consensus.' *BMC Psychiatry*, **18**(1), p. 281.

Zdun, S., (2011), 'Immigration as a trigger to knife off from delinquency? Desistance and persistence among male adolescents from the Former Soviet Union in Germany', *Criminology and Criminal Justice*, **11**(4), pp. 307–323.

Zimmerman, M.A., Bingenheimer, J.B. & Notaro, P.C., (2002), 'Natural mentors and adolescent resiliency: A study with urban youth', *American Journal of Community Psychology*, **30**(2), pp. 221–243.

Chapter 3

Theorising peer mentoring as a critical relational practice

Identity, pedagogy and collective politicisation

Whilst desistance scholarship offers a useful theoretical framework to hypothesise peer mentoring as a change process, and indeed has enabled a favourable context for peer mentoring to develop, peer mentoring is not *just* about leaving crime behind, it is also a process of learning, a form of coming together or solidarity and a political social activity. This chapter therefore draws upon wider interactionist theories to acknowledge multiple dynamics in mentoring relationships. In doing so it offers a theoretical framework to ground the analysis which follows. As attempts to define the practice are currently bounded by the limits of criminological literature, the chapter reaches to other disciplines to open out the analytical terrain, drawing upon the fields of education, sociology and theology. Despite disciplinary and explanatory diversity, each theory employed is congruent with *symbolic interaction*, that is:

> That human beings act toward things on the basis of the meanings that the things have for them... that the meaning of such things is derived from, or arises out of, the social interaction that one has with one's fellows... [and] that these meanings are handled in, and modified through, an interpretive process used by the person in dealing with the things [s]he encounters.
>
> (Blumer, 1969: 2)

Peer mentoring is not an independently measurable entity, but mentors and mentees *construct* its meanings in interaction with the experience, with other individuals and through interpretation. An interactionist perspective sheds light on mentoring in its complexity, not just as a way of supporting desistance, reducing reoffending or numerous other functional claims that have been made, but also as a practice that employs identity politics, has features of critical pedagogy, relies upon notions of fraternity or sorority and potentially politicises people.

Whilst several themes run through the [peer] mentoring literature, there is no coherent theory of peer mentoring by criminalised people. Approaches led by criminalised people potentially complement the aims of existing rehabilitation models, such as the risk-need-responsivity (RNR) model (Andrews & Bonta, 2010), by offering fewer antisocial associates and a supportive work situation (Lebel, Richie & Maruna, 2015: 111), and the Good Lives Model (Ward & Gannon, 2006; Ward & Marshal, 2004), in terms of gaining a sense of meaning, purpose (Lebel et al., 2015) and self-worth (Perrin, 2017), but there are more features to mentoring in this field than those explicitly related to offending and desistance. This chapter develops a fuller theory, arguing that there are four core precepts which underpin this work; precepts that can be traced throughout the literature but have not yet been formally drawn together or recognised. These are as follows: *The Identity Precept*, which considers mentoring as identity work; *The Pedagogical Precept*, which conceives of mentoring as a critical educational activity; *The Fraternity or Sorority Precept*, which has regard for the collective nature of the practice and *The Politicisation Precept*, which recognises the often-politicised nature of such contexts. This framework not only recognises efforts to help people change or 'desist', but also some of the manifold objectives of the practice, which have not been fully acknowledged to date.

The identity precept

The concept of identity is recognised as central to moving away from crime. The formation of a new identity can be central to an offender 'Making Good' (Maruna, 2001), and desisters often experience subjective changes in self and identity (McNeill, 2006: 46). There are also indications that peer mentoring may involve *identity work*. Brown and Ross (2010: 38) suggest that 'the narratives offenders construct around themselves, their circumstances and their future goes to the issue of human capital and would also be a reasonable process target for mentoring relationships'. Similarly, McNeill (2006) argued that: 'if sustained desistance requires a narrative reconstruction of identity, then it seems obvious why relational aspects of practice are so significant' (McNeill, 2006: 49). Peer recovery groups, such as Alcoholics Anonymous, encourage 'a transformation of [group member] identities, from drinking non-alcoholics to non-drinking alcoholics' (Holland, Skinner, Lachicotte & Cain, 1998: 66). Identity is therefore framed as an aspect of self which is central to desisting from crime and which can be positively shaped by interactions with peers or mentors. However, just *how* these social processes work is worthy of further scrutiny. This section theorises peer mentoring as identity work based upon three central elements: *mimetic desire* (Girard, 1977), *situated social performance* (Goffman, 1963) and *shared language* (Bernstein, 1971).

Identity as mimetic desire

Rene Girard's theory of mimesis (1962) is completely congruent with any practice reliant upon role modelling and identity. For Girard, identity does not emerge in isolation but rather it is preceded by desire, moreover, desire does not reside within the individual, but is shaped by social models:

> If desire is only mine, I will always desire the same things... to have mobility of desire... the relevant difference is imitation; that is the presence of the model or models... Mimetic desire is [what makes it possible for us to] construct our own, albeit inevitably unstable, identities.
>
> (Girard, 2010: 58)

Imitating the desires of others is theorised as key to changes in identity. In Girard's model, 'we do not desire to change spontaneously, but according to another person; we imitate the Other's desire' (Doran, 2008: xv). Mimetic models (or role models) are therefore fundamental to *what* people come to desire and *who* they become: 'the mimetic model directs the disciple's desire to a particular object by desiring it [her/] himself. That is why we can say that mimetic desire is rooted neither in the subject nor in the object, but in a third party whose desire is imitated by the subject' (Girard, 1977: 180). This dynamic is palpable if unarticulated within peer mentoring. Mentoring is constituted of mentees (intended 'disciples'), desired behaviour change (the object) and mentors (the third party). Mentors are positioned as 'role models' (Kavanagh & Borrill, 2013; Finnegan, Whitehurst & Denton, 2010; Parkin & McKeganey, 2000), suggesting implicitly that mentees will come to desire that which they see within their mentors (models). Desire to desist from crime, in these terms, is not inherent in a mentee from her or his own side, nor is there anything inherently desirable about 'going straight', but mentees require a model to direct their desire. The peer mentor's task is to activate mimetic desire in mentees. The *reformed offender* as role model constitutes a lived invitation to become: 'desire to desist, as have I'.

However, *peer* mentors are also positioned as role models based on a constructed point of connection, usually that their previous experiences of offending make them more *credible*. It is claimed that 'ex-offender' mentors have a 'credibility that statutory agencies don't often have' (Nellis & McNeill, 2008: xi) and that 'offenders are more likely to relate to a mentor who has previously been in prison' (The Princes Trust, 2008: 4). Shared similar past experiences are theorised to generate credibility and admiration. This aspect too is congruent with Girard's conception of mimetic desire. For Girard, the mimicker (mentee) selects a model that s/he admires and respects; 'if [s]he had not done so, [s]he would hardly have chosen him[her] as a model in the first place' (Girard, 1987: 290). It is reasoned that: '[w]e desire what we see others desire, and if we admire other people, our desire for what they want is all the sharper' (Hull, 2008: 594). The *status* of a mimetic model (mentor), as perceived by the protégé (mentee) is, therefore, regarded as important as the presence and actions of that model.

For Girard (1991), people can adapt their identity. Indeed, identity constantly shifts as a result of individuals selectively mimicking the desires of those whom they admire and respect. Importantly however, this is not a predictable process. People do not *always* imitate what they desire in another, but often experience an urge not to imitate:

> When we imitate successful rivals, we explicitly acknowledge what we would prefer to deny – their superiority. The urge to imitate is very strong, since it opens up possibilities of bettering the competition. But the urge not to imitate is also very strong. The only thing that the losers can deny the winners is the homage of their imitation.
>
> (Girard, 1991: 240)

Thus, power relations are integral to Girard's thesis. To mimic is to defer to, to pay 'homage'. Girard sees this process as essential in the human drive towards self-betterment, but he also argues that we reject this theory of self because it contradicts the dominant discourse in a modern world, which is 'arch-individualistic' (Girard, 2010: 58). Whilst our desires, indeed our very identities, are intrinsically linked to the social world we observe, this is not an aspect of ourselves we are comfortable with: 'the mimetic quality of child-hood desire is universally recognized. Adult desire is virtually identical, ex-cept that (most strikingly in our own culture) the adult is generally ashamed to imitate others for fear of revealing his lack of being' (Girard, 1977: 155). So, role models (mentors) may actually inspire a strong urge (in mentees) to become something *other* than what is modelled. This could lead to a mentee rejecting the modelled desire to 'go straight', as the intention of a mentee to deny homage is so strong. The very presence of mimetic models therefore introduces the potential for resistance to the offered ideal. In addition to the potential for rejected examples, there is a need to consider the ethics of en-couraging imitated desire through *ideal* models. Consider, for example, the recollections of bell hooks, as she recalls her experiences as a black scholar entering predominantly white institutions:

> Nonconformity on our part was viewed with suspicion... those of us from marginal groups who were allowed to enter prestigious, predomi-nantly white colleges were made to feel that we were not there to learn but to prove that we were the equal of whites. We were there to prove this by showing how well we could become clones of our peers.
>
> (hooks, 1994: 5)

hooks highlights how aspects of self can be subtly devalued or relegated as people are offered ideal models, whether these are implicit or explicit. In hooks' account these models are implicit, peer mentors are more explicit. People are overtly positioned as mentees (protégés) and offered mentors (models). Within this dynamic of presumed superiority and lack is potential for mentees to feel a similar pressure to become the 'clones of their peers'.

Whereas Girard (1987) theorises the mimetic processes underpinning identity, mentoring works to exploit such processes. Indeed, Girard himself argued that 'everything that we know under the titles of apprenticeship, education and initiation [to which I would add mentoring] rests on this capacity for mimesis' (Girard, 1987: 290). Whilst other approaches to rehabilitation, such as 'offender management' or cognitive behavioural work, promote desistance as a desirable *end* to be attained, peer mentoring invites desire for desistance by offering *models* who have already achieved it in the hope their desire will come to be shared. Like Girard, peer mentoring 'replaces an object-oriented conception of desire… with an intersubjective or "inter-individual" conception predicated on the power of the social' (Doran, 2008: xv). Nonetheless this process is problematic. Whilst mimesis can result in mimicked desire it can also result in rejected models, an urge not to imitate, dependent upon the will of the protégé (mentee). Furthermore, the presence of ideal models may serve to devalue aspects of the person on the 'receiving' side of the exchange.

Identity as situated performance

Whilst Girard's ideas are relevant to identity-based aspects of peer mentoring, his work is more concerned with desire than identity specifically. Erving Goffman (1963, 1961, 1959), however, is principally concerned with identity. For Goffman, identity is performative: people perform a variety of roles, they take on institutional definitions of identity and their character can be inferred from who their time is spent with. However, these roles and directions are far from stable and require interpretation:

> When the individual does move into a new position in society and obtains a new part to perform, he is not likely to be told in full detail how to conduct himself… he will be given only a few cues, hints and stage directions, and it will be assumed that he already has in his repertoire a large number of bits and pieces of performances that will be required in the new setting.
>
> (Goffman, 1959: 79)

Being 'socialised' to desist requires the transmission of 'pieces of expression' (Goffman, 1959: 79) (from mentors) and invention (from mentees). As a result: 'There is no essential character behind one's acts', rather 'the individual is free to perform, project and manage a variety of official and unofficial selves' (Hardie-Bick & Hadfield, 2011: 16). Identity, here, is a complex, multifarious set of performances, which take direction from a variety of sources. In this light, mentoring relationships become just one of several sites of stage direction and interpretive performance by mentors and mentees. Within the mentoring space, both mentors and mentees must look for hints to their role performance and fill the gaps from their side.

To complicate the interaction further, performances are subject to a social audience who have the power to shape the identity of the performer. Goffman (1963: 132) highlights, for example, how 'the stigmatized individual defines himself as no different from any other human being, while at the same time he and those around him define him as someone set apart'. The existing perceptions of the social audience, therefore, set the parameters of credibility in the performance being viewed. This feeds into the performance itself. A peer mentor's (or desisting mentee's) performance is only likely to be as successful as its audience decides it to be. Crucially however, there are two 'audiences' to consider here. Peer mentors constitute a social audience offering feedback to mentees as to whether the identity performance is successful (Asencio & Burke, 2011). On a broader level society constitutes an audience and within society 'a criminal conviction – no matter how trivial or how long ago it occurred – scars one for life' (Petersilia, 2003: 19). No matter how well an 'ex-offender' performs the desister role, of being 'no different', they may continue to be viewed as different by those around them. Where a social force as powerful as stigma is at work, the freedom to perform is limited. The social audience already has a strong perception of a person's pre-defined character and indeed often avoids contact on this premise. The very anticipation of 'mixed contact' between people who are stigmatised and people who are not can 'lead normals and the stigmatized to arrange life so as to avoid them' (Goffman, 1963: 23). This serves to undermine any performance on the stigmatised actor's part before it has begun. As a result, there is a sacrifice to be made: '[a]mong his own, the stigmatized individual can use his disadvantage as a basis for organizing life, but he must assign himself to a half-world to do so' (Goffman, 1963: 32). Whilst peer mentoring may offer an opportunity for criminalised people to belong, find purpose, and 'organise life', indeed it creates a valuable opportunity for people who often find it difficult to obtain work otherwise (Clinks & MBF, 2012), it can also be a restricting practice, one in which mentors are necessarily identified by past offending. As a result, they are seen as targets for bullying or pressure to pass drugs, mobile phones or information (Boyce, Hunter & Hough, 2009; Devilly, Sorbello, Eccleston & Ward, 2005) and face difficulties in relation to access and criminal history clearance (Clinks & MBF, 2012). In Goffman's terms, they are consigned to a 'half world'. There is also another problem faced by those aiming to *employ* their stigma:

> In making a profession of their stigma, native leaders [e.g. peer mentors] are obliged to have dealings with representatives of other categories, and so find themselves breaking out of the closed circle of their own kind. Instead

of leaning on their crutch, they get to play golf with it, ceasing, in terms of social participation, to be representative of the people they represent.

(Goffman, 1963: 39)

In aiming to reduce the border between stigmatised and normal, the 'native leader' becomes lost in the wasteland: no longer representative, but also not 'normal' (Goffman, 1963). Collins and Evans (2007: 3) have argued that acquiring expertise is 'a social process – a matter of socialization into the practices of an expert group – and expertise can be lost if time is spent away from the group'. This fragile space is potentially one which peer mentors come to inhabit. As they do so they are potentially doubly disadvantaged, perceived as 'risky' by criminal justice service providers *and* potentially detached/out of touch by their peers and therefore not representative. This bind is recognised by Scott, Doughty and Kahi (2011: 188) who frame peer support is a 'liminal occupation', a state of being 'in-between' two identities, which results in unease as people are drawn in two directions at once. This tension is explored further in Chapters 5 and 8 as observers ask questions about mentors' credibility and their close alignment with punitive criminal justice systems.

Goffman and Girard both imagine the self as dependent upon social interactions for its shape. For Girard this shape is born of mimetic desire, for Goffman the process is more of a dialectic performance correlated with situational routine and audience. Peer mentors and mentees, viewed in Goffman's terms, are essentially social performers. The mentee, as potential *desister,* receives direction from situational rules and social cues; including the 'stage directions' provided by peer mentors. However, performances of identity also require individual improvisation, the mentee therefore needs to interpret what is expected of *desister* and *client* roles and manage these expectations. Goffman also illustrates how audiences help to define these performances. Because peer mentors straddle the border between 'offender' and 'desister' they meet potential problems in terms of how their new identity performance is interpreted by those around them, which may undermine their position as 'role models' in the eyes of both professional and lay observers.

Identity as defined and constrained by language

Whilst Girard and Goffman see identity as intertwined with the social – with models and the performing of modes – Basil Bernstein (1971) views identity as constituted through language, arguing 'it is through specific linguistic codes that relevance is created, experience given a particular form, and social identity constrained' (Bernstein, 1971: 146). Class relations are integral to his thesis. In his provocative work *Class, Codes and Control* (1971), Bernstein contends that there are 'entirely different modes of speech found within the middle class and the lower working class' (Bernstein, 1971: 78). The lived realities of people from different class backgrounds are seen as fundamentally different because the very language, which constitutes that reality has observable variations. Bernstein asserts that 'the typical, dominant speech mode of the middle class… facilitates verbal elaboration of subjective intent' (1971: 78), whilst the 'lower' working class are:

> …limited to a form of language use, which although allowing for a vast range of possibilities, provides a speech form which discourages the speaker from verbally elaborating subjective intent and progressively orients the user to descriptive, rather than abstract, concepts.
>
> (Bernstein, 1971: 79)

This early work of Bernstein draws attention to the capacity for language to both express and constitute a category of identity (in this case social class). This sentiment can also be traced within peer mentoring literature. Turner and Shepherd (1999), for example, make sense of peer education in terms of 'subculture theories', drawing upon Cohen (1955), who argued that 'delinquents developed subcultures which promote values and behaviour which were oppositional to mainstream culture', and Miller (1958) who argued that 'working class culture is oppositional to middle class culture' (Turner & Shepherd, 1999: 242). These 'subculture theories' are applied to four elements of peer education, namely that peers are a 'credible source of information', that peer education 'formalizes an already established means of sharing information and advice', that education by peers 'may be acceptable when other education is not' and that 'peer education can be used to educate those who are hard to reach through conventional methods' (Turner & Shepherd, 1999: 242). Whilst subculture theories centre on social class, the peer mentoring literature more commonly implies that the language of *lived experience* and *professional expertise* is what differs. Devilly et al. (2005: 231), for example, argue that peers 'are deemed more credible sources of information because they have experienced similar struggles and are, therefore, able to "speak the same language"'. Carl Cattermole's (2019) reflective account of prison and its aftermath offers two completely different glossaries of language used by prisoners and imprisoners (pp. 181–186). Other writers, whilst not referencing language specifically, point to mentoring reducing the inaccessibility of professional services, through '"outreach workers" linking individuals with local services that they would otherwise fail to access' (Newburn & Shiner, 2006: 27) or the 'targeting of mentoring for those variously identified as "disaffected", "disengaged", "non-participating", or "hardest to help"' (Colley, 2002: 9). The clear implication here is that non-peers or professional interveners are not connecting with their intended clients or are even speaking a different language.

The notion that the knowledge of socially similar others has more credibility than professionally constructed knowledge is also one which Bernstein aims to make sense of. He argues that theories of learning (in North America) have been influenced by psychological theories, which place an overwhelming emphasis upon the significance of the early years of the child's life. These ideas 'are likely to view problems of educability as arising out of interactions which are considered to be deficient, inadequate or even pathological' (Bernstein, 1971: 274). As a result, 'much of the research into "who is able to learn what" was carried out by psychologists whose intellectual training and whose own socialisation led them to define the problem in a limited way' (Bernstein, 1971: 274). He goes on to suggest that:

> It was only with the radicalising of American academics through Vietnam, the rise of Black Power, through the exposure of the failure of the American urban school, that fundamental questions were raised about the political implications of forms of education during the late sixties.
>
> (Bernstein, 1971: 274)

Bernstein juxtaposes the dominant discourse about how people learn with movements to challenge this dominance. In doing so he contends that accepted 'professional' truths are open to the challenge that the social world can be experienced and communicated differently by people from different social backgrounds. Moreover, difference is not necessarily indicative of deficit, but can expand understanding. This argument is echoed by those attempting to explain the emergence of peer mentoring. These explanations privilege *personal insight* into prison life, which offers ex-offenders 'a *credibility* that statutory agencies don't often have' (Nellis & McNeill, 2008: xi; emphasis added). Peers are claimed to have *specific knowledge* about risk and realistic strategies to reduce risk (Devilly et al., 2005: 223; emphasis added). This quiet but insistent privileging of lived experiences tacitly challenges notions of deficit inherent in dominant forms of intervention. It also has the potential to shift from pathological versions of 'criminal' deficit and towards deficiencies in the social and penal order. Bernstein also recognised, however, that variations in language codes are not limited to different classes or different status positions, but are also situational:

> The speech used by members of an army combat unit on manoeuvres will be somewhat different from the same members' speech at a padre's evening. Different forms of social relations can generate quite different speech–systems or linguistic codes.
>
> (Bernstein, 1971: 145)

People therefore relay meaning through codes, which differ by setting as they do social strata. Indeed, a similar linguistic division was also recognised by Goffman in the context of the asylum:

> An institutional lingo develops through which inmates describe the events that are crucial in their particular world. The staff, especially its

lower levels, will know this language, too, and use it when talking to inmates, reverting to more standardized speech when talking to superiors
and outsiders.

(Goffman, 1961: 55)

If language bears a print of social class and situated experience and these
prints carry and constitute meaning, this may explain why criminalised
people claim to *relate* to people with shared histories and why their peers
find them 'credible'. Common experience leads to common language and
elements of a common reality. Whilst Bernstein's work helps to make sense
of this key connecting element within peer mentoring, he is not without
criticism. His early work 'was highly controversial because it discussed
social class differences in language that some labelled a deficit theory'
(Sadovnik, 2008: 21). Indeed, Labov argued that 'Bernstein's views are
filtered through a strong bias against all forms of working-class behaviour
so that middle-class language is seen as superior in every respect' (cited in
Bernstein, 1971: 273). Bernstein, however, responded to these criticisms
by arguing:

> In a fundamental sense, a restricted code is the basic code. It is the code
> of intimacy which shapes and changes the very nature of subjective ex-
> perience, initially in the family and in our close personal relationships.
> The intensifications and condensations of such communication carry us
> beyond speech, and new forms of awareness often become possible.
>
> (Bernstein, 1971: 275)

For Bernstein, it is not that middle-class codes of speech are superior to lower
working-class codes, but that they operate in linguistically and therefore con-
ceptually different ways. Moreover, this difference allows for exclusionary
practice:

> Bernstein argued that different social classes used different 'codes' in
> their language, and the middle/upper classes developed 'elaborate' codes
> which restricted access to the education system they devised and ran.
>
> (Rowlingston & McKay, 2012: 195)

By this reasoning, in order to minimise inequality of opportunity between
social classes, there is a need to recognise the different codes in operation
and how they can be exclusionary. Peer mentoring quietly makes a similar
claim. By insisting that mentors have experiential credentials, which are as
valuable as academic credentials and that they speak a particular 'language',
its advocates suggest there is something excluding about the reality imposed
by expert forms of understanding. Whilst Bernstein's theory of language has
met with controversy, his central thesis that language codes differ in different
social contexts and settings, and indeed that this has a direct bearing on the

possibilities of social identity, are relevant to peer mentoring. These ideas help us to consider how language is perceived and used in mentoring relationships. Bernstein also alerts us to the potential for subtle processes of social control and personal limitation where administrators of education employ different language techniques to some of their 'beneficiaries'. Indeed, as mentoring itself is a form of education, any theoretical work must also acknowledge pedagogical processes.

The pedagogical precept

Whilst the importance of identity is relatively well recognised, less has been written about peer mentoring as a form of critical education. The 'pedagogical precept' proposed here explores the principles of teaching and learning, which underpin peer mentoring. One of the important and overlooked ways this practice can be theorised is as a process of social learning. A pedagogical precept denoted by forms of 'intervention', whilst not yet theorised, is arguably the most dominant principle of peer mentoring which can be traced in the literature to date. The job of the mentor is to draw upon the personal experience of going straight, to 'steer' mentees and to convey educational messages (UNODC, 2002), to run 'programmes' (MoJ, 2011) and to help with practical tasks (Hunter & Kirby, 2011). The job therefore is to educate. The desired outcomes are generally changes in the mentee, including reductions in re-offending; aggression; and drug use and/or improved attitudes, behaviours or academic achievement. Despite being grounded in ideals of transformative intervention, however, peer mentoring can also be conceived as having a more radical character. It permits into the field of criminal justice a voice of experience, which has long been relegated in the construction of truths about crime and change:

> [K]nowledge generated outside scientific discourses such as lived experiences, autobiographies and memories can be silenced, 'subjugated or disqualified'... prisoners' version of 'the truth' is located at the bottom of the hierarchy of knowledge – subjugated, disqualified, or 'muted' altogether.
> (Ballinger, 2011: 110)

Through peer mentoring the (ex-)prisoner's version of 'the truth' is elevated; it is central to the intervention. This moves 'beyond the cognitive deficit model to harness the strengths residing in peer support networks' (Weaver, 2012: 407). However, this radical potential co-exists with a focus which remains upon 'offenders' as recipients, as subjects who require improvement with the help of morally superior others. It therefore sustains the corrective, normative ethos, which is already dominant in criminal justice interventions.

The work of critical educator Paulo Freire is helpful in terms of theorising this tension. Freire's critique explored how normative *teaching* conveys unacknowledged power relations. As a result, he proposed that pedagogy must 'be forged with, not for, the oppressed' (1970: 30), that learning must not be: 'explaining to, but rather dialoguing with people about their actions' (1970: 35). Freire's critique fundamentally questions the construction of experts and receivers within educational practices. He calls for a rejection of the established 'banking' concept of education, which turns students into 'containers', into 'receptacles' to be 'filled' by the teacher (Freire, 1970: 53) in favour of 'libertarian education', which 'must begin with the solution of the teacher-student contradiction, by reconciling the poles of the contradiction so that both are simultaneously teachers and students' (Freire, 1970: 53). Freire contends that: 'The banking approach to adult education... will never propose to students that they critically consider reality' (1970: 55), whereas: 'To exchange the role of depositor, prescriber, domesticator, for the role of student among students would be to undermine the power of oppression and serve the cause of liberation' (Freire, 1970: 56). Freire therefore advocates that we abandon 'the educational goal of deposit making and replace it with the posing of the problems of human beings in their relations with the world' (1970: 60). This indeed appears to be one of the premises of peer mentoring:

> peer relationships are unique because they offer a degree of mutuality that enables both individuals to experience being the giver and receiver of key functions, in contrast to a traditional mentoring relationship where the mentor specialized in the role of guide or sponsor.
>
> (Ensher, Thomas & Murphy, 2001: 423)

Here a 'peer' is a person of equal position, as distinct from a person who shares a similar past. Applied to a criminal justice context, peer mentoring potentially enables people to 'feel like masters of their thinking and views of the world explicitly or implicitly manifest in their own suggestions and those of their comrades' (Freire, 1970: 105). Rather than having their future goals 'banked' by *expert* others, mentees can explore the possibility of an alternative future with peers who are living this reality. Freire did indeed reference mentoring specifically as a form of learning and argued that the mentor's task is a 'liberatory' one. It is not to 'encourage the mentor's goals and aspirations and dreams to be reproduced in the mentees, the students, but to give rise to the possibility that the students become the owners of their own history' (Freire, 1997: 342). This is echoed in claims that peer mentoring can increase a sense of agency, by enabling recipients to feel autonomous and resolve their own problems without professional assistance (Shelter, 2010; Pollack, 2004).

Such ideals are not without criticism, however. Roger Lancaster (1988: 199) 'saw Freire's analysis as a kind of "orientalism" that casts the poor as inanimate and inert, almost prereflective, predialogic "things" devoid of all subjectivity' (cited in Scheper-Hughes, 1992: 531). Freire's mission to liberate

the oppressed was claimed by Lancaster to have been subject to the same patterns of hierarchical imposition that he aimed to overcome:

> Freire proposed literacy as the vehicle for establishing creative dialogue,
> insofar as the illiteracy of rural Brazilians in the modern state was a
> source and symbol of their "muteness". The irony (or the final "insult")
> was Freire's suggestion that the silent oppressed had to be "taught" to
> surrender their passivity and their fear of taking direct action. Freire's
> radical pedagogy was marred, Lancaster suggested, by a false notion of
> dialogue, insofar as it depends on the role of the "teacher-vanguard"
> to enter the imprisoned community from without to initiate reflexive
> speech, to rupture the silence of the oppressed, and to release the long-
> trapped flow and exchange of ideas, language, and critical thinking.
>
> (Cited in Scheper-Hughes, 1992: 531)

This is a useful critique. Whilst peer mentoring can be viewed as an attempt to open 'creative dialogue', it might equally constitute a form of
paternalist awakening inspired by a more 'enlightened' other: 'an initiative
consisting of trained individuals volunteering to support people with specific or multiple needs to provide practical advice and guidance' (Clinks,
2012: 8). Chapter 9 reveals that such paternalism is as visible in how mentors are trained, prepared for, or governed in the role, as it is in how
mentees are mentored.

Problems with the egalitarian ideal

Lancaster's (1988) critique gets to the heart of an issue, which will be a recurrent theme in this study, that is, the legitimacy of identity positions which
appear to have crossed a border. The 'ex-offender', for example, has been an
offender and is now a *desister*. Her or his lived reality straddles two identity
positions; they can relate to being both. Similarly, Paulo Freire was part of
the oppressed poor in Brazil but became a prominent teacher and theorist.
His knowledge of lived reality, too, straddled two very different identity positions. Whilst Lancaster is partially correct to identify a 'teacher-vanguard'
element to Freire's argument (wherein he positions himself as an external
teacher initiating and releasing those currently less able), he misses the significance of Freire's own history. What marks him out for Lancaster (1988) is his
crossing the border from dispossessed learner to recognised theorist, which
then highlights a tension. When do 'the oppressed', powerless or stigmatised,
by empowering themselves, leave the shared struggle, or even come to be
viewed as part of the oppression? Is the border of two identities a space from
which one can legitimately speak from and to both sides of the border, or will
tensions of voice arise? To use Goffman's terms (1963: 39) it may be inevitable
that 'native leaders... instead of leaning on their crutch, they get to play golf

with it, ceasing, in terms of social participation, to be representative of the people they represent'. A potential problem with straddling two perceived identity positions (be it 'pauper' and 'theorist' or 'offender' and 'mentor'), however, is that it may weaken the credibility or authenticity of the message for some listeners. Regardless of whether learners within critical pedagogy need to be 'taught to surrender their passivity' (Lancaster, 1988: 199), it is clear that protégés in this model are not inert receptors, but necessarily active agents. Indeed, Freire argues that:

> No pedagogy which is truly liberating can remain distant from the oppressed by treating them as unfortunates and by presenting for their emulation models from among the oppressors. The oppressed must be their own example in the struggle for their redemption.
>
> (Freire, 1970: 36)

To a degree peer mentoring exemplifies this ideal. 'Ex-offenders', as stigmatised 'others', come to occupy spaces of power within the educational exchange when they become mentors; unseating expert models and setting their own example. This represents a potential dissolution of the power dynamic Freire critiques. Simultaneously however, Freire's arguments problematise peer mentoring. First, whilst peers do appear to offer a sense of mutuality or equity not present in more hierarchical, directive educational relationships, peer mentoring remains a space where people perform a more structured educational role than in non-structured peer relationships. There is a focus, for example, on 'endorsing "healthy" norms, beliefs and behaviours... and challenging those who are "unhealthy"' (UNODC, 2002), often as part of a broader criminal justice intervention (MoJ, 2011). The sense of mutuality is therefore undermined in both aim and context. Second, peer mentoring carries an implicit expectation that mentees come to emulate their mentors. Whilst striving for a more equal learning plane than traditional educational forms, peer mentoring nonetheless offers models to emulate and assumes that mentees require intervention by a superior other. In this case, the mentor is rendered superior by virtue of having mastered 'going straight', rather than in terms of social status and resources. It therefore maintains a hierarchical approach to knowledge acquisition. Moreover, there is an obscure third-party present within this hierarchy. Criminal justice peer mentoring does not exist independently, but services are almost always required to seek funding for their work. To do so they often need to fit the agendas and targets of external funders, which may result in 'drift' from the original vision (Buck & Jaffe, 2011). This is a critique that has been recognised in the context of youth work where, 'the practice of mentoring increasingly reflects class interests, particularly the intrusion of powerful political, institutional and business priorities into supposedly dyadic relationships' (Colley, 2001: 179). Colley argues that there have been four distinct historical stages in the development of mentoring, which have shifted it from 'dominant groupings reproducing their own power, to subordinate groupings reproducing their own oppression' (Colley, 2002: 257). It is helpful to consider Colley's analysis in detail in order to assess the context in which today's peer mentoring emerges.

Colley considers mentoring through classical pedagogical models. She argues that the first historical stage of mentoring (the Homeric stage) resides in mythology and involves 'the (all) powerful [Greek God Athene] mentoring the powerful [King's son Telemachus] to ensure the continuation of the nascent patriarchy and the suppression of matrilineal social forms' (Colley, 2002: 264). Stage two (the Classical stage) is characterised by 'quasi-parental' relationships between exceptional individuals. It is 'activity carried out by the powerful on behalf of the powerful, in order to preserve their dominant social status... Its essence is thus an intra-class and gendered reproductive function, the transmission of cultural capital' (Colley, 2002: 264–265). Stage three (the Victorian stage) identifies middle-class mentors befriending working class families in order to improve them by presenting a moral example. It is seen as 'a direct instrument of domination of one class over another with the same essential goal of preserving the status of the ruling class' (Colley, 2002: 266). The fourth and final (Modern) stage, ushered in by New Labour's social exclusion agenda 'has become openly associated with the moral aim of altering the attitudes, beliefs, values and behaviour of the targeted group... in line with employment-related goals determined by welfare-to-work policies' (Colley, 2002: 267). In terms of personnel, this work resembles the 'weak mentoring the weak' as non-professional staff, with less qualifications and training and lower pay mentor socially excluded people (Colley, 2002: 267–268).

Considered in the light of Colley's history, peer mentoring utilises underprepared (usually unpaid) staff undertaking emotionally demanding work with relatively powerless protégés, whilst subtly directed by the monies and missions of powerful stakeholders. In a criminal justice context, much of the 'power' to spend monies and direct 'missions' currently lies with state or private agencies. The recent (failed) 'Transforming Rehabilitation' experiment (see Corcoran & Carr, 2019) awarded the majority of prime rehabilitation contracts to large private corporations (MoJ, 2014), whilst several charities were cut adrift losing 'sources of referral, professional and interpersonal contacts and their place in local criminal justice networks' (Corcoran et al., 2019: 105). Although Probation in the UK has now been renationalised, 'innovation' partnerships with the private or voluntary sector remain a key objective (HMPPS, 2019). It is unclear, yet, whether peer mentoring in such a context will offer those with lived experience an equitable voice within criminal justice, or whether mentoring will merely become an affordable 'innovative' add-on to marketised and regulatory forms of offender management.

The works of Freire and Colley highlight tensions inherent in peer mentoring as a pedagogical project, specifically, the unspoken power asymmetries created by pedagogical practice. Peer mentoring offers role models and aims to deposit information – thus resembling a banking concept of education; it also resembles a 'weak mentoring the weak' model, which may serve to perpetuate the oppression of subordinate groups. However, it is also a practice which strives to bring about reform and implies a commitment to critical dialogue: '[w]e work to provide ways that enable unheard voices; to make a difference, to urge policy-makers and people with power who make decisions to listen' (User Voice, 2014). Peer mentoring is therefore currently engaged in a difficult balance between banking received, status quo knowledge and critically challenging received truths.

The first two precepts (*Identity* and *Pedagogy*) proposed here represent prevailing themes in current understandings of peer mentoring. They position mentoring as an intervention upon the individual, be it in order to influence identity shift or teach new skills. Both underlying aims concur (in focus at least) with dominant discourses about criminality, that is, that 'the offender' is flawed and needs external intervention to bring them back into line with the ideals of social conformity. The next two principles that this chapter introduces represent less dominant, underlying themes within the claims for peer mentoring, which are present nonetheless. The *Fraternity or Sorority Precept* and the *Politicisation Precept* both actively challenge the assumption that 'the offender' is lacking. These precepts suggest that peer mentoring is not simply concerned with individual change, but also social change, a practice which aims to shape the social view of 'offenders'.

The fraternity or sorority precept

Notions of brotherhood or sisterhood run through the peer mentoring literature, from concepts of 'Big brothers, Big sisters' and 'Buddies' in early US studies (Grossman & Tierney, 1998; O'Donnell, Lydgate & Fo, 1979) to more recent conceptions of female mentors who fashion entire communities outside of prison walls to offer emotional support (Collica, 2010). The fraternity or sorority precept acknowledges these foundational, familial ideals and processes of people finding community or solidarity with 'folks like themselves' (hooks, 1993: 77). These are often folks of the same gender, as, for example, in mentoring projects specifically for women (see Rumgay, 2004). However, there is more to such identifications than gender alone. They can be more accurately described as myriad forms of 'resistance building – the notion that peers can form solidaristic groups to protect themselves' (Pawson, 2004: 52). Chapter 4 will introduce a research field which identifies peer-hood in diverse ways. 'Peers' will be conceived of as *ex-offenders, community members, female offenders, gang-leavers* and *care leavers*, amongst others. In all the fieldwork sites, however, the act of mentoring as a peer appears to involve much more than just offering special insight, gaining trust or being an inspiration. It also appears to involve bonding with others who share a common experience and using this bond to allow space for marginalised perspectives. Jordan (1992) frames such processes as *relational resilience*:

> Joining others in mutually supporting and meaningful relationships most clearly allows us to move out of isolation and powerlessness. Energy flows back into connection, joining with others is a powerful antidote to immobilization and fragmentation. It is thus an antidote to trauma. Moreover, the ability to join with others and become mobilized can further efforts towards a more just society.
>
> (Jordan, 1992: 9)

Weaver and Weaver (2016: 225) point to the centrality of reciprocity or mutual exchange in the desistance process, arguing that solidarity or a sense of 'we-ness' enables support without dependence achieved through interdependence and trust. Members of a user-led fraternity or sorority can assert a perspective on crime and desistance because they have lived through particular experiences. In this way the precept shares something with feminist standpoint epistemology, which: 'identifies women's status as that of victim and then privileges that status by claiming that is gives access to understanding about oppression that others cannot have' (Stanley & Wise, 1993: 91). Standpoint epistemology supposedly 'makes possible a view of the world that is more reliable and less distorted than that available to capitalist or to working class men' (Stanley & Wise, 1993: 91). Whilst peer mentors and mentees are not (always) clearly identified in terms of a victim status, peer mentoring does privilege the offender's, female offender's, care leaver's, or gang leaver's status, claiming it gives access to an understanding that others cannot have. To quote a respondent of Boyce et al. (2009: 29): 'I'm able to understand and be empathic towards my client group, because a lot of their situations I've been in myself'. The practice therefore offers up forms of *criminalised standpoint epistemology*. It positions peer mentors and mentees as members of a collective. Their role is also to create a space for voices and truths, which may not be recognised or evident outside of first-hand experience. The common voice of the mentoring fraternity or sorority need not just be a 'female' or 'male' voice or even an 'ex-offender' voice, but a voice from any marginalised standpoint. The power of shared standpoint, for otherwise unacknowledged perspectives, has been highlighted by Stanley and Wise (1993), who argued, in the context of obscene phone calls they received on a lesbian group contact number:

> The only people who immediately accepted our reactions as valid-for-us were other women who had similarly experienced such reactions from men; and these were mainly other lesbians. If other women have shared similar experiences then they're willing to accept ours as valid; and if they haven't then they are much less willing to do so.
>
> (Stanley & Wise, 1993: 129)

Whilst this context differs from peer mentoring, the underpinning assumption is the same: that people who have not shared similar experiences do not afford the lived experience validity. Hence 'prisoners' version of "the truth" is located at the bottom of the hierarchy of knowledge' in professional circles (Ballinger 2011: 110) and recovering inmates are 'more capable of establishing credibility and demonstrating understanding [amongst peers] compared to hired treatment staff' (Fletcher & Batty, 2012: 6).

Experience and validity are intricately linked. If an audience cannot relate to a position, they may not achieve understanding. The achievement of validity is not solely dependent upon shared or recognised experiences, however, but also upon power relations: 'Those people with less power, those people without power – the oppressed – are more likely than those with power to find their accounts of reality discredited by others' (Stanley & Wise, 1993: 147). Given the power of criminal stigma the 'ex/offender' may feel that s/he faces a social field where 'valid-for-us' truths are highly restricted. Peer mentoring by contrast, not only makes valid-for-us truths possible, but central. The problem with employing standpoint in this way, is that it 'can slip into essentialist arguments' (Henry & Milovanovic, 1996: 85). Essentialism is 'most commonly understood as a belief in the real, true essence of things, the invariable and fixed properties which define the 'whatness' of a given entity' (Fuss, 1989: xi). To create a criminalised standpoint is therefore to suggest there is a true and unified essence of the criminal experience, when this is evidently not the case. Above the more general 'anti-essentialist poststructuralist feminist' concern with 'resisting any attempt to naturalise human nature' (Fuss, 1989: xi), a problem with reformed offenders employing essentialist arguments is that: '"Experience" emerges as the essential truth of the individual subject, and personal "identity" metamorphoses into knowledge... Exclusions of this sort often breed exclusivity' (Fuss, 1989: 113–115). This is a concern shared by Spalek (2008: 13): 'it would be a mistake to view the collectivisation of identities in a solely positive way, since group identities are formed and reinvigorated through the "threat and practice of exclusion"'. To draw upon experience as a claim to knowledge can therefore exclude those who do not share that experience:

> The politics of experience sometimes takes the form of a tendency amongst both individuals and groups to 'one down' each other on the oppression scale. Identities are itemised, appreciated and ranked on the basis of which identity holds the greatest currency at a particular historical moment and in a particular institutional setting. Thus, in an Afro-American Studies classroom, race and ethnicity are likely to emerge as the privileged items of intellectual exchange, or, in a Gay Studies classroom, sexual 'preference' may hold the top notch on the scale of oppressions.
>
> (Fuss, 1989: 116)

In the context of peer mentoring, workers who are not ex-offenders often find their claims to knowledge relegated beneath those with a history of offending: 'Only offenders can stop re-offending' (User Voice, 2019, emphasis added). Such hierarchising excludes other perspectives. bell hooks encourages that we consider these criticisms more closely however. Her counter-argument is that charges of essentialism tend to be directed at already marginalised groups who have already had to struggle for a voice of recognition, thus such criticisms can compound their invisibility:

> I am suspicious when theories call this practice harmful as a way of suggesting that it is a strategy only marginalized groups employ... [This] leaves unquestioned the critical practices of other groups who employ the same strategies in different ways and whose exclusionary behavior may be firmly buttressed by institutionalized structures of domination that do not critique or check it. At the same time I am concerned that critiques of identity politics not serve as the new, chic way to silence students from marginal groups.
>
> (hooks, 1994: 82–83)

For hooks, essentialism becomes a valid strategy to try and counter such negation:

> Looked at from a sympathetic standpoint, the assertion of an excluding essentialism on the part of [people] from marginalized groups can be a strategic response to domination and colonization, a survival strategy that may indeed inhibit discussion even as it rescues those students from negation.
>
> (hooks, 1994: 83)

Thus, whilst ex-offenders may employ essentialism in ways which appear to exclude others, they are not alone in employing such a strategy. The *essentialising* of offenders is commonplace outside of peer mentoring narratives. Maruna, for example, argues that 'academic criminology has at times acted as an active coproducer of the discourse of criminal essentialism' (Maruna, 2001: 6). To be too critical of adopted essentialism within emerging ex-offender voices may, therefore, serve to silence a group with a marginal voice; a group whose truth is already written for them in essentialist terms by others. Viewed sympathetically, the essentialism employed by ex-offender peer mentors emerges as a strategic response to the professional, risk culture dominated, colonisation of their lived experiences to this point. However, whilst making essentialist claims to knowledge may serve the purpose of reclaiming voice and may establish a valid position from which to speak, the problem, as hooks highlights, is that as a strategic response it is as 'inhibiting' as it is 'rescuing'. Essentialism creates a fiction of unified experience, which can be

as restrictive to the emergence of diverse voices as externally imposed exclusions, yet it is part of the complex reality of peer mentoring. This book
will pay close attention to the manifold ways and contexts in which subject-
position is deployed. Chapters 6, 7 and 9, for example, will explore how essentialism materialises via expressions of personal worth, self-validation and
personal dignity alongside forms of alterity, claims of distinction from and
criticisms of others.

Politicisation precept

A fourth way that peer mentoring can be theorised is as an act of consciousness-
raising or politicisation. Consciousness-raising provides a means for challenging oppression in solidarity with others who identify the same way (Gilchrist,
Bowles & Wetherell, 2010: 22).

> Thus, communities of identity develop as pressure groups and social
> movements, campaigning against different forms of discrimination and
> offering mutual support. Claiming the relevant identity in order to be
> part of these networks allows people to enjoy positive affirmation of their
> experience, contribute to collective action and may open up new insights
> into how to gain opportunities in an unfair world.
>
> (Gilchrist et al., 2010: 22)

The politicisation precept recognises the personal-political facet of peer mentoring and makes sense of peer mentoring as a form of collective action.
Coordinators and mentors capitalise upon emerging peer voices to raise new
forms of awareness, be it by engaging those who have experience of the
criminal justice system in bringing about its reform (User Voice, 2014) or
in the context of recovery from addiction, 'community education' shifting
'pathology-focused discussions within the community to solution-focused
discussions' (White, 2009: 24). Indeed, Maruna argues that:

> The next chapter of the desistance story will largely be written by de-
> sisting ex-prisoners themselves... Reframing the understanding of de-
> sistance as not just an individual process or journey, but rather a social
> movement, in this way better highlights the structural obstacles inherent
> in the desistance process and the macro-social changes necessary to suc-
> cessfully create a 'desistance-informed' future.
>
> (Maruna, 2017: 6)

The fraternity/sorority precept is a necessary precursor for this element as
it establishes the common position from which action and shared purpose
can emerge. Indeed, forming a fraternity or sorority, although perhaps not
consciously so, constitutes political action in itself. Identifying with others

through the construction of an ex-offender experience constitutes what hooks (1994) terms 'identity politics', which emerge she argues: 'out of the struggles of oppressed or exploited groups to have a standpoint on which to critique dominant structures, a position that gives purpose and meaning to struggle' (hooks, 1994: 89). Like Freire she holds that 'critical pedagogies... necessarily embrace experience, confessions and testimony as relevant ways of knowing, as important, vital dimensions of any learning process' (hooks, 1994: 89). Politicisation is already nascent therefore in the adjacent precepts of critical pedagogy and fraternal standpoint. The 'politicisation' precept itself refers to a more deliberate, organised aim. Peer mentoring in this light is understood as part of a voluntary sector or civil society space, which has aims additional to functional or practical assistance:

> Civil society is a space where ordinary people enter into dialogue about power, privilege and rights; come together to develop and express local cultural, economic and gender identities and needs in ways that go beyond voting or consuming; act collectively to make demands on the state... and proactively seek to fulfil their own interests and needs with others who share these interests and needs.
>
> (Sandler & Mein, 2010: 169)

Peer mentoring is understood here not just as an interpersonal practice, but as part of a larger 'social movement' of reformed offenders:

> For... groups with stigmatised identities, social movements and equality campaigns have been vital in affirming pride in different dimensions of identity and creating the momentum for increased integration and acceptance. Over the past few decades identity politics, based on collective self-organisation, have built both self-esteem and community empowerment for many people experiencing disadvantage and oppression.
>
> (Gilchrist et al., 2010: 22)

In this model, peer mentoring personnel not only provide a service based on 'shared interests and needs' (Sandler & Mein, 2010), but also behave as public advocates; promoting the integration and acceptance of those they see as oppressed or misrepresented. Their aims are to establish new understandings on a broader stage, to secure more effective resources or services and to challenge discrimination. For example, many voluntary sector providers, including *St Giles Trust, The Princes Trust, The Prison Reform Trust* and *User Voice*, campaign to raise awareness of the positive potential of reformed offenders and to improve housing and employment opportunities for them. Similarly, every one of the projects in this study are involved in some form of consciousness-raising activity, be it through publishing academic articles, organising or speaking at conferences, contributing to multi-agency forums or challenging professional partners (see Chapters 4 and 9).

Despite this emphasis on social activism, or consciousness-raising as an associated practice, mentoring itself perpetuates assumptions about the status and role of 'beneficiaries'. The role of the mentee in this model is to be a 'client'. On the one hand, peer mentoring questions the existing order of criminal justice, particularly the social exclusion of offenders and the demotion of their voices. For mentees, however, peer mentoring retains elements of hierarchy, paternalism and *speaking for*, which appear to be being fought against. In this sense, it is not a critical practice but upholds a 'client'-based model. Some of the theorists already considered in this chapter cast interesting light on the politicisation precept. Goffman, for example, examined the notion of the stigmatised speaking on behalf of their peers:

> [A]nother of their [representatives of the stigmatized] usual tasks is to appear as 'speakers' before audiences of normals and of the stigmatized; they present the case for the stigmatized... no matter how small and how badly off a particular stigmatized category is, the viewpoint of its members is likely to be given public presentation of some kind.
>
> (Goffman, 1963: 37–38)

Shared experience of stigma therefore affords political legitimacy; the stigmatised identity can be used as a tool for political action. As highlighted earlier, however, by 'professionalizing' their stigma in this way, speakers risk 'ceasing, in terms of social participation, to be representative of the people they represent' (Goffman, 1963: 39). This is redolent of Lancaster's critique of Freire's ideal typical teacher. Where Lancaster (1988: 199) saw Freire as a 'teacher-vanguard' entering the imprisoned community from without, Goffman identifies a *speaker-vanguard* partially exiting the community from within. Where Freire loses some of his credibility as a speaker by crossing an imagined line between the socially included and excluded, the peer mentor potentially loses some of their credibility to speak by crossing the same imagined line between socially excluded and included in order to become an intervener. Furthermore, in both cases the concern is that the power of the individuals being spoken to or for is undermined, potentially consolidating their oppression.

A return to Freire's own work challenges this sense of pessimism. Freire reasoned that an individual's associates are central to their perception of the possibility for change. He argued that 'yearning to be free' from the structure of domination in which people are immersed 'can be transformed into reality only when the same yearning is aroused in their comrades' (1970: 29). Peer mentoring can be read to provide such a context, not just on an individual level, but at the level of the group. It is a space wherein the yearning of comrades (peers) to communicate alternative truths is made visible. Peer mentors have the potential to act as an 'oppositional community' (Ferguson, 1996: 121), a network of 'people who share a critique of the existing order and who choose to identify with and engage in some material and/or political practices to show forth this critique' (Ferguson, 1996: 121).

Communal critique

The critique which peer mentoring offers is that crucial voices are missing from criminal justice. The material political practice, which makes this case is mentoring; expressing the voice of lived experience and offering help on this basis. Ferguson argues that without the existence of such communities fewer people would be able to make 'a reconstitutive leap' (Ferguson, 1996: 122), a theoretical and practical change. To illustrate her point, she uses the example of speaking against bodily objectification:

> I have adopted a goal to redefine beauty as meaning health rather than normalized body objectification... For such strategies to have any possibility of being effective they must be collective and ethico-political... I can only succeed in my goal to redefine beauty as health rather than make-up, if other women are also engaged in the same self-strategy. Otherwise, the normalized social meaning ("She has really let herself go, hasn't she?") will be taken to be the meaning of my refusal to wear make-up, whether I like it or not!!.
>
> (Ferguson, 1996: 116)

Ferguson therefore adopts a different perspective on the power of communal intention than Freire, yet their arguments reach a compatible conclusion. For Freire, the oppressed subject can be paralysed by an absence of yearning for change among his or her peers. His/her position in the social order therefore seems inevitable and s/he remains oppressed. For Ferguson, even if a subject has a personal yearning for change, a lack of a collective recognition among peers can limit the realisation of their individual intention. Both perspectives point to the importance of community, of group solidarity to the establishment of positioned truths. These theoretical arguments have relevance for the settings in this study. Take, for example, a prisoner who spent much of his childhood in local authority care (this group features in Chapter 4). He has a belief that his experience of care featured in his journey to prison and wants to see changes to the care system on this basis. If he feels isolated in this view or feels that his peers have not reached a similar determination, he is unlikely to speak his truth and more likely to view his situation as unfortunate but inevitable. If on the other hand he has determined to speak his truth, to make the case for this reality, but the audience who hears him is invested in another reality, for example – that plenty of children leave care and do not go to prison, so responsibility lies solely with the individual – then his truth is undermined; it loses its power in the face of the dominant discourse. What may break through both obstacles however is the presence of an 'oppositional community'. If the same prisoner joins with others (e.g. 'care leaver' mentors) who value his truth and incorporate it into the discourse of their fraternity it gains new power. He now speaks from a position of collective truth. However, Ferguson is also keen to stress the limits of working with one aspect of identity in this way:

> [A] view of the human subject as an embodied conscious process with multiple aspects and contextualized identities implies that identity politics based on an essentialist singling out of just one of these aspects to reconstitute will not successfully empower individuals. Rather, we will require many networks and coalitions, membership in many oppositional communities.
>
> (Ferguson, 1996: 122–123)

And so we return to the limits of essentialism. Whilst speaking collectively from one identity position may be momentarily empowering, indeed, it may offer a vehicle for establishing previously unacknowledged perspectives, it also neglects the multiplicity of human subjectivity. It relies upon a degree of conformity to a singular identity and of identical experiences within that identity. The way out of this dilemma, Ferguson suggests, is to acknowledge that identity is multifarious and that subjects will require many networks to identify with. In other words, she asserts that identity is intersectional (Crenshaw, 1991). Chapter 5 will examine identity within peer mentoring as dynamic and multifaceted.

This section has argued that a politicisation precept underlies criminal justice peer mentoring and that the work represents not just personal intervention, but also socio-political action. This element begins to counter Colley's concern that 'mentoring aims to "fit" people into society as it exists, rather than equipping them with a critical understanding of society or any means by which they might seek to change it' (Colley, 2002: 268). In other words, a passive view of mentoring gives way to more active possibilities. However, the success, or strength, of this precept remains unclear at this moment. Indeed, Colley's critique gets to the heart of the ambiguity on which this precept stands; peer mentoring at once appears to aim to fit people into society *and* equip them with means by which they might seek to change it. These are not always compatible goals. By sanctioning peer mentoring, the criminal justice system allows for a partial suspension of the divisive structure, for more '"free and familiar contact between people" who would usually be separated hierarchically' (Vice, 1997: 152) and between and groups who had previously had moralistic labels assigned, such as: *offender or manager, helper or client*. Such mixing presents a real challenge to the ordered role constructions, which support authoritarian and punitive justice responses. However, mentoring also instils discipline and aims to effect personal change. It is much more likely to be these features that render it attractive to commissioners in the criminal justice system. In this light, the suspension of constraints does not represent a radical shift, but a concession which permits a diluted form of quasi-professionalism. Peer mentors are at risk of being co-opted as cheaper, less well-trained and supervised replacements for expensive professional justice staff. Not a revolution then, but the testing of personnel margins, of stigma and division on limited and safe ground. Limited inclusion is permitted, but with no space for critique.

Most ex-offender peer mentors are volunteers, whilst there are some examples of paid mentors; as will become clear, they are often employed part time and receive low pay. It is these people whose voices are currently being granted validity whilst simultaneously their claims to experiential knowledge serve to *other* or discredit the knowledge of Probation Officers and Social Workers. This is expedient given that the privatisation and de-professionalisation of criminal justice (and social) services have been actively pursued. Peer mentoring can be read as the radical emergence of previously muted voices and as a challenge to the marginalisation of offenders, but it also serves to undermine paid professionals and provide a lower-cost workforce (often in their place). This is auspicious for a justice marketplace intent on reducing costs and maximising business profits.

This chapter has constructed four precepts, which I argue underpin criminal justice peer mentoring, but which are not formally or overtly drawn upon. The intended contribution is to open these possibilities up. These precepts provide a framework for a theoretical reading. *The Identity Precept* positions the ex-offender identity itself as the active element in this process. Past identities are viewed as a precursor to trusting relationships, whilst current identities provide inspirational models. Girard, Goffman and Bernstein offer theories which make sense of such 'identity work' in different, but pertinent ways. For Girard, identity is premised upon mimetic desire, individuals desire that which they see others desire, in particular those others who they respect. Peer mentoring therefore offers up 'role models' with the implied intention that mentees come to mimic the desire of their mentors to 'go straight'. Whilst mentoring may result in mimicked desire however, it may also result in rejection of the proffered model. Furthermore, the presence of ideal models may serve to devalue the person on the 'receiving' side of the exchange. For Goffman, identity is constituted by performances, which take direction from a variety of sources and settings. Mentors therefore receive theatrical direction from the rules, cues and 'stage directions' of mentors; and their resulting performance is received by an audience. Yet given the stigma of criminality the social audience already has a strong perception of an ex-offender's character, which can undermine their performance. Goffman's notion that identity is formed of a variety of selves also destabilises fixed notions of what it means to be a peer, increasing the potential for mismatches between the intended identity message and the performance as read by the recipient. For Bernstein, identity is constituted through language and social class. The language codes of class position can express and constitute a category of identity. Code variations are not limited to class, however, but are also situational. People with convictions may therefore 'relate' to people with shared histories because they share common elements of language and its resulting reality. The *Pedagogical Precept* positions peer mentoring as an educational process, one which is critical in aim and pedagogic practice, but which nonetheless maintains more familiar hierarchical elements, both in terms of a tendency towards correctional interpersonal intervention and externally set funding targets.

The *Fraternity or Sorority* and *Politicisation precepts* both challenge interventionist assumptions of deficiency. These precepts indicate that peer mentoring is not just aimed at individual change but also at social change, at promoting acceptance of 'offenders' as positive resources in their own right. The *Fraternity or Sorority Precept* constructs peer mentoring as a process of finding community or solidarity, one which will allow space for hitherto unacknowledged perspectives. The practice therefore offers up forms of criminalised standpoint epistemology wherein experience and validity are intricately linked. The problem is that such a stance can become essentialist, breeding exclusivity. However, as essentialising offenders is already commonplace, essentialism within peer mentoring can be read as a strategic response. The *Politicisation Precept* underpins peer mentoring as an act of consciousness-raising or politicisation. Mentors and coordinators behave as public advocates promoting integration and understanding. Shared experience of stigma affords political legitimacy and group expressions of such shared perspectives help to establish new truths. Whilst speaking collectively from one identity position may be empowering, it also neglects the multiplicity of human subjects and relies upon a myth of uniformed experiences; potentially neglecting the uniqueness of each mentee. As political action, peer mentoring may present a solid challenge to authoritarian and punitive justice, or it may simply represent pacification through the granting of limited power. Not a revolution then, but the safe testing of margins as punitive legislation, privatisation and continued stigmatisation rolls on. The aim of this book is not to 'test' any of these precepts or theoretical positions, but to draw upon them to shed light on current practices within criminal justice settings. Whilst these perspectives are not seen to encompass the full complexity of peer mentoring, and indeed there will be rich and diverse readings available outside of these boundaries, they do provide some new ways of thinking about mentoring and offer a useful framework for fuller theoretical consideration.

Acknowledgements

This chapter has adapted material from the following work:

Buck, G., (2017), "'I wanted to feel the way they did": Mimesis as a situational dynamic of peer mentoring by ex-offenders', *Deviant Behavior,* **38**(9), pp. 1027–1041.

I am thankful to the publishers for their permission.

References

Andrews, D. A., & Bonta, J. (2010). The psychology of criminal conduct (5th ed.). Cincinnati, OH: Anderson Publishing.

Asencio, E.K. & Burke, P.J., (2011), 'Does incarceration change the criminal identity? A synthesis of labelling and identity theory perspectives on identity change', *Sociological Perspectives,* **54**(2), pp. 163–182.

Ballinger, A., (2011), 'Feminist research, state power and executed Women: The case of Louise Calvert'. In: Farrall, S., Sparks, R. & Maruna, S., (Eds.), *Escape routes: Contemporary perspectives on life after punishment.* Abingdon, Oxon: Routledge.

Bernstein, B.B., (1971), *Class, codes and control.* Volume 1- *Theoretical studies towards a sociology of language.* Reprint, St Albans: Paladin, 1973 edition.

Blumer, H., (1969), *Symbolic interactionism: Perspective and method.* Reprint, University of California Press, 1986 edition.

Boyce, I., Hunter, G. & Hough, M., (2009), *The St Giles trust peer advice project: Summary of an evaluation report.* London: The Institute for Criminal Policy Research, School of Law, King's College. Available at: http://eprints.bbk.ac.uk/3794/ [Accessed August 2019].

Brown, M. & Ross, S., (2010), 'Mentoring, social capital and desistance: A study of women released from prison', *Australian & New Zealand Journal of Criminology (Australian Academic Press),* **43**(1), pp. 31–50.

Buck, G. & Jaffe, M., (2011), 'Volunteering in criminal justice'. Seminar Report. *ESRC Seminar Series: The Third Sector in Criminal Justice.* Keele: Keele University.

Cattermole, C., (2019), *Prison: A survival guide.* London: Ditto Press.

Clinks, (2012), *Volunteer peer support: A volunteering and mentoring guide.* London: Clinks.

Clinks and MBF, (2012), *Supporting offenders through mentoring and befriending: Clinks and MBF survey findings September 2012.* Available at: www.2ndchancegroup.org/wp-content/uploads/2014/06/Clinks-and-MBF-survey-report-findings-final-version-Sept-2012.pdf [Accessed August 2019].

Cohen, A.K. (1955), *Delinquent Boys: The Culture of the Gang.* New York, Free Press.

Colley, H., (2002), 'A "rough guide" to the history of mentoring from a Marxist feminist perspective', *Journal of Education for Teaching: International Research and Pedagogy,* **28**(3), pp. 257–273.

Colley, H., (2001), 'Righting rewritings of the myth of Mentor: A critical perspective on career guidance mentoring', *British Journal of Guidance and Counselling,* **29**(2), pp. 177–197.

Collica, K., (2010), 'Surviving incarceration: Two prison-based peer programs build communities of support for female offenders', *Deviant Behavior*, **31**(4), pp. 314–347.

Collins, H. & Evans, R., (2007), *Rethinking expertise*. London: University of Chicago Press.

Corcoran, M. & Carr, N., (2019), 'Five years of transforming rehabilitation: Markets, management and values', *Probation Journal*, **66**(1), pp. 3–7.

Corcoran, M.S., Maguire, M., & Williams, K. (2019), Alice in Wonderland: Voluntary sector organisations' experiences of Transforming Rehabilitation. *Probation Journal*, **66**(1), 96–112.

Crenshaw, K., (1991), 'Mapping the margins: Intersectionality, identity, and violence against women of color', *Stanford Law Review*, **43**(6), pp. 1241–1300.

Devilly, G.J., Sorbello, L., Eccleston, L. & Ward, T., (2005), 'Prison-based peer-education schemes', *Aggression and Violent Behavior*, **10**, pp. 219–240.

Doran, R., (Ed.), (2008), *Mimesis and theory: Essays on literature and criticism, 1953–2005*. California: Stanford University Press.

Ensher, E.A., Thomas, C. & Murphy, S.E., (2001), 'Comparison of traditional, step ahead, and peer mentoring on proteges' support, satisfaction, and perceptions of career success: A social exchange perspective', *Journal of Business and Psychology*, **15**(3), pp. 419–438.

Ferguson, A., (1996). 'Can I choose who I am? And how would that empower me? Gender, race, identities and the self.' In: Garry, A. & Pearsall, M., (Eds.), *Women, knowledge and reality: Explorations in feminist philosophy*, (2nd Edn.). London: Routledge.

Finnegan, L., Whitehurst, D. & Denton, S., (2010), *Models of mentoring for inclusion and employment: Thematic review of existing evidence on mentoring and peer mentoring*. London: Centre for economic and social inclusion.

Fletcher, D. & Batty, E., (2012), *Offender peer interventions: What do we know?* Sheffield Hallam University: Centre for Economic and Social Research. Available at: www.shu.ac.uk/research/cresr/sites/shu.ac.uk/files/offender-peer-interventions.pdf [Accessed August 2019].

Freire, P., (1997), *Mentoring the mentor: A critical dialogue with Paulo Freire*. New York: Peter Lang.

Freire, P., (1970), *Pedagogy of the oppressed*. Reprint, London: Penguin, 1996.

Fuss, D., (1989), *Essentially speaking: Feminism, nature and difference*. New York: Routledge, 1990 edition.

Gilchrist, A., Bowles, M. & Wetherell, M., (2010), *Identities and social action: Connecting communities for a change*. London: Community Development Foundation.

Girard, R., (2010), 'A theory by which to work': The mimetic mechanism'. In: Girard, R., de Castro Rocha, J.C. & Antonello, P., (Eds.), *Evolution and conversion: Dialogues on the origins of culture*. London: Continuum International Publishing, pp. 56–95.

Girard, R., (1991), 'Innovation and repetition'. In: Girard, R. & Doran, R., (Eds.), (2008), *Mimesis and theory: Essays on literature and criticism, 1953–2005*. Stanford, CA and London: Stanford University Press, pp. 230–245.

Girard, R., (1987), *Things hidden since the foundation of the world*. London: Continuum.

Girard, R., (1977), *Violence and the sacred*. London: Continuum, 2005 edition.

Girard, R., (1962), 'Marcel proust'. In: Girard, R. & Doran, R., (Eds.), (2008), *Mimesis and theory: Essays on literature and criticism, 1953–2005*. Stanford, CA and London: Stanford University Press, pp. 56–70.

Goffman, E., (1963), *Stigma: Notes on the management of spoiled identity.* Middlesex: Penguin.

Goffman, E., (1961), *Asylums: Essays on the social situation of mental patients and other inmates.* Reprint, London: Penguin, 1991.

Goffman, E., (1959), *The presentation of self in everyday life.* Reprint, London: Penguin, 1990.

Grossman, J.B. & Tierney, J.P., (1998), 'Does mentoring work? An impact study of the Big Brothers Big Sisters program', *Evaluation Review*, **22**(3), pp. 403–426.

Hardie-Bick, J.P. & Hadfield, P., (2011), 'Goffman, existentialism and criminology'. In: Hardie-Bick, J.P. & Lippens, R., (Eds.), *Crime, governance and existential predicaments.* New York: Palgrave Macmillan.

Henry, S. & Milovanovic, D., (1996), *Constitutive criminology beyond postmodernism.* London: Sage.

HM Prison and Probation Service (HMPPS). (2019), *The proposed future model for probation: A draft operating blueprint.* London: HMPPS.

Holland, D., Skinner, D., Lachicotte, Jr., W. & Cain, C., (1998), *Identity and agency in cultural worlds.* Cambridge, MA and London: Harvard University Press.

hooks, b., (1994), *Teaching to transgress: Education as the practice of freedom.* New York; London: Routledge.

hooks, b., (1993), *Sisters of the yam black women and self-recovery.* London: Turnaround.

Hull, J., (2008), 'Religion, violence and religious education'. In: De Souza, M., Durka, G., Engebretson, K., Jackson, R. & McGrady, A., (Eds.), *International handbook of the religious, moral and spiritual dimensions in education (Vol. 1).* Dordrecht, The Netherlands: Springer Science & Business Media.

Hunter, G. & Kirby, A., (2011), *Evaluation summary: Working one to one with young offenders.* London: Birkbeck College.

Jordan, J., (1992), *Relational resilience.* The Stone Center Papers, Wellesley College, Wellesley, MA.

Kavanagh, L. & Borrill, J., (2013), 'Exploring the experiences of ex-offender mentors', *Probation Journal*, **60**(4), pp. 400–414.

Lancaster, R.N., (1988), *Thanks to God and the revolution: Popular religion and class consciousness in the new Nicaragua.* New York: Columbia University Press.

LeBel, T.P., Richie, M. & Maruna, S., (2015), Helping others as a response to reconcile a criminal past: The role of the wounded healer in prisoner reentry programs. *Criminal Justice and Behavior*, **42**(1), pp. 108–120.

Maruna, S., (2017), 'Desistance as a social movement', *Irish Probation Journal*, **14**, pp. 5–20.

Maruna, S., (2001), *Making good; how ex-convicts reform and rebuild their lives.* Washington, DC: American Psychological Association.

McNeill, F., (2006), 'A desistance paradigm for offender management', *Criminology and Criminal Justice*, **6**(1), pp. 39–62.

Miller, W.B. (1958), Lower class culture as a generating milieu of gang delinquency. *Journal of Social Issues*, **14**(2), 5–19.

Ministry of Justice (MoJ), (2014), *The transforming rehabilitation programme: The new owners of the Community Rehabilitation Companies, 18/12/2014.* London: Ministry of Justice. Available at: www.gov.uk/government/uploads/system/uploads/attachment_data/file/389727/table-of-new-owners-of-crcs.pdf [Accessed August 2019].

Ministry of Justice (MoJ), (2011), *Making prisons work: Skills for rehabilitation review of offender learning.* London: Department for Business, Innovation and Skills. Available at: https://assets.publishing.service.gov.uk/government/uploads/system/uploads/

attachment_data/file/230260/11-828-making-prisons-work-skills-for-rehabilitation. pdf [Accessed January 2016].

Nellis, M. & McNeill, F., (2008), Foreword. In: Weaver, A., (Ed.), *So you think you know me?* Hampshire: Waterside Press.

Newburn, T. & Shiner, M., (2006), 'Young people, mentoring and social inclusion', *Youth Justice,* **6**(1), pp. 23–41.

O'Donnell, C.R., Lydgate, T. & Fo, W.S.O., (1979), 'The buddy system: Review and follow up', *Child Behaviour Therapy,* **1**(2), pp. 161–169.

Parkin, S. & McKeganey, N., (2000), 'The rise and rise of peer education approaches', *Drugs: Education, Prevention and Policy,* **7**(3), pp. 293–310.

Pawson, R., (2004), *Mentoring relationships: An explanatory review,* Working Paper 21. Leeds: University of Leeds.

Perrin, C., (2017), *The untapped utility of peer-support programs in prisons and implications for theory, policy, and practice.* Doctoral dissertation, Nottingham Trent University.

Petersilia, J., (2003), *When prisoners come home: Parole and prisoner reentry.* New York: Oxford University Press.

Pollack, S., (2004), 'Anti-oppressive social work practice with women in prison: Discursive reconstructions and alternative practice', *British Journal of Social Work,* **34**(5), pp. 693–707.

Princes Trust, (2008), *Making the case: One-to-one support for young offenders.* Princes Trust, Rainer, St Giles Trust, CLINKS.

Rowlingston, K. & Mckay, S., (2012), *Wealth and the wealthy: Exploring and tackling inequalities between rich and poor.* Bristol: The Policy Press.

Rumgay, J., (2004), 'Scripts for safer survival: Pathways out of female crime', *The Howard Journal of Criminal Justice,* **43**(4), pp. 405–419.

Sadovnik, A.R., (2008), 'Contemporary perspectives in the sociology of education'. In: Ballantine, J.H. & Spade, J.Z., (Eds.), *Schools and society: A sociological approach to education* (3rd Edn.). Chicago: Pine Forge Press, pp. 20–29.

Sandler, J. & Mein, E., (2010), 'Popular education confronts neoliberalism in the public sphere: The struggle for critical civil society in Latin America'. In: Apple, M.W., (Ed.), *Global crises, social justice, and education.* Abingdon, Oxon: Routledge.

Scheper-Hughes, N., (1992), *Death without weeping: The violence of everyday life in Brazil.* Berkeley and Oxford: University of California Press.

Scott, A., Doughty, C. & Kahi, H., (2011), '"Having those conversations": The politics of risk in peer support practice', *Health Sociology Review,* **20**(2), pp. 187–201.

Shelter, (2010), *In their own words - Shelter's peer education services for young people,* London: Shelter.

Spalek, B., (2008), *Communities, identities and crime.* Bristol: Policy Press.

Stanley, L. & Wise, S., (1993), *Breaking out again feminist ontology and epistemology.* London: Routledge.

Turner, G. & Shepherd, J., (1999), 'A method in search of a theory: Peer education and health promotion', *Health Education Research,* **14**(2), pp. 235–247.

United Nations Office on Drugs and Crime (UNODC), (2002), *Mentoring definition.* In: Finnegan, L., Whitehurst, D. & Denton, S., (Eds.), (2010), *Models of mentoring for inclusion and employment: Thematic review of existing evidence on mentoring and peer mentoring.* London: Centre for economic and social inclusion.

User Voice (2019). *User voice website.* Available at: www.uservoice.org [Accessed August 2019].

User Voice, (2014), *Our story.* Available at: www.uservoice.org/our-story/ [Accessed: August 2019].

Vice, S., (1997), *Introducing Bakhtin.* Manchester: Manchester University Press.

Ward, T., & Gannon, T. (2006), Rehabilitation, etiology, and self-regulation: The Good Lives Model of rehabilitation for sexual offenders. *Aggression and Violent Behavior,* **11**, 77–94. doi:10.1016/j.avb.2005.06.001

Ward, T., & Marshall, W.L. (2004), Good lives, aetiology and the rehabilitation of sex offenders: A bridging theory. *Journal of Sexual Aggression,* **10**(2), 153–169.

Weaver, B., (2012), 'The relational context of desistance: Some implications and opportunities for social policy', *Social Policy & Administration,* **46**(4), pp. 395–412.

Weaver, B. & Weaver, A., (2016), 'An unfinished alternative: Toward a relational paradigm'. In: Trotter, C., McIvor, G. & McNeill, F., (Eds.), (2016), *Beyond the risk paradigm in criminal justice.* London: Palgrave, pp. 221–239.

White, W.L., (2009), *Peer-based addiction recovery support. History, theory, practice, and scientific evaluation.* Philadelphia: Great Lakes Addiction Technology Transfer Center.

Chapter 4

The research field

The UK voluntary sector in criminal justice is made up of around 1,700 organisations (Mullen, 2018), with incomes ranging from 'none whatsoever' to in excess of £5 million, although 51% of the sector reported an annual turnover or income of £150,000 or less (Centre for Social Justice, 2013: 7). Most criminal justice voluntary organisations have few employees. A quarter (24%) said they had no full-time equivalent employees; whilst 69% reported having ten or fewer (Centre for Social Justice, 2013: 7). The peer mentoring landscape is similarly diverse. In 2013, Sova reported stark contrasts in peer mentor numbers across criminal justice in England and Wales (Willoughby, Parker & Ali, 2013: 7). Some areas had no reported peer mentors, most others were considerably below 50%, whilst Wiltshire (92%) and Oxfordshire (71%) recorded high percentages of peer mentors amongst mentor populations (Willoughby et al., 2013: 7). What we know about peer mentoring to date is generally based upon the work of larger charitable organisations (see, e.g. The Social Innovation Partnership, 2012; Princes Trust, 2008), quite possibly because they have the staff numbers and funds to support research. Given that 'most' criminal justice organisations have few employees, however, this study also includes some of the very smallest examples.

Dominant truths about offender rehabilitation

Prior to undertaking this study, I was employed as a Youth Justice Social Worker. My professional training was predominantly shaped by generalising truths, which positioned 'offenders' as rational subjects making poor choices. The result was a dominant discourse, which held that solving *the crime problem* required specialist experts effecting behavioural changes in flawed subjects. The claims to knowledge within this discourse, however, as highlighted in Chapter 2, were often based on distant quantifying practices (Spalek, 2008; Gelsthorpe, 2006). In contrast, this study sought to consider how mentoring was meaningful to participants, not just because such views can get lost within dominant functional evaluations, but also because so little was known about the micro-dynamics and subjective experiences of mentoring relationships.

This *constructionist* approach (Crotty, 1998) is compelling for understanding peer mentoring as it allows us to recognise multiple and situated meanings, rather than narrowing down the diverse manifestations in practice. For example, understandings of what constitute a 'peer' and a 'mentor' are variable, they depend upon individual perspectives and social settings. To try and objectively measure the nature and outcomes of such diversity collectively, risks not paying full attention to the variances. As a result of a diverse, multiply constructed field, coupled with an increasing objectification of the people within it, the decision was taken to adopt qualitative methods.

Qualitative methods

Research methods which stand outside the lived experience of deviance or criminality can perhaps sketch a faint outline of it, but they can never fill that outline with essential dimensions of meaningful understanding (Ferrell & Hamm, 1998: 10). A qualitative approach enabled exploration of the meanings that participants themselves attached to mentoring, in the context of the meanings that they attached to desisting from crime. Mixed methods were adopted, including forty-four in-depth *interviews* with key players, these included eighteen peer mentors, twenty mentees, four mentoring coordinators and two Probation staff. Interviews formed the primary method given they facilitated answers to all four of the initial research questions (how does peer mentoring work in practice; what sense is made of peer mentoring by the people delivering and using services; what relationship, if any, does peer mentoring have to 'desistance'; and what is the impact of a shifting voluntary sector context on their role and relationships with clients, the community and other services and partners?). *Observations* of voluntary sector practices were also undertaken, including recruitment, training and supervision of volunteers, and (group) mentoring activities. These provided a supplementary perspective of mentoring in practice and insight into the shifting voluntary sector context. Finally, *Documentary analysis* of organisation literature was undertaken (e.g. promotional material, evaluations and reports). These documents outlined the origins and rationale of programmes from the perspective of those delivering them, they also illustrated the voluntary sector context and relationships with partners. This mixed method approach is *ethnographic,* in that it balances 'detailed documentation of events with insights into their meaning to those involved' (Fielding, 2008: 267).

Sources of data – project selection

A 'purposive sampling method' (Denscombe, 2014: 41) was adopted, meaning projects were 'hand-picked' – through internet searches and conference networking – based on their relevance to the issue being investigated and their knowledge of the topic. This was enhanced using 'Snowball sampling', a technique where participants already recruited (in this case project coordinators) helped to locate other participants (i.e. providers) who they know (Babbie, 2011: 208). Projects were only contacted if they were operating in the voluntary sector and delivering peer mentoring in a criminal justice context. In order to gain 'depth information' of a snapshot in time and place (Major & Savin-Baden, 2010: 15) the search for data sources was limited to the North West of England, but multiple sites were included to try and reflect some of the diversity of peer mentoring practices. Seven projects eventually took part, their staff numbers ranging from one to thirty. All participants' names have been replaced with pseudonyms, as have the names of projects to maintain anonymity.

Project 'Peer'

Project 'Peer' provides peer mentoring to people subject to community supervision. Whilst mentees take part on a voluntary basis, mentoring is supplementary (and sometimes integral) to court ordered supervision, some of the complexities of which will be discussed in Chapter 9. The history and aims of the project were:

> A shared vision in which volunteers became part of the support package offered to offenders.... Our Mentors will act as experienced guides, trusted allies and advocates whilst encouraging pro-social behaviour modelled on their own.
>
> (Project 'Peer' Flyer)

Funding was provided by the local Crime and Disorder Reduction Partnership (CDRP) on the proviso that the Probation Service initially had managerial oversight. Operations were managed by two salaried coordinators, who had histories of substance addiction and long-term imprisonment, respectively. Their office was located within the Probation Service, an arrangement which caused significant unease initially, given that the two coordinators potentially had access to personal records of past personal associates. Both the Probation manager and coordinators described a difficult early 'bedding in' period where the new staff had to gain the trust of their colleagues and their manager had to carry the risk of confidentiality breaches or 'things going wrong'. By the time my fieldwork commenced, however, the mentors had been in post for twelve months. All of the above parties perceived that the peer mentoring service was now fully embedded, and it certainly appeared that the mentoring managers were regarded as trusted colleagues by Probation staff. Project 'Peer' had a team of twenty-five to thirty volunteer mentors, many but not all of whom, had a history of involvement in the criminal justice system. This was because of a slight shift in approach since inception:

> In the past I've felt that experience [of offending] would count for most, but from the last two years I've kind of learned that that is not necessarily

the case, just being genuine and sincere is more important, but yeah a mixture of both, depending on the individual needing a mentor.

(Adam, Mentoring Coordinator)

The original intention to only recruit volunteers with personal experience of drugs or crime therefore shifted to also include volunteers from a variety of backgrounds. Most volunteers offered one-to-one mentoring and some offered group peer support.

Project 'Facilitate'

Project 'Facilitate' is a charity which offers mentoring as a supplementary and voluntary activity for women who are subject to (or post) state punishment. Women-specific projects were deliberately included to avoid the approach to criminology which 'ignores women and girls in conflict with the law or simply treats sex as a variable to be included in complex statistical analyses' (DeKeseredy, 2011: 28). Project 'Facilitate' 'provides fresh opportunities for women who are jobless and have a criminal record to learn new skills and find employment' (Project 'Facilitate' Information Pack). They claim that:

A unique feature of the service will be the opportunity for some participants to receive special training and personal development support and work alongside our professional staff in delivering the service. Peer facilitators will be key members of the [...] team. They will pass on valuable life skills learning, advice and advocacy support to other women ex-offenders at risk of re-offending and those struggling to adapt to life on the outside.

(Project 'Facilitate' Information Pack)

Project 'Facilitate' differed from the other projects in that *all* of their facilitators (mentors) were simultaneously active service users themselves. Mentors each had their own 'project worker' to assist with any difficulties *they* had and to supervise their facilitation work. The rationale for this was twofold; it offered women still subject to criminal justice interventions an opportunity to help others and to 'increase their employability', whilst ensuring they were fully supported and supervised. It also offered women using the charity the 'assistance of those who have experience of the criminal justice system' (Project 'Facilitate' Manager). Referrals to the service (for both facilitators and mentees) came from the Probation Service and other community partners (such as the Job Centre or Women's Centre). The project also accepted self-referrals, often through word of mouth.

During the fieldwork period the project had twelve volunteers. They also provided a three-day training course for new volunteers twice yearly. Many of the trainee volunteers had been users of the service themselves. Indeed, it was the project's intention that women enter as 'service users' and leave having volunteered and increased their 'social and employment capital'. All mentoring at 'Facilitate' was undertaken on a one-to-one basis. Project 'Facilitate' was funded for three years through a national grant making body. As this period was nearing an end, they sought funding from other sources, which made demands upon the time of the manager and staff in addition to the demands of delivering the service. It also caused significant anxiety among the staff and volunteer group as there was no guarantee they would have jobs within the coming six months. This situation is not uncommon to small voluntary sector projects who often find themselves focused on 'chasing the funding' (Seddon, 2007: 58). As a footnote, Project 'Facilitate' did secure further funding, but not before their two support workers secured alternative employment positions elsewhere in the face of pending unemployment. Whilst the service continued, therefore, there was an impact in terms of staffing consistency.

Project 'Safe'

Project 'Safe' is a young women's peer mentoring project attached to a community youth programme. They offer mentoring to young women who are involved with, exiting or at risk of criminality and exploitation, but their work is separate from formal criminal/youth justice sanctions. 'The programme was initially conceived as a response to the emerging concerns of young women's' involvement in gang-activity and the abusive relations that some young women may endure' (Project 'Safe' Evaluation Report). It is important to note that the term 'gang' has been problematised as a descriptor of the activity of young people, not least because the application of a gang label does not always fit with the understanding of those labelled and does little to explain contexts of inequality or lack of legitimate opportunities. Indeed, uncritical acceptance of the term has served to 'marginalise and isolate some ethnic minority communities' (Smithson, Ralphs & Williams, 2013), given the emergence of a 'wave of United States-inspired gang injunctions and dedicated multi-agency and policing units [which] disproportionately target young, ethnic minority males from already socially excluded, marginalized and heavily policed neighbourhoods' (Smithson et al., 2013: 125). Respondents in this study reiterated some of these concerns as will become clear in later chapters. Nonetheless Project 'Safe' points to the 'growing numbers of young people identified as gang-involved' in addition to the 'dearth of information or evidence relating to the involvement of young women in gangs' (Project 'Safe' Evaluation Report). Project 'Safe' was particularly concerned:

> that a proportion of young women defined as a 'gang-concern' have experienced sexual violence and exploitation by gang members [and that]

there remains very few appropriate interventions for young women who are 'at risk' of gang-involvement.

(Project 'Safe' Evaluation Report, 2012: 3; see also Berelowitz, Firmin, Edwards & Gulyurtlu, 2012)

Project 'Safe' was established by a community member who took it upon herself to address this problem. She secured funding from a social housing provider and recruited a small group of 'peer mentors', all of whom had been involved with, or had knowledge of, local gang-related issues. Referrals came from schools and from the local gang management unit to a 'group-work programme provided and delivered by specialist and peer practitioners' (Project 'Safe' Evaluation Report). Mentors built relationships with young women on the course and provided post-course mentoring where required. Peer mentors were paid employees, described as a deliberate attempt to acknowledge and reward the value of the experience young mentors bring. They also had monthly supervision sessions with volunteer 'Aspirational Mentors'. Aspirational mentors were described as 'successful, professional or inspirational' adult women from the local community (Project 'Safe' Coordinator), who volunteer to support the work of the project. Their role was to provide reflective supervision, advice and guidance and to nurture the aspirations of mentors. They were positioned as role models, given that many of the women held senior management positions within statutory or community sector settings. The intention was to counter the 'poverty of aspiration' young people can face if their life experience has left them feeling de-motivated (Project 'Safe' Information Booklet, 2012).

Project 'Care'

The aim of Project 'Care' was to understand why people who have been 'looked after' by the local authority as children, are over-represented in the criminal justice system and to provide 'peer' mentoring for this group. *The Prison Reform Trust* points out that 'Less than 1% of all children in England were looked after [in March 2011, but] half the children held in young offender institutions are, or have been previously, looked after [and] 27% of the adult prison population had once been in care' (Blades, Hart, Lea & Willmott, 2011: 1). Project 'Care's' specific intention was to employ mentors with experience of both the care and prison systems, believing that these experiences offered unique knowledge and credibility:

Mentoring is about having the best interests of those they are supporting at heart... Mentors need to know what it takes to overcome adversity and offer hope [and] demonstrate how you can use your own life experiences to support and inspire others.

(Project 'Care' Flyer)

Project 'Care' received grant funding to run a three-year peer mentoring pilot. The full-time coordinator of the project identified himself as both an ex-offender and a care leaver and described his work as 'user led practice'. Whilst Project 'Care' was only in the formative stages of setting up peer mentoring during the fieldwork phase, the manager agreed to be interviewed and agreed that I could observe their volunteer training as it developed. This offered a unique opportunity to see a new project in development from the outset, but also presented unique problems. The biggest potential obstacle to researching the work of 'Care' was that they were unable to proceed with their training and delivery as planned. Their original plan was to consult with potential mentors and mentees about the type of challenges they face and the type of service they would like to see, to deliver a jointly produced training course and to deliver one-to-one 'through the [prison] gates' mentoring. Whilst they were able to hold 'consultation events' with care leavers in both prison and community settings, and eventually adapt their approach to facilitate peer support groups, they met significant barriers to training and 1-1 provision. In terms of *training*, they found it difficult to recruit enough potential volunteers from their very specific pool of potential recruits. Whilst they were in touch with many care leavers as a charity, and with some care leavers who had a criminal history, not all of these people were interested in becoming mentors. Rather, most of the people the charity usually worked with had support or advocacy needs of their own. Similarly, lots of the people who expressed an interest in volunteering did not meet the criteria of being an ex-offender care leaver. These problems highlight a limitation of the biographical qualification for peer mentors, which is that some projects cannot adequately recruit. In terms of *through the gate* work they met an additional barrier. The aim was for volunteer mentors to meet clients in prison settings in the months prior to release in order to build a relationship, then provide a one-to-one mentoring service 'through the gates' and beyond. However, gaining access to some prisons proved to be a bigger barrier than anticipated, given that the manager and potential volunteers – necessarily – had criminal records. They therefore met resistance to gaining entry on security grounds. This obstacle will be discussed in greater detail in Chapter 9. The changes that Project 'Care' underwent in the early stages of operation offer a fascinating insight into the hurdles that new services can face at their inception.

Some late additions!

Whilst forty interviews with staff and recipients from the above projects were eventually obtained, there was a period when it appeared there would be a lack of sufficient respondents. One recruited project ceased operation altogether due to a decision by their London-based head office to reallocate funds to another geographical area, whilst another experienced delays in delivery. During sampling and recruitment however, I did meet several individuals who, whilst working individually or in very small projects, who clearly had valuable perspectives to offer in terms of the local field.

Project 'Learn'

I met *Phil* at a conference when he was delivering a youth inclusion programme on behalf of a non-profit housing association. His programme was 'designed to challenge young people's attitudes about crime and change negative lifestyles' (Project 'Learn' website). Phil identified himself as an ex-offender, his role was to deliver personal development work with young people and mentor them based upon his own experiences. He had also previously delivered peer mentoring to groups in adult prison settings, having been invited back informally after his own release. Furthermore, he had offered one-to-one support to local adult prisoners coming 'through the gate'. He therefore had an in-depth understanding of peer mentoring in several guises. Phil was interviewed individually in his capacity as a peer mentor.

Project 'Work'

Georgie had recently gained employment as a director of a community re-settlement project, which utilises volunteer peer mentors. She previously used the same service as a mentee following her release from prison. The project Georgie works for (Project 'Work') 'provides resettlement and support services for ex-prisoners... Each beneficiary is allocated a volunteer "befriender" at pre-release stage' (Project 'Work' Website). Many, but not all, of Project 'Work's' volunteers are ex-offenders. *Nick*, who manages the project, explained that this is because 'they know what they're talking about and have a life experience closer to their mentee; they are also often keen to put something back and take on a positive pro-social role'. Project 'Work' did not have enough active peer mentors to provide the numbers initially wanted from each setting, but were keen to speak to the research; Georgie and Nick were therefore interviewed about their experiences. They not only shed light on a coordinator and mentor perspective within a small organisation, but Georgie also illustrates some of the challenges of changing role from service user to staff.

Project 'Team'

Keisha was initially wary of contributing to research as she had had some negative experiences of her ideas being appropriated (these will be explored in Chapter 8). However, during recruitment networking, Keisha's name was forwarded by a local youth project leader as 'someone you need to speak to'. Having answered her many questions about the research aims and publication plans, Keisha agreed to be involved. She wanted to advocate for peer mentoring whilst raising awareness of the difficulties of delivery when you have a criminal record. Keisha established Project 'Team' after being released from prison. Project 'Team' is a peer mentoring service working 'to deter young people from a life of crime to prevent negative outcomes amongst young people' (Project 'Team' Website). Keisha and her business partner were inspired to mentor young people, having spent a significant period of their own young adulthoods in prison. The project delivers workshops 'designed to promote positive behaviour and encourage positive change' (Project 'Team' Website). They also provide one-to-one mentoring, advice and support and family advocacy. Keisha was interviewed in her capacity as a peer mentor.

What emerged is not a tidy cohort of respondents, but a data set reflective of the shifting local picture encountered, which includes some very small parts of the sector, and some of the different interpretations of 'peer mentoring'. For example, whilst all respondents considered that they were undertaking peer mentoring in the voluntary sector and all recognised value in recruiting ex-offenders as mentors, not all mentors had to be ex-offenders; not all mentors had to be volunteers; and not all mentors called themselves mentors. These differences will be revisited throughout the book.

Interview respondents

In larger settings, the 'purposive sampling method' (Denscombe, 2014: 41) was continued in that coordinators were asked to recruit a sample of mentors *and* mentees to enable insight into experiences on both sides of the relationship. An advantage of using coordinators as 'gatekeepers' (Remenyi, Swan & Van Den Assem, 2011: 67) was that they had prior knowledge of respondents' personal wellbeing and capacity, providing a layer of safeguarding. A challenge was that gatekeepers were employed as Project Managers and therefore interested parties with the opportunity to select people based on organisational/personal agendas. To minimise intermediary influence, sampling was enhanced using direct advertising within projects. This included the distribution of posters and leaflets around offices and group work rooms. 'Snowball sampling' was also employed whereby members of the 'target population' were asked 'to locate other members of that population who they happen to know' (Babbie, 2011: 208). I also spoke to people informally, in the group sessions that I observed, about their experiences in both group and one-to-one settings.

In order to avoid compulsion (however implicit), I made the request to participate directly to all respondents following introduction by project managers and full information, including the right to withdraw was personally explained. Semi-structured interviews were selected to offer 'more opportunity for dialogue and exchange between the interviewer and interviewee' (Noaks & Wincup, 2004: 79). Four key questions were asked of *all* mentors and mentees: What is peer mentoring? Why are peer mentors volunteers? What does 'going straight' involve? Does peer mentoring have anything to do with going straight? These not only offered a guide for the interview, but also allowed space for any 'follow up ideas' (Crowther-Dowey, 2007: 102) that the respondents had. Often these four prompts were all that was needed for the hour-long interview. Where respondents gave shorter responses or did not develop points from their own side, a bank of additional prompts was available to encourage the discussion. These were similar for both mentors and mentees, differing only to acknowledge the different positions of mentor and mentee (e.g. what happens if *mentees* don't attend/what happens if *you* don't attend?). Eighteen interviews were completed with mentors from across the projects, and twenty interviews with mentees. In addition, the opportunity was taken to interview four project coordinators, offering insight into the origins of projects and the practicalities of service provision. Finally, the opportunity was taken to interview two Probation Officers who referred in to one of the projects, which gave valuable insight into the perspectives of a partner agency; and into the compromises made over differences in approach. Debriefing took place with all participants, which involved summarising the main points discussed and how these might be presented. It allowed interviewees to correct any factual errors or withdraw statements if they wished. Few interviewees disagreed with summaries, although some did re-emphasise the points they considered most important. Additionally, debriefing allowed for any distress to be identified and any concerns about disclosure and confidentiality to be addressed.

Observation sources and practices

Every site invited me to their workplace and four allowed me to visit at least one external partner or setting where their work is carried out. I completed two separate volunteer training courses as a participant (overt) observer, spent time in office spaces, used meeting rooms for interviews and accessed communal areas. I also observed a number of peer-led group activities, several volunteer recruitment interviews and uniquely, a supervision session between a coordinator and a peer mentor. One organisation also invited me to attend their multi-agency conference focusing on effective ways of helping young women involved in youth violence.

> It is usually fairly important for the researcher to scrutinize the structural layout of the areas in which the behaviour to be studied takes place... physical characteristics almost always reflect social characteristics (as well as conditioning social behaviour).
>
> (Corbetta, 2003: 247)

As I built relationships with coordinators and staff, I was able to informally observe settings, including the physical appearance of offices and rooms, the local areas in which they were based and the administration practices and social cultures within offices. I did not observe one-to-one mentoring in any of the settings, which would have been both ethically problematic and a poor source of data, given my presence as a researcher would have been so disruptive to the relationship. I was also already getting descriptive accounts of this practice from interviews. The places I did observe illustrated the social settings of peer mentoring, the formal interactions and also allowed access to social actor's 'definition on the situation' (Corbetta, 2003: 285). Given I was a participant observer (albeit overt) in group and training settings, I was able to access a wealth of what would have been otherwise hidden data, such as whispered feelings about content and facial expressions of discomfort or pleasure at different points. See Chapter 9 for specific examples of this. My presence as an observer of planned activities, as I will reflect on more fully later, also allowed me invaluable additional access to a wealth of data relating to the culture and character of organisations.

A major problem with observational work is that 'The presence of the observer may change the nature of the interactions being observed' (Hall, 2008: 205). Indeed this 'social desirability bias (SDB)' or 'the tendency for individuals to present themselves in a favourable or socially desirable manner' (Hall, 2008: 205) could arguably have been at work in interviews too. As with interviewing, however, the task of the observer who is mindful of social construction is not to seek the objective truth of a situation, as this is ultimately viewed as unobtainable; rather the task is to critically approach the narratives available with an awareness of power agendas and the ways in which texts came to be constructed.

Proceeding ethically

I was very aware of the complex power asymmetries and potential for exploitation in the research setting and took steps to minimise these. The informed consent of all participants was sought and participants were fully informed of the purposes of the research and the proposed use of research findings. Participation in interviews and observations of practice was fully voluntary and all respondents were informed orally and in writing that they had the right to withdraw from the research at any point and to decline to answer any questions. The decision was made to anonymise individuals and projects to enhance the likelihood and accuracy of responses (Maxfield & Babbie, 2015: 63) and to offer protection to people and organisations if somebody said something which others found critical. Participants were advised that their answers, discussions, names and any identifying details about organisations would be anonymised carefully to avoid unintended disclosure. However, whilst identities would be protected within the study, participants were advised prior to interview of the researcher's obligation to report to the authorities any current criminal activity, involvement in terrorism or planned harm to themselves or others.

Research with criminalised people requires an understanding that of-fending is intertwined with complex needs and vulnerabilities. Even in the absence of overt manipulation, participants may have felt coerced to take part simply by being asked, given they were under the management of a system which heavily dissuades non-participation. I aimed to minimise this potential by talking with agency gatekeepers about the importance of vol-untary inclusion. I also spent time at the beginning of each interaction mak-ing clear that participation is a choice and there would be no judgement or consequence if people decide they do not want to take part. To maintain a duty of care towards respondents who may be distressed by discussions, all participants were issued with a leaflet detailing local helplines and services. Additional safeguards were implemented at Project 'Safe', due to the young age of respondents (13–14), which could impact upon their understanding of the implications of contributing to research (in terms of personal disclo-sures and the risk of recognition); or what impact research findings may have (on the services they use). To minimise these risks, I continually consulted with gatekeepers about respondent suitability and obtained parental consent where participants were under the age of 18 (with the prior knowledge and consent of potential participants). Having practised as a Social Worker with young people, I employed transferrable skills and sensitivities. I am aware, for example, that many young women on the periphery of gang activity are sexually exploited by gang members. I was very clear about my duty to in-form the authorities if ongoing abuse was disclosed. As an extra safeguard, all interviews with young people took place at the charity's centre or at the young person's school to ensure they had familiar staff support nearby if the discussions caused them distress.

Given the high levels of poor literacy amongst criminalised people (Cad-dick & Webster, 1998) and high rates of dyslexia (Kirk & Reid, 2001), I verbally explained all written information regarding the implications of re-search and did not proceed unless assured they were understood. All written information was 'dyslexia friendly' (Price & Skinner, 2007) including pastel coloured paper. I also produced pictorial versions of information sheets.

Reflexivity – the context of analysis

It is important to note that prior to embarking on this study I was working in a youth offending team and was therefore not an 'objective' observer (Den-scombe, 2010: 88) – if indeed such a thing exists (Crotty, 1998). I had also experienced peer mentoring as a Social Worker in a charity tackling child sexual exploitation and it was these experiences that motivated my research. The first time I assisted with a peer-led intervention, two young women shared a conversation about their harrowing and violent experiences of child sexual exploitation. I watched in fascination as through tears, laughter and trauma-filled honesty the younger of the two dropped some of her shame and self-hatred and the elder grew in stature and compassion. The conversation was an experiment, a 'pilot', yet it had such a profound impact on both parties that peer mentoring was implemented on a broader scale across the service. I recall this history to be clear about my own starting point as a researcher, but also to be clear about the need for reflexivity. I was aware that my first impression of peer mentoring had been favourable, I was also aware that I had witnessed peer mentoring in practice on a one-to-one basis, yet would not be doing so in this study. I therefore needed to separate out my own impressions from how respondents were describing their experiences and in order to do so I would need analytical tools, which would remain close to respondent narratives *and* allow me to separate out my own assumptions. Elements of *grounded theory*, critical *discourse analysis* and Gilligan's *listening guide* were helpful here and will be discussed more fully below. Before doing so, it is also relevant to note that this personal history was not just a possible influence to be managed, but also a helpful tool. I was a relative 'insider' when approaching voluntary sector agencies having worked in similar settings myself. I was therefore familiar with the 'habitus' (Bourdieu, 1980: 53) or durable dispositions common to this field. I was 'uniquely positioned to understand' the workings of these settings, to gain access and to engage with gatekeepers (see Kerstetter, 2012). However, there are very few cases 'in which someone can be characterized as a complete insider or a complete outsider', rather 'the 'space between' is usually characterized as a multidimensional space, where researchers' identities, cultural backgrounds, and relationships to research participants influence how they are positioned within that space' (Kerstetter, 2012: 101). This was a complexity I identified with as I went about the business of *managing my identities* within the various research settings.

A major test was leaving behind the Social Worker habitus when faced with a respondent's distress. One young woman was tearful during interview about years 'wasted' following an exploitative introduction to heroin as a child, yet she was also communicating loss and frustration that her mentoring relationship had been too hastily terminated, at a time when she felt the support was most needed. The young woman went as far as to say it made her feel like committing a crime again to get the support. As a Social Worker, my learned response to her narrative would be: reflectively listen, explore alternative problem-solving skills and consequential thinking, educate the young woman on her rights in relation to accessing support and to advocate on her behalf for a more staged and supported ending. Indeed, I could hear these responses being played out in my head as she spoke. As a researcher, however, I had more recently been schooled in the importance of non-directional listening and therefore felt an inner conflict about how to respond. I uneasily settled for reflecting on the content and feelings and for information sharing:

> I would like you to ask could you have some support, maybe not at the level you had – but just to bridge that gap until you go into detox…

I don't think there's anything wrong with picking up a phone to a manager and saying: 'can I just give you some feedback for how I'm feeling?' You never know what might happen, you're not saying anything bad about anybody who you've worked with, I'm not hearing that. What I'm hearing is that you're feeling like you want something else and the manager just seems like the right person to go to.

Following the interview, however, my inner conflict did not subside. Had I said and done enough to ease this young woman's distress and assist her in securing the service she desired at such a crucial time in her recovery? Had I said and done enough to prevent her acting on her temptation to offend again? Should I speak with the coordinator about my concerns or would this unnecessarily breach confidentiality? Alternatively, had I already said *too much*, potentially influencing this young woman's response to the service and in turn their performance of endings whilst I was still only in an early stage of my fieldwork? After reflection in supervision I fed back my concern about 'end points' generally to this project at the end of the first batch of interviews, thus maintaining individual confidentiality. I also had to accept that my role in this setting was not to effect individual change or advocate on an individual basis.

Data analysis

Interviews were transcribed verbatim, allowing me to get 'close' to people's stories. Transcribing was 'as much a form of interpretation and analysis as... a technical activity' (Fraser, 2004: 188). Quotations were 'cleaned up' (Nespor & Barber, 1995) to render them understandable to a wide audience. Connecting phrases such as 'um', 'like', and 'you know?' were omitted unless this would have been detrimental to the meaning of the quote. Whilst there are concerns that 'such editing distorts what people said' I would agree with Nespor and Barber (1995: 56), that 'far from being markers of "authentic" speech, these are artefacts of interview practices'. Observation data was recorded by hand contemporaneously in field diaries and later typed up. These typed diaries included separate sections, which recorded my own observations, impressions and comments. In order to analyse the amassed data I drew upon techniques of *thematic analysis*, critical *discourse analysis* and Gilligan's *listening guide* method.

Thematic analysis, or analysis through the identification of common themes, 'involves making choices about what to include... [and] implies some degree of repetition' (King & Horrocks, 2010: 149). The thematic analysis of interview data was influenced by the *grounded theory* approach, which encourages researchers to remain 'open to the data' in order to 'discover subtle meanings and have new insights' (Charmaz, 2014: 137). King and Horrocks (2010: 153) describe one system of analysis using three stages of coding: *descriptive coding, interpretive coding* and *overarching themes*. In the context of this research, descriptive work involved reading through transcripts and diaries, highlighting material and adding brief comments; interpretive work involved creating clusters from these markers and beginning to interpret meaning in relation to the research question. Overarching themes then emerged to form the shape of chapters. For example, the recurrent *description* of the importance of shared experiences was then *interpreted* in terms of asserting submerged voices. This led to an *overarching* theme of *identity*, which not only encompassed this finding, but also the descriptions of peer mentoring involving elements of translation between identity positions (see Chapter 5 for full discussion).

Critical discourse analysis (CDA) is 'essentially a form of textual analysis. Typically, it involves (a) finding a regular pattern in a particular text or a set of texts... and then (b) proposing an interpretation of the pattern, an account of its meaning and ideological significance' (Cameron, 2001: 137). In practice, analysts look at the text as a whole; the genre; framing; what is foregrounded/omitted; what is taken for granted; what connotations are used and is the register formal or informal? The aim is to uncover often hidden evidence to make a case for how meaning is made. Whilst useful for highlighting unspoken dynamics (see, e.g. the taken-for-granted-ness of gendered forms of mentoring in Chapter 9), there are concerns that CDA positions analysts as superior to speakers, implying that with the correct analytical process, a critical version of truth superior to the speakers can be gotten at, or as Stanley and Wise (1993) argue:

> Data are elicited by the researcher, who then evaluate them in relation to her assessment of the participant's competence in 'properly' understanding what is going on... one of the major ways in which power is exercised in research situations.
>
> (Stanley & Wise, 1993: 115)

To address this imbalance, elements of Gilligan's 'voice method' or 'listening guide' method were also employed (Kiegelmann, 2009). This method attempts to include a fuller representation of the researcher's position in the analysis. The method lays out 'three steps as a way of entering and coming to know another person's inner world, in the context of the research relationship' (Kiegelmann, 2009: 11). These steps are listening for plot, for the 'I' voice and for contrapuntal voices. Gilligan offers very practical advice on how to listen for and record each of these features and in doing so, she offers an open approach to the problem that much analytical work is 'hidden' and subjective. She suggests, for example, that alongside listening for plot:

> [T]rack your responses to the other person and what they are saying, making these explicit so as to avoid projecting them onto others or acting them out in various ways. Objectivity then becomes a matter not of

avoiding relationship but paying attention to relationship, not silencing yourself but distinguishing your voice from that of the other person.

(Kiegelmann, 2009: 11)

She also suggests that analysts create 'I poems' from data by taking 'each I phrase... that occurs and list to them in sequence ("I want, I know, I don't know, I think ...")' She argues that these can 'often prove to be remarkably revealing, picking up an associative logic that runs under the logic of the sentence and capturing what people know about themselves, often without being aware of communicating it' (Kiegelmann, 2009: 11). The benefit of such openness is that:

> By making explicit the connections between evidence and interpretation, other researchers can see how you arrived at the understanding you have come to and also explore different paths. Reliability, reframed within a relational understanding of the research process, means checking one's listening against that of others, especially people whose backgrounds or cultures may lead them to pick up what you have missed or misheard.
>
> (Kiegelmann, 2009: 11)

This kind of reflective ethnographic practice is not without criticism, however, as there are concerns that the scientific gaze becomes skewed towards researcher at the expense of the researched (Taylor & Winquist, 2001). There was a need to remain focused upon the research question, therefore, and listen closely to the people describing their experiences. Data are presented in Chapters 5–9, interwoven with analyses which resulted from engaging these techniques. As some of this data has already been published elsewhere (Buck, 2019a, 2019b, 2018, 2017, 2014), unpublished material is foregrounded.

This chapter began by introducing a research field which is relatively unknown. Indeed, the number of 'peer' mentoring projects in operation is difficult to quantify given the diversity of practices and the short-term or poorly funded nature of many services. In turn, criminology has been conceived of as prioritising statistical analyses over what is meaningful to 'offenders' (Gelsthorpe, 2006). Certainly, quantifiable understandings of 'what works' in addressing individual deficit have most informed the training of Probation and Youth Justice staff in recent decades. In response to these contexts this study sought to employ mixed qualitative methods to uncover what practices mean to those involved. This chapter has sought to be clear about methods selected, sources selected, and tools of analysis used, in order that the reader is clear about how knowledge has been constructed. In aiming for transparency, the chapter has already uncovered some key issues related to peer mentoring. These include the challenges of delivering services within an insecure funding environment, the problem of recruiting volunteers from a small pool of expertise and the diversity of activities that constitute 'peer mentoring'. Each of these issues will be explored in greater detail in the following chapters.

Acknowledgements

This chapter has adapted material from the following works:

Buck, G., (2019), 'Politicisation or professionalisation? Exploring divergent aims within UK voluntary sector peer mentoring', *The Howard Journal of Crime and Justice*, **58**(3), pp. 349–365.
Buck, G., (2017), "I wanted to feel the way they did": Mimesis as a situational dynamic of peer mentoring by ex-offenders. *Deviant Behavior*, **38**(9), pp. 1027–1041.

I am thankful to the publishers for their permission.

References

Babbie, E., (2011), *The basics of social research* (5th Edn.). Belmont, CA and London: Wadsworth Cengage Learning.
Berelowitz, S., Firmin, C., Edwards, G. & Gulyurtlu, S., (2012), "I thought I was the only one. The only one in the world": The Office of the Children's Commissioner's inquiry into child sexual exploitation in gangs and groups: Interim report.
Blades, R., Hart, D., Lea, J. & Willmott, N., (2011), *Care - a stepping stone to custody? The views of children in care on the links between care, offending and custody*. London: Prison reform trust.
Bourdieu, P., (1980), *The logic of practice*. Reprint, California: Stanford University Press, 1990 edition.
Buck, G., (2019a), 'Mentoring'. In: Ugwudike, P., Graham, H., McNeill, F., Raynor, P., Taxman, F., Trotter, C., (Eds). *Routledge companion to rehabilitative work in criminal justice*. Abingdon, Oxon: Routledge.
Buck, G., (2019b), "'It's a tug of war between the person I used to be and the person I want to be": The terror, complexity, and limits of leaving crime behind', *Illness, Crisis & Loss*, **27**(2), pp. 101–118.
Buck, G., (2018), 'The core conditions of peer mentoring', *Criminology & Criminal Justice*, **18**(2), pp. 190–206.
Buck, G., (2017), "'I wanted to feel the way they did": Mimesis as a situational dynamic of peer mentoring by ex-offenders. *Deviant Behavior*, **38**(9), pp. 1027–1041.
Buck, G., (2014), 'Civic re-engagements amongst former prisoners', *Prison Service Journal*, **214**, pp. 52–57.
Caddick, B. & Webster, A., (1998), 'Offender literacy and the probation service', *The Howard Journal of Criminal Justice*, **37**(2), pp. 137–147.
Cameron, D., (2001), *Working with spoken discourse*. London: SAGE.
Centre for Social Justice, (2013), *The new probation landscape: Why the voluntary sector matters if we are going to reduce reoffending*. www.centreforsocialjustice.org.uk/core/wp-content/uploads/2016/08/landscape.pdf [Accessed August 2019].

Charmaz, K., (2014), *Constructing grounded theory* (2nd Edn.). London: Sage.

Corbetta, P., (2003), *Social research: Theory, methods and techniques.* London: Sage Publications.

Crotty, M., (1998), *The foundations of social research: Meaning and perspective in the research process.* London: Sage.

Crowther-Dowey, C., (2007), *An introduction to criminology and criminal justice.* Hampshire: Palgrave Macmillan.

DeKeseredy, W.S., (2011), *Contemporary critical criminology.* Abingdon, Oxon: Routledge.

Denscombe, M., (2014), *The good research guide: For small-scale social research projects* (4th Edn.). Berkshire: McGraw-Hill Education (UK).

Denscombe, M., (2010), *Ground rules for social research: Guidelines for good practice* (2nd Edn.). Berkshire: Open University Press.

Ferrell, J. & Hamm, M.S., (1998), *Ethnography at the edge: Crime, deviance, and field research.* Boston, MA: Northeastern University Press.

Fielding, N., (2008), 'Ethnography'. In: Gilbert, G.N., (Ed.), *Researching social life* (3rd Edn.). Los Angeles, CA; London: Sage.

Fraser, H., (2004), 'Doing narrative research analysing personal stories line by line', *Qualitative Social Work*, **3**(2), pp. 179–201.

Gelsthorpe, L., (2006), *What is criminology for? Looking within and beyond', plenary speech presented at the British Society of Criminology conference.* University of Strathclyde, Glasgow, unpublished presentation. Cited in: Spalek, B., (2008), *Communities, identities and crime.* Bristol: Policy Press.

Hall, R., (2008), *Applied social research: Planning, designing and conducting real-world research.* South Yarra: Palgrave Macmillan.

Kerstetter, K., (2012), 'Insider, outsider, or somewhere in between: The impact of researchers' identities on the community-based research process', *Journal of Rural Social Sciences*, **27**(2), pp. 99–117.

Kiegelmann, M., (2009), 'Making oneself vulnerable to discovery. Carol Gilligan in conversation with Mechthild Kiegelmann', *Forum Qualitative Sozialforschung/ Forum: Qualitative Social Research*, **10**(2). pp. 1–19

King, N. & Horrocks, C., (2010), *Interviews in qualitative research.* Los Angeles, CA: Sage.

Kirk, J. & Reid, G., (2001), 'An examination of the relationship between dyslexia and offending in young people and the implications for the training system', *Dyslexia*, **7**(2), pp. 77–84.

Major, C.H. & Savin-Baden, M., (2010), *An introduction to qualitative research synthesis: Managing the information explosion in social science research.* Abingdon, Oxon: Routledge.

Maxfield, M. & Babbie, E., (2015), *Research methods for criminal justice and criminology* (7th Edn.). Stamford, CT: Cengage Learning.

Mullen, J., (2018), *What the future probation reforms mean for charities.* Available at: www.civilsociety.co.uk/voices/jessica-mullen-what-the-future-probation-reforms-mean-for-charities.html [Accessed August 2019].

Nespor, J. & Barber, L., (1995), 'Audience and the politics of narrative'. In: Hatch, J.A. & Wisniewski, R., (Eds.), *Life history and narrative.* London: Falmer Press.

Noaks, L. & Wincup, E., (2004), *Criminological research: Understanding qualitative methods.* London: Sage.

Price, G. & Skinner, J., (2007), *Support for learning differences in higher education, the essential practitioners' guide*. Stoke on Trent: Trentham Books.

Princes Trust, (2008), *Making the case: One-to-one support for young offenders*, 23 June 2008: Princes Trust, Rainer, St Giles Trust, CLINKS.

Remenyi, D., Swan, N. & Van Den Assem, B., (2011), *Ethics protocols and research ethics committees: Successfully obtaining approval for your academic research*. Reading: Academic Publishing International.

Seddon, N., (2007), *Who cares? How state funding and political activism change charity*. London: The Institute for the Study of Civil Society.

Smithson, H., Ralphs, R. & Williams, P., (2013), 'Used and abused the problematic usage of gang terminology in the United Kingdom and its implications for ethnic minority youth', *British Journal of Criminology*, **53**(1), pp. 113–128.

Spalek, B., (2008), *Communities, identities and crime*. Bristol: Policy Press.

Stanley, L. & Wise, S., (1993), *Breaking out again feminist ontology and epistemology*. London: Routledge.

Taylor, V.E. & Winquist, C.E., (2001), *Encyclopaedia of postmodernism*. London: Routledge.

The Social Innovation Partnership, (2012), 'The WIRE (Women's Information and Resettlement for Ex-offenders) Evaluation Report'. London: The Social Innovation Partnership. Available at: www.stgilestrust.org.uk/misc/Support%20for%20vulnerable%20women%20leaving%20prison%20full%20report.pdf [Accessed August 2019].

Willoughby, M., Parker, A. & Ali, R., (2013), *Mentoring for offenders: Mapping services for adult offenders in England and Wales*. London: Sova.

Part Two

Making sense of peer mentoring

Chapter 5

The importance of identity to peer mentoring

Reconstructions of identity, or changes in self-identity, are important aspects of maintaining desistance from crime (Burnett & Maruna, 2006; McNeill, 2006; Maruna, 2001). Peers may be particularly well placed to assist with such identity shifts, given that their appraisals are often more readily internalised (Asencio & Burke, 2011) and they can recruit their contemporaries into 'a new figured world, a new frame of understanding' (Holland, Skinner, Lachicotte & Cain, 1998: 66) using the personal story as a 'cultural vehicle for identity formation' (Holland et al., 1998: 71). Peer mentors are, therefore, potential co-authors helping mentees to imagine and live out new identity stories. This chapter demonstrates that identity shift is not just prompted by the presence of peers undergoing changes, but rather it is preceded by desire (Girard, 1977). Mentees often come to mimic the desires of their mentors whom they admire and respect. However, identity is also conceptualised in terms of performance and external audiences (Goffman, 1963, 1961) as mentors recount differing levels of successful identity transformation in the face of social stigma. The chapter also employs Bernstein's (1971) theory that language is central to social identity by illustrating how peer mentoring often involves translating the spoken word. Respondents suggest that mentors and mentees use shared forms of language, which differ to those used by figures of authority and as a result identity is employed as a resource for translating the social world. Finally, the chapter considers whether knowledge which draws upon a particular identity position breeds essentialist exclusivity (Fuss, 1989), or whether it is an important strategy to prevent the silencing of people from marginal groups (hooks, 1994). A third position is forwarded, which calls for an inclusion of excluded voices within practices based upon *dialogue*.

The chapter begins by tracing claims of authenticity in respondent narratives. Mentors and their advocates often employ the 'ex-offender' identity as an authentic position from which others can learn. This identity position is constructed as a useful resource, which can inspire self-improvement and facilitate new forms of communication. Peer mentors often claim a non-authoritarian standpoint, constructing peer-to-peer relationships as horizontal rather than hierarchical, yet the chapter concludes by highlighting a number of barriers faced by mentors as they attempt to employ identity in these ways, given that external perceptions do not always reinforce individual efforts.

Claims to authenticity

Personal experience of crime and desistance is claimed to offer peer mentors an *authentic standpoint,* which facilitates bonding with mentees (Princes Trust, 2012), offers a credibility that statutory workers do not have (Nellis & McNeill, 2008) and enables 'authentic empathy' (Portillo, Goldberg & Taxman, 2017: 320). Peers also have specific knowledge of life inside and outside of prison, which can be helpful to those in the criminal justice system (Devilly, Sorbello, Eccleston & Ward, 2005). Respondents in this study often agreed with these claims and so buttressed the ex-offender standpoint upon which such statements rest, however, they often did so in ways which excluded other forms of knowledge. Ben, for example, is using a peer mentoring service attached to his Probation Office. He valued knowledge drawn from lived experiences above that which is gained from theoretical learning:

> It does seem to work better when you've actually been there, that's how I personally feel anyway. Somebody who's just read it from a book isn't the same as [someone who has] actually been there and done it.
>
> (Ben, Mentee)

Similarly, Fiona, a mentee using the same service argues:

> You can't learn [experience], you can pick pointers up, but you can't get that life skill, that extra that you need that completes it. You can't get it unless you've seen it, been there, got somewhere, you know?
>
> (Fiona, Mentee)

One problem with this stance is that it suggests a true and unified essence of the *criminal* experience. This rests upon essentialist beliefs in the 'true essence of things, the invariable and fixed properties which define the "whatness" of a given entity' (Fuss, 1989: xi) when clearly, experiences of crime and change are different for different individuals. In addition to abridging diverse experiences 'exclusions of this sort often breed exclusivity' (Fuss, 1989: 113–115). They suggest that people without lived experiences of crime have nothing to offer in mentoring settings. Adam, however, a peer mentoring project manager, challenged this assumption:

> In the past I've felt that experience [of offending] would count for most, but from the last two years I've kind of learned that that is not necessarily the case, just being genuine and sincere is more important.
>
> (Adam, Mentoring Coordinator)

Whilst there are counter views to the primacy of the ex-offender experience and indeed problems with the premise, the claimed importance of shared offending experience was a dominant theme in mentor and mentee narratives and therefore requires attention. Such shared experience was repeatedly presented as a *privileged* form of knowledge, wherein desistance from crime and the criminal justice system itself can only be fully understood if they have been experienced. Phil, for example, mentors adults in prison and young people in the community having spent a number of years in prison himself. He explains:

> The advantage is I've faced many of those barriers that they're [mentees] likely to encounter and obviously come through them, more importantly. So, you know, through that reflective practice I'm able to share that experience with them and prepare them.
>
> (Phil, Mentor)

Similarly Lin, who mentors adults in a community setting having spent a number of years in the criminal justice system for 'alcohol related offences', described peer mentoring as:

> Somebody that's had a similar experience or similar problem to me, but found a way to overcome it and then they would guide their client or their peer, by their own experiences.
>
> (Lin, Mentor and previously a Mentee)

Julie mentors adults in a community rehabilitation setting and has been subject to a number of community sentences. She considers that she has:

> A good [understanding] of the criminal justice system because I've been there myself. Also other things in my past, ye know, like getting in trouble, having horrible ex-boyfriends, other things have happened to me and I think I use that knowledge to guide them in the right way sometimes.
>
> (Julie, Mentor)

Phil, Lin and Julie all assert that mentors with personal experience have an understanding of barriers, systems and problematic relationships that they can draw upon to prepare and guide people. 'Reflection' upon the tactics learned from experience are essential to this model. These speakers describe forms of learning which rely upon the experiences of 'human beings in their relations with the world' (Freire, 1970: 60). They also suggest that this reflective understanding is not currently being utilised in existing approaches. This position was supported by a Probation manager who worked alongside one peer mentoring service:

> All of our ex-offender staff [peer mentors who went on to paid Probation roles] changed because of their own connections, not Probation. That's not

to say that Probation doesn't help, but that there are other strategies available outside professional understanding.

(Probation Manager)

These narratives aim to afford people with experiences of crime an authenticity because they have overcome barriers. They do not privilege what Pollack
(2004: 697) terms 'professional understandings' or 'deficit based constructions', but 'behaviour is contextualised' (Pollack, 2004: 697). Of course, not
all professional Probation staff subscribe to interventions which aim to correct individual deficit. Indeed, as will become clear in Chapter 9, not all peers
always avoid such models themselves. Nevertheless, there is an assertion of
voice present here, which aims to undermine professional knowledge; this
will be explored further below.

Undermining professional knowledge

Mentors and mentees alike often created a hierarchy of knowledge through
which they passionately relegated knowledge *not* based on personal experience:

Workers, in this building [probation officers]… they haven't got a clue
what they're talking about. They're sat in that chair and I'm not being
big-headed; they just don't know what they're talking about, they've
learnt it all out of a book.

(Fiona, Mentee)

Some of them [Probation staff] just don't know what they're talking
about, who've not been there. Alright they might have read it in books,
but you're not going to know unless you've been there done it, in my
eyes anyway.

(Don, Mentee)

There is an emotive *othering* of knowledge sources taking place, whereby
'books' and formal learning are demoted in favour of the sensed, the felt, the
experienced. Indeed, there is also an othering of the people who rely upon
such formal knowledge. Probation Officers and related professionals 'haven't
got a clue/ don't know'. These discursive constructions often reach further
than the knowledge base of professionals to include their assumed personal
histories. Toni, for example, was recruited as a peer mentor for a women's
employment project having previously used the service herself whilst on
Probation:

I think it's far better than going into like the Job Centre and someone
who's never done anything or experienced anything, you know, had a
wonderful life, saying: 'just get on with it; you've got to do it'.

(Toni, Mentor)

Toni assumes that there are significant differences between her own life experiences and those of the people tasked with helping her. As a result, she
views their strategies as unrealistic. Katy, a mentor at the same project, expressed a similar sentiment; she perceived that the professional helpers in her
life had degrees of social, educational and practical separation from her own
experience, which her peers do not:

> Someone who could have been brought up with a silver spoon in their
> mouth, and gone through college and university, and five minutes out of
> university, have to get a map out to find where you are and want to sit
> and tell you how to deal with your life and cope with things. Well no: 'go
> away I'm not listening to you!' With a peer it's equal, it's on the same level.
>
> (Katy, Mentor)

Lin, who has used a range of peer and professional services and now volunteers as a mentor herself, expresses a similar perception of professional distance and peer connection:

> With someone else like *the man in the suit* I'd just think 'you haven't got a
> clue, what do you mean?' And it would make me feel angry and resent-
> ful towards them, but if I get it off a peer I think, well, they know what
> they're on about and I trust their comments.
>
> (Lin, Mentor and previously a Mentee)

These speakers caricaturise professionals and officials by inverting the props
and associations of professionalism, or more accurately of social superiority –
the wonderful life – the silver spoon – the man in the suit. Attributes associated with
formal learning and professionalism are relegated below lived understandings of facing barriers, having 'horrible boyfriends' and overcoming problems. Peers who have 'been there' are elevated above people (particularly
professionals) who they assume have not. The peer mentor identity is, in
this sense, partly 'formed and reinvigorated through the threat and practice
of exclusion' (Spalek, 2008: 13). However, this exclusion is targeted at those
in positions of authority. Underlying these practices is a 'spirit of carnival…
the symbolic destruction of authority and official culture and the assertion
of popular renewal' (Arnds, 2008: 70). The carnival motif is a helpful one in
terms of theorising the techniques of inversion which are employed by mentors and mentees here. Mikhail Bakhtin (1965) saw the carnival as 'temporary liberation from the prevailing truth and the established order; it marked
the suspension of all hierarchical rank, privileges, norms, and prohibitions'
(Bakhtin, 1965: 10). Whilst peer mentoring is not intended to be temporary
and does not wholly achieve suspension of rank and privilege, as will become clear throughout this book, the mentors and mentees speaking here do
employ strategies, which challenge the established order and call for a symbolic destruction of professional authority. Indeed, like the carnival, there are

moments when peer mentoring represents a fracture of the established order. Peer mentors with convictions enter spaces and roles that were previously only open to professional officers, resulting in more *free and familiar* contact between 'ex-offenders' and the non-criminalised. These border crossings, along with a rhetorical inversion of expertise signifiers, attempt to undermine established approaches to 'rehabilitation', which have been experienced as hierarchical and excluding. In contrast, as demonstrated further below, peer mentors are constructed as non-authoritarian.

The non-authoritarian/non-hierarchical identity

The limited literature on peer mentoring does begin to acknowledge a commitment to egalitarianism. Boyce, Hunter and Hough (2009: vi), for example, see peer-led work as 'a counterbalance to the widespread belief that programmes are something that are "done" to offenders by specialists', whilst Kavanagh and Borrill (2013: 14) state that mentoring can be 'empowering in both prison and probation settings', in contrast to 'previous experiences of feeling powerless'. Respondents in this study advanced this narrative, arguing that mutuality and parity between mentor and mentee are vital elements of the mentoring relationship. Katy, for example, in dismissing the 'silver spoon' privilege of professionally trained interveners (above) also argued that: 'with a peer it's equal, it's on the same level' (Katy, Mentor). This perception of equality, of horizontal rather than hierarchical relationships, was persistent. In many of these narratives mentors with convictions are positioned not *just* as experts with unique experiential knowledge but also, crucially, as unpatronising 'equals'. Steve, for example, an ex-prisoner who volunteered as a peer mentor and now works as a paid Probation employee, frames his own past experience as a 'levelling' factor:

> [My mentees said] you're straight down the line, but you don't come across as if you think you're better than us... So I think that's why a lot of them tell me about their past and their upbringing, because I can relate to it.
>
> (Steve, Mentor and previously a Mentee)

Brad, a volunteer mentor with a long criminal history, employs a similar levelling strategy:

> Just being on the same sort of level as these young lads and knowing where the ones that have been in care come from, ones with drug habits come from, knowing where ones that have been in trouble with the police, problems with parents. I can relate to that, when I was nineteen I had problems.
>
> (Brad, Mentor)

Moreover, Brad sees his role as specifically managing the power dynamic present within formal criminal justice exchanges:

> If you go in hot handed like a probation officer, or anybody really that deals with them in these sorts of situations, they are all authority figures. It's about being the intermediary – in between that authority figure.
>
> (Brad, Mentor)

Brad recognises that 'heavy-handed enforcement strategies run the risk of adversely effecting [mentees'] attitudes… [that] oppressive enforcement critically damages the legitimacy of that authority' (Robinson & McNeill, 2008: 438). He sees his own role as a conciliator, mediating the potential damage of such an approach. He aims to be *on a level* in terms of both approach and status in order to achieve legitimacy. There are also echoes of Goffman's 'mixed contacts' between the stigmatised and 'normals' here (1963: 25). Goffman argued that 'during mixed contacts, the stigmatised individual is likely to feel that he is 'on', having to be self-conscious and calculating about the impression he is making' (Goffman, 1963: 26), a perception that can be traced in Steve's words (above). Common experience levels the ground, offering a space free from 'the sort of patronizing you get from straight people' (Goffman, 1963: 26). A mentor who has lived understandings of crime is perceived to level the power dynamic between helper and helped, or between worker and client. Here, peer mentors are *not* distant experts patronising mentees as flawed subjects and dictating change, but companions *relating* to known challenges and barriers. These mentors describe a joining of forces with their mentees on an equal footing. This representation of peer mentoring shares some characteristics of 'libertarian education', whereby 'people to come to feel like masters of their thinking and views of the world explicitly or implicitly manifest in their own suggestions and those of their comrades' (Freire, 1970: 105). Mentoring is thus represented as a form of shared problem solving, rather than the banking of actuarially assessed improvements by a superior professional. Shared problem solving is about:

> Getting on a level with the people, with the audience, so it's not like a teacher model where it's a teacher talking down to the pupil, it's more like on a level.
>
> (Phil, Mentor)

I wouldn't want to be seen as being above them, or better than them. You know? It's non-judgmental, we are sort of equals and we're doing this together. It's a 'we thing'… If they see you or think of you as being better than them, then you're relationship is not going to work… It's 'us', well a partnership really, to help each other… So being able to meet with someone who's not going to put them down all the time and say 'you should have been here – you should have done this'.

(John, Mentor)

Being 'on a level' does not just refer to having shared experiences or a sense of shared identity therefore, but it refers to collaborative relationships, which are distinct from 'intervention' in the normative sense. This dynamic was not just voiced by mentors, but also by mentees. Lin, for example, attended a peer-led alcohol recovery group and one-to-one peer mentoring. She explains:

I felt more comfortable talking to my peers, because they weren't official people. I felt like they were on my level and I didn't have to worry about what I was saying, worry about their reaction... It wasn't authoritative, I didn't feel like I was getting looked down on. I was made to feel really relaxed and at ease, which obviously helps you to open up more then, if you feel like that.

(Lin, Mentor and Previously a Mentee)

Will and Paul, mentees at a mentoring service attached to the Probation Service perceive a similar lack of hierarchy within their one-to-one mentoring relationships:

A probation officer only knows what you tell them, and take that on belief, whereas a mentor has been there and done it. So if you speak to them, they know if you're speaking crap or not, it's like a proper conversation... No hesitation or anything, it's hard to explain... Just someone to talk to, like a mate or something, it's mad. [They] still have a badge round [their] neck, but not proper official, [they] talk on a level to you.

(Will, Mentee)

Not to be too in your face about things, like down to earth, relaxed... Not give you un-useful information. It's like [mentor name], he doesn't chat shit to you, he won't tell you to do something he wouldn't do himself. That's a good quality to have.

(Paul, Mentee)

These mentees describe experiences of mutual recognition, of parity with their mentors. Mentors are not perceived here as official, but like 'mates', offering suggestions they themselves would or have used, which results in feelings of ease. Importantly, however, this parity is also valued because it differs so much from what has been known before, because it is *not* a relationship with disciplinary consequences for saying the wrong thing, or which requires people to say 'the right thing' even if it is not the truth of an experience; and because it is not 'in your face' or interrogative. Peer mentoring relationships based upon such collaborative ideals potentially allow more trusting, open and peaceable exchanges. These articulations communicate desires not only for levelling the power disparity between helper and helped, but also for relationships where personal experiences can be explored with less judgement and adverse consequences.

The limits of parity

Whilst these speakers call for open and comfortable relationships wherein relaxed discussions can take place, for non-authoritative, 'proper' and open conversations, respondents also spoke of restrictions to such exchanges within current criminal justice settings. In the relationships they described outside of mentoring, mentors and mentees often felt *unheard*, *dehumanised* and *deconstructed*. Keisha, for example, mentors young people in the community; she came to this work after being released from prison and feeling that her voice was unheard by the resettlement services she was referred to:

> There's no voice for the people... People just get lost in the system, do you know what I mean? And it's sad, because most people that do want to make the change, and can't, go back into crime.
>
> (Keisha, Mentor)

This demotion of personal voice, as argued in Chapter 2, can be seen as a consequence of the 'professional nature' of justice services, which have increasingly deprived 'offenders' of a voice in their own narrative. To quote Ballinger again:

> [K]nowledge generated outside scientific discourses such as lived experiences, autobiographies and memories can be silenced, 'subjugated or disqualified'... prisoners' version of 'the truth' is located at the bottom of the hierarchy of knowledge.
>
> (Ballinger, 2011: 110)

People subject to formal criminal justice processes experience a devaluation of their voices given the *superior* knowledge held by those in 'the system'. As Freire argued, however:

> Pedagogy which begins with the egoistic interests of the oppressors (an egoism cloaked in the false generosity of paternalism) and makes of the oppressed the objects of its humanitarianism, itself maintains and embodies oppression. It is an instrument of dehumanization.
>
> (Freire, 1970: 36)

Freire argues that 'any attempt to treat people as semihumans only dehumanises them. When people are already dehumanized, due to the oppression they suffer, the process of their liberation must not employ the methods of dehumanization' (1970: 49). Interestingly his proposed antidote to dehumanisation is 'dialogue' (1970: 49). This is a notion that will be returned to. For the moment, however, it is important to recognise that the experience of dehumanisation is often familiar to people who have been subject to 'criminal justice'. Indeed, a surprising theme emerged from the interviews with both mentors and mentees in which they referred to themselves and each other in *non-human* terms:

> In a prison setting that's quite *dog eat dog*, offenders go into survival mode... some people just need to speak humanely to other people which doesn't always happen in prison, a humane conversation.
>
> (Phil, Mentor)

> Jail is *not for people*, jail doesn't rehabilitate you... *it's like a cattle market.*
>
> (Will, Mentee)

> I told this woman at college (about my conviction) and she just looked at me like she'd just *stepped in me,* and it was a horrible feeling.
>
> (Eve, Mentee)

> When I got referred to that place [a resettlement charity] they thought there was nothing wrong with me because *the bag looked clean,* the bag never had two teeth missing, you know? Because people stereotype don't they?.
>
> (Keisha, Mentor)

The dehumanising effects of prison have been noted before. Scraton (2009: 73–74), for example, pointed to the dehumanisation reported by many prisoners:

> There were constant references by guards to animal descriptions ('beast,' 'dog,' 'maggot') and to waste ('scum,' 'dross,' 'shit')... [As a result] Prisoners experienced loss of identity, lack of respect and personal humiliation.

Morin (2015) also noted how:

> Caging humans requires producing them as animalistic first... Prison inmates themselves turn to animal imagery to express the dehumanizing effects of isolation and exposure in the prison. Many express shame and anger at being caged in view of other that position them like animals in a zoo.
>
> (Morin, 2015: 75)

It is quite possible therefore that the speakers here have internalised such messages and come to see themselves and their contemporaries in animalistic or non-human terms. However, two of the four voices above are not referring to prison experiences, but to the judgements people make of them in the community. The 'dirtying power' (Bouson, 2000: 131) of such animalistic representations therefore appears to run deeper than direct insults or experiences. These speakers appear to feel their humanity diminished, simply by being gazed on as an 'offender'. This can be compounded by professional assessment frameworks. Tools such as OASys (the national adult Offender Assessment System) and ASSET (the national Youth Justice Assessment Profile), create 'an artificial individual constructed from ticking boxes' (Durnescu, 2012: 206). Identity in these contexts does not exist in terms of a situated, felt, holistic experience, but as an 'objective', selective and often electronic assessment. However, 'categorizing human identity into axis grids and risk instruments is an act of deconstruction of subjectivity' (Aas, 2004: 387). It breaks complex individuals down into signs or indices and is a partial picture, incomplete in terms of the lived and felt human experience. Steve, for example, explains how he and his mentee had little faith in the processes that the prison service and Probation employ:

> When you're in prison you're just a number... What good is it doing, him coming in here [probation] for half an hour chat with you and then he goes... 'I'll just blag my way through, I'll just attend the appointments, do what I've got to do... like I have done with all my probation appointments', like I have all my life.
>
> (Steve, Mentor and previously a Mentee)

Hope, a mentor in a young woman's gang intervention project, similarly critiques such decontextualised categorisation:

> Professionals need to get people with [personal] experience and not just people to tick a few boxes... To get us in to show them little things they may be missing, it might change people's perspective, but at least they'll learn and we'll all get the same thing we want, which is progression and change.
>
> (Hope, Mentor)

'Box ticking' and assessment 'appointments' are derided within these accounts; they are reframed as blocking activities, which mask underlying truths of an experience rather than uncovering them. As experiences are appropriated into managerial formats respondents see such representations as lacking the full picture. Moreover, people who have their subjectivity deconstructed for instrumental purposes and their life history artificially reconstructed through formal assessment, come to see the people doing the deconstructing as 'not having a clue'. Peer mentors, in contrast, often seek to recognise the holistic experience of people involved with crime, to recognise them as human:

> You're dealing with a human being and when you're dealing with a human being it has its own mind.
>
> (Keisha, Mentor)

> We are able to work on enhancing and empowering them as individuals, and as humans, and part of society, because at moment they're outcasts.
>
> (Hope, Mentor)

> Some people just need to speak humanely to other people, which doesn't always happen in prison, a humane conversation… We always have to get titles, why can't we just be humans?.
>
> (Phil, Mentor)

In contrast to box-ticking and risk instruments, these aims for peer mentoring are grounded in subjectivity; they position lives as lived experiences rather than measurable, quantifiable components: 'She said this is your life, where do you want to take it? Take a step at a time, you start to think 'oh yea I forgot this is my life' I've been so lost in everything else for ages' (Georgie, Mentee). If increasingly professionalised knowledge of 'offenders' has led to a denial of subject voice, a decontextualising of identity and a deconstruction of subjectivity, then peer mentoring can be read as a powerful riposte to the authority of professionals and their tools by asserting the need for human-level engagement.

Identity as a resource to inspire self-improvement

This chapter has argued that mentors and their advocates often construct an ex-offender identity as an authentic position, one which differs significantly from that of the authoritarian professional; and which can assist in building relationships which potentially have greater parity. However, peer mentoring also relies on positioning ex-offenders as role models. The offering of role models rests upon the assumption that people will emulate that which they see in others. Rene Girard (1962) offered a theoretical foundation for this premise, arguing that 'mimetic desire'– imitating the desires of those we admire – is what makes it possible for us to construct 'our own, albeit inevitably unstable, identities' (Girard, 2010: 58). This premise, however, rests upon an intrinsic hierarchy between mentor and mentee because imitation explicitly acknowledges superiority (Girard, 1991: 240). Discourses which frame peer mentoring as non-authoritarian, therefore, serve to mask this otherwise discernible hierarchy. Despite this apparent contradiction, one of the strongest claims made about relationships based upon shared past experiences was that they can *inspire* people to change:

> If I'm looking to deter young people from crime, I've got to be that positive change, to make them know that I've made it…I made a change. It wasn't easy but look what I've done. I've got to inspire people.
>
> (Keisha, Mentor)

> They can see people like myself and [the coordinators], and several other mentors that have come from an offending/ drug using background, and can say 'Well look they've done it, why can't I do it? They've gone straight; they've sorted their lives out, they've got good jobs why can't I do it?' That's basically, the basic idea behind it. If people see you, and say: 'You can do it, why can't I do it?' in their own mind.
>
> (Brad, Mentor)

These perspectives offer further support for claims that peers can be effective inspirational role models (South, Bagnall & Woodall, 2017; Hunter and Kirby, 2011; Boyce et al., 2009) and offer credence to policy aims to make 'good use of the old lags in stopping the new ones' (Grayling, 2012). Accounts of inspirational mentors also fit with Girard's (1962; Girard & Doran, 2008) theory that people come to mimic the desires of those they admire:

> I wanted to feel the way they did, they weren't beaming out happiness, but they weren't sad, they was that content in their life they were offering to other people, to help them and I wanted to be able to do that.
>
> (Georgie, Mentee)

> To meet people who were just as twisted as I was, they've gone through change, having to change my own view on the world… You see somebody for yourself go through them changes and be like a positive member of the community, you know it's possible.
>
> (Lin, Mentor and previously a Mentee)

> Because I can see her… Like, what she was telling me about her school life, I thought that about mine, and then now looking at her where she is. I think it's a good experience, because she's got far with her life… I just think they're inspiring.
>
> (Karina, Mentee)

People are inspired by peer mentors because they *admire* them. They mimic their desire for self-improvement. Importantly, they also *see* the change which is expected. It becomes visible. They 'learn enough pieces of expression to be able to 'fill in' and manage' (Goffman, 1959: 79). However, there appears to be more to these accounts than simply imitated desire or directed performance. Rather mentors appear to provide inspiration in subtly different ways. Whilst all appeared to recognise and respond to the invitation to 'look what I've done, you can too', the voices of these mentees also illustrate the complexity of inspiration when at work in different subjects. For Lin, her role model facilitated a shift in perspective, indeed she 'changed her view on the world' and in doing so introduced the *possibility* of newness, a map to redemption when none had seemed possible. For Karina it was important to *see* someone who has not only prospered, but who crucially had also been in a similar place to her. This allowed her to relate more easily to potential within herself. Success was not something that just happened to others, but to people *like her.* For Georgie, the process of being inspired most clearly resonated with the notion of imitated desire: 'I wanted to feel the way they did'. The object of desire inspired in her is not specifically 'going straight' however, or even just a feeling of 'happiness', but rather it is the desire *to give to others:* 'they were offering to other people... I wanted to be able to do that'. Future self-projection is key to these narratives; mentors are not just inspirational because they are admirable, or offer pieces of direction, but because they offer a template of a future life, which appears attainable regardless of problematic histories. Hucklesby and Wincup (2014) argue that this dynamic could be particularly valuable:

> Mentoring projects have so far concentrated their efforts on enhancing instrumental/ secondary goods replicating much of the work undertaken by prisons and probation services (Farrall, 2004). Instead, they could make a unique contribution to criminal justice by assisting offenders to construct visions of 'good lives' free from offending.
>
> (Hucklesby & Wincup, 2014: 16)

For the speakers in this study, inspiration does not simply require a model to construct a 'vision', but a model who has faced similar challenges and has found a new route; who now has something to give. This notion of giving is one I want to stay with for a moment. A significant number of mentees, like Georgie, came to share the desire of their mentors to volunteer or to give:

> [Mentor name] is now working for probation; I'd like to do that. I'd love to work with ex-offenders and people with drug problems, cos like I said, who's the best person to talk to? Someone who's been there and done it. I'd like to do something like that, like [mentor name].
>
> (Don, Mentee)

> One of the lads [mentees], I was telling him how I've changed, he said: 'I could do your job', I said 'you could do my job – maybe in a few years get rid of your probation order', 'Yea, yea I could do'.
>
> (Brad, Mentor)

This pattern could be interpreted as a form of reciprocity in that mentees persistently described a wish to help in the ways they had been helped by their mentors. However, it also resembles Girardian mimesis, given that mentees come to imitate their mentors' desire to help, '[t]he mimetic model directs the disciple's desire to a particular object by desiring it himself... mimetic desire is rooted...in a third party whose desire is imitated by the subject' (Girard, 1977: 180). Mentees mimic (learn) desire for the thing their mentors most visibly want – the desire to mentor others, or to *give*. Whilst this process is not perhaps the intended aim of peer mentoring projects, it is not a problematic dynamic. Quite the contrary given that Uggen and Janikula (1999) found 'real reintegration requires more than physical re-entry [... it also involves] "earning" one's place back in the moral community' (in Burnett & Maruna, 2006: 84). If peer mentoring results in mentees becoming volunteer helpers, it encourages a number of subtle processes, which underpin and maintain desistance. Mentees become involved with an activity that decreases their chances of arrest (Burnett & Maruna, 2006: 88) and demonstrates their moral reparation. More than this however, it offers a platform for mentees to re-frame their past in new ways: 'who's the best person? / I could do that'. This resembles a feature of 'secondary desistance' (Burnett & Maruna, 2006: 94), wherein people can distinguish 'between the 'old me', that is the self who had offended, and the 'new' or 'real me', that is a person who is caring towards others and able to use his/her shameful past in order to help others' (Burnett & Maruna, 2006: 94). It also helps mentees to gain a sense of social and emotional wellbeing – 'better myself... make me feel better'. There are clear articulations here that the ex-offender identity offers inspiration, this point will be returned to *and problematised* in Chapter 8.

Identity as a resource for translating the social world

This chapter has presented several ways in which mentors and mentees utilise shared offending histories. They position authoritarian professionals as *other*, enabling relations that are more egalitarian. However, peer mentors have also been described – by both themselves and their mentees – as privileged; as role models from whom those still involved with crime can draw inspiration. This tension between parity and privilege is also present in one of the most surprising themes to emerge in this study: that shared past experiences can be important for helping people to *translate* the social world. Translation here operates at two different levels – making meaning and linguistic comprehensibility.

Notions of translation can be traced in the existing literature on peer approaches. Peer mentoring for 'lower socioeconomic urban students... involves translating and transmitting the academic culture and values into concepts and actions the mentee can understand and employ' (Morales,

Ambrose-Roman & Perez-Maldonado, 2016: 122–123). Peers are also 'deemed more credible sources of information because they have experienced similar struggles and are, therefore, able to "speak the same language"' (Devilly et al., 2005: 231). Mentoring is framed as a process of reducing the inaccessibility of professional services, be it through '"outreach workers" linking individuals with local services that they would otherwise fail to access' (Newburn & Shiner, 2006: 27) or the 'targeting of mentoring for those variously identified as "disaffected", "disengaged", "non-participating", or "hardest to help"' (Colley, 2002: 9). These efforts allude to the fact that different individuals can conceive of the same social experiences wholly differently; that they may be speaking a different language. People who have spent lengthy or repeated periods in prison, for example, described feeling excluded from the technical realities and demands of everyday life:

> I've been in and out of jail for most of my life, so like opening a bank account and going online, doing a CV, that's never been a priority for me before. It's a bit of a pain in the arse doing it on your own when you don't know how to. [Mentor name] being there, you know how to do it, has really helped me.
>
> (Paul, Mentee)

> Maybe that person [the mentee], like myself, went to prison at a time where social networking weren't booming, and come out to Smart phones and texting. So this is all new operating, and it's important for the person that's going to be mentoring to understand that.
>
> (Keisha, Mentor)

Paul and Keisha required more than a role model, then, they also argue that mentoring has a role to play in *translating* the social world, in explaining the practical requirements of job seeking and using technology, in rendering these things knowable. Mentoring here involves transmitting the norms of mainstream inclusion to those who have been physically excluded and who consequently 'don't know how' to do specific administrative tasks that may be required of them; or are overwhelmed by technological advances, which have happened in their absence. This kind of translation of unfamiliar tasks and resources is perhaps something we would expect to see in relation to mentoring activity given that practical benefits 'such as help with benefit claims, dealing with frustrations, housing or employment' (Princes Trust, 2012: 4) have already been reported. Moreover, peers have been argued to have 'specific knowledge' (Devilly et al., 2005: 223). Translations of *speech*, however, were a less expected finding:

> [My mentor] helps me explain things better to the doctor [GP], cos sometimes I don't know what words to use... So they help me, you know?

Any form filling, any forms, I'm no good at spelling, struggle to read sometimes.

(Fiona, Mentee)

She [mentor] came with me when I applied for [University...] she does a lot of speaking on my behalf... I'm doing it part time because I am on benefits... that's something I wouldn't have known about until [mentor] phoned up on my behalf... she knows the ins and outs.

(Janet, Mentee)

There was official kind of language that we could use... if there's people that struggle to understand it would be left to us to judge... add a bit of humour [...the informality] is a really good thing for building up relationships.

(Ellie, Mentor)

There appears to be a language barrier at play in professional settings, which limits communication. The task of the mentor is to *translate* professional processes and forms of speech to mentees and to speak on behalf of mentees to professionals. There is an obvious parallel here with Bernstein's theoretical contention (in Chapter 3) that there are different modes of speech found within the middle class and working class (Bernstein, 1971: 78). Bernstein argued that 'the typical, dominant speech mode of the middle class... facilitates verbal elaboration of subjective intent' (1971: 78), providing a barrier to the lower working class whose speech 'discourages the speaker from verbally elaborating subjective intent and progressively orients the user to descriptive, rather than abstract, concepts' (Bernstein, 1971: 79). This reading seems to be partially endorsed by both Fiona and Ellie who imply that professional settings employ unknown, complex forms of *talk*. However, there are some problems with this reading. To suggest that mentees speak in 'simpler' terms than the professionals they encounter, without adequate words, is to assume a universality of mentees' linguistic capacity. It also invites the 'deficit theory' criticisms levelled at Bernstein in which he is accused of viewing one group as tacitly superior to another (Sadovnik, 2008). Indeed, even if these criticisms are countered with the same response that Bernstein used – that the pattern observed is not *deficit*, but conceptual *difference* – we still have a problem. The task of the peer mentor in these situations is not to translate mentees' formulation of the world, but to translate into and from *more elaborate* forms into simpler ones. Put more simply, the mentee's voice is relegated in an unfavorable hierarchy; their words are either taken and made to fit those of the medic (in Fiona's case), or shaped by the perspectives of others, such as the mentor, whose message needs to be communicated in simpler terms (in Ellie's case). The social progression of mentees therefore requires that they accept, or must trust, *others framing of the world*, whether those of 'professional'

or mentor. In neither example is the voice of the mentee elevated to equal
authority:

> What's been missing from some social care for ever and a day has been
> that user perspective, it's all been tokenistic, we need to have that user
> perspective as central and as respected.
>
> (Lol, Mentoring Coordinator)

This notion of mentoring as bridging a linguistic space is not wholly disempowering however. Indeed Hope, a mentor in a young woman's gang
intervention project, articulates some of the complexities of this theme well.
She begins by describing how selfhood and by extension 'peer-hood' has a
linguistic character:

> I never change my language, my language is me, and who I am, and
> where I'm from. When I'm in a professional setting I know I have to
> change the way I speak, in order to get in touch with different people.
> But you know, you are who you are and a lot of kids find they can't relate,
> because a lot of professionals use big words. Whereas, for me, I just get
> on that level and that's how I talk to them and whereas that might not be
> classed as a professional thing to say, if it works: why not?.
>
> (Hope, Mentor)

For Hope, language is wholly entwined with identity: 'my language is me';
it is also interwoven with personal history: 'where I'm from'. Yet she sees a
fundamental mismatch between the language used by the 'kids' she works
with and 'professionals' tasked with helping them. They cannot relate, they
cannot get 'in touch'; there is a tangible barrier (despite both groups being
English speakers), a use of 'big words', which requires translation. As before,
there is a strong echo of Bernstein here. Where Bernstein saw a middle class
characterised by elaboration and a lower working class discouraged from verbal elaboration (Bernstein, 1971: 78–79), Hope implies that professionals use
exclusive speech with people who communicate on a different 'level'. Hope
herself does not specify class as the dividing barrier here, yet her clarification
below, in which she recalls her experience as a trainee teacher, is replete with
references to 'posh' and 'urban' and wholly expressive of social stratification:

> They [trainee teachers] would have just turned up and expected the kids
> to listen, but when you don't have that relationship and your teacher uses
> a different language a lot of urban children misread well-spoken people
> for posh. It's automatically 'you can't understand where I come from' and
> as a child you put those barriers up... For me, enhancing and empow-
> ering an individual is so important, because there are too many people
> in a professional sense that will write kids off... If they [teachers] don't

understand these kids, it's easier to take the easy option, because it takes too much time and effort to work with these kids. Because it's done over a period of time and that's how you develop that relationship.

(Hope, Mentor)

Interestingly, whilst Hope initially frames herself as something of an interlocutor, it is not translation *explicitly* (whereby meanings are expressed in another word, term or medium) that Hope advocates here. She is not suggesting that mentors translate the words of professionals to 'urban' children using different terms, or even that they translate the words of these children to professionals. Rather she calls for acknowledgement of differences in language and the mutual exclusions which take place as a result of a failure to recognise such differences. In doing so she calls for a levelling of the relationship between the two discussants and for relationships that do not position children as inferior to professionals because they cannot be understood or speak in different ways. She also suggests that patient relationship-building may be a tool for connecting and empowering both parties. What we appear to have returned to then, is a call for inclusiveness of voice. In her call to 'get in touch', to not 'write kids off' and to 'develop that relationship' in language that makes sense, Hope echoes Freire's call for a method 'based on dialogue, which is a horizontal relationship between persons' (Freire, 1974: 42). For this to happen however an awareness of excluded voices must arise:

[A]s a professor... I had to teach people what a small group of white intellectuals had decided was knowledge... it dawned on me that [the arguments and stories] might just be dreams, reflections of the conceit of a small group who had succeeded in enslaving everyone else with their ideas... [W]e must start learning from those we have enslaved for they have much to offer and, at any rate, they have the right to live as they see fit even if they are not as pushy about their rights and their views as Western conquerors have always been.

(Feyerabend, 1993: 263–265)

This indicates that for communication within criminal justice to improve, there needs to be more open dialogue between parties, dialogue which respects the voices, histories and perspectives of those subject to interventions. This point will re-emerge in Chapter 7. For now, however, the potential of peer mentoring, as described here, is not necessarily to translate the language of professionals, of that small group with dominant ideas, but to model communication based on open dialogue. For educated experts to continue 'banking' (Freire, 1970: 53) the known answers to *the crime problem* with those who are experiencing it, without really listening or engaging in critical dialogue is merely to maintain the status quo; to maintain the power imbalances inherent in criminal justice and perhaps even to stifle change. What peer mentors appear to be asserting, through observations of language differences and mis-communications, is that there is a need for a more dialogical communication (Bakhtin, 1984) about crime, communication that includes those people who have perceived criminality as a lived reality *in addition* to those working in theoretical or professional realms. This theme of translation, or more accurately 'horizontal' communication, calls for efforts at mutual understanding. These are issues that criminology has not yet fully appreciated as constructive influences in the change process. Peer mentoring, by promoting the inclusion of an 'ex-offender' perspective, calls us to task on this.

Problems with common identity claims

Throughout this chapter respondents have constructed and buttressed an 'ex-offender' identity. This is an identity defined by past experiences of crime, which is claimed to facilitate understanding, egalitarianism, connection and inclusiveness. It is important to note, however, that the potential and importance of this identity position was not universally supported. This section will therefore explore two specific problems with employing an ex-offender identity. First, it will highlight the difficulties people faced in having their 'ex-offender' identity recognised and second, it will draw attention to views that shared experience of offending is not imperative to peer mentoring. Despite the claimed importance of visible ex-offender role models, peer mentors often referred to specific difficulties in making the transition from 'offender' to ex-offender volunteer, because their identity shift was undermined by stigma. Cat, for example, is a mentor at a women's employment project. In addition to volunteering as a mentor she also volunteers at another charity; whose client focus is not ex-offenders. It was here that she met with difficulty:

> I told the head person [of the charity] I've got a conviction, they were fine, but I'm sick of tip toeing round people so I told [my colleagues] and that's when the shit hit the fan, they asked me to stand down.
>
> (Cat, Mentor)

Janet is also a volunteer mentor at a women's employment project and has a second voluntary job at a local hospice. Whilst she did not recount any direct discrimination, this was clearly a fear for her:

> I work for a hospice as well and I didn't want to tell them [that I'm a peer mentor], I think they have this impression that all the really bad criminals get together and discuss different things and it's just not like that.
>
> (Janet, Mentor)

Both women speaking here were engaged heavily in voluntary work for local charities yet, in these contexts too, they spoke of forms of exclusion or fear of exclusion. They described a sense of *inauthenticity*, of being continually outside and needing to hide. This ambivalence is rarely discussed in the optimistic evaluations of and indeed hopes for mentoring as an approach, yet it highlights how uniquely challenging this work can be for people who are trying to be open about their past criminal histories. Surprisingly, this sense of inauthenticity was also voiced by 'offenders' themselves: 'How can he help me? I've burgled houses with him!' (Peer Group Member). Indeed, this scepticism that past experience could be positively reframed to help others was also communicated by Don, himself an advocate of peer mentoring:

> Some say about [mentor name], he's a fucking nob working here. They know him, know what he was like, he used to run everything round here, now he's working for probation, it can put some people off. I know a few, they say: 'You'll never guess who they want me to go and see? He's telling me after what he's done!'.
>
> (Don, Mentee)

The difficulties described by the mentors above in making the transition from 'offender' to volunteer, of being viewed by their self-defined present rather than their risk defined pasts, recurs. This time, however, it is their *peers* expressing doubt and concern. In Goffman's terms, these observers: 'develop conceptions, whether objectively grounded or not, as to the sphere of life-activity for which an individual's particular stigma primarily disqualifies him' (Goffman, 1963: 66). They are unable to see their criminalised peers as authentic mentor figures as the stigma of criminality is too strong. Interestingly, however, both the sceptical group member and Don's associate do not just draw upon collective notions of criminal stigma here, but rather they draw upon *lived memories* of their peers as 'offenders'. They therefore struggle to believe they now have a credible voice, which can assist rehabilitation. 'Peers' who knew a mentor's criminal history, either personally or by reputation, can vividly bring to life a remembered identity and in doing so at least partially dismiss the new identity, which the mentor assumes. The problem this poses for mentoring approaches built around identity is that there is as much potential for rejection of the model as there is imitation of the model:

> The urge to imitate is very strong, since it opens up possibilities of bettering the competition. But the urge *not* to imitate is also very strong. The only thing that the losers can deny the winners in the homage of their imitation.
>
> (Girard, 1991: 240)

Whilst these sceptical perspectives were much less dominant than the prevailing view (that ex-offender mentors are well positioned to gain the trust and admiration of their peers) my respondents were largely accessed via gatekeepers. The 'group member' quoted above was notably one of the speakers that was not chosen *for* me, but who consented to his peer-led recovery group being observed at my request. It is therefore a possibility that such views are more prominent than I was able to access through selection processes involving gatekeepers.

The second potential problem for mentors who utilise their ex-offender identity to appeal to potential mentees was a small current of resistance to the notion that shared experience is a crucial factor. Jen, for example, was referred to Project 'Facilitate' by her Probation Officer. Her view was that 'experience [of offending] is not important' rather what appealed to her about mentoring was that 'there's a focus on getting a job and I need that focus, they give practical help too' (Jen, Mentee). Jen implies that such practical assistance can be offered effectively by mentors who are not ex-offenders. Gina and Fiona, both passionate advocates of peer mentoring and the importance of shared experience, also suggest that experience *in itself* may not be enough:

> I think it would be valuable if they had [personal experience] yea, but I don't think it's a necessary... I think you've got to be a certain type of person, I mean, I think it would be valuable but I don't think it's compulsory.
>
> (Gina, Mentee)

> It sounds strange because there's people, mentors that have been on stuff [illegal drugs], but the few that I've met, I don't know they don't seem to be ready.
>
> (Fiona, Mentee)

People may therefore have relevant personal experiences but not yet be *ready* to help others. To be 'ready' to help, Fiona, Gina and Jen imply that additional skills, approaches or levels of awareness are required. This theme will be explored more fully in Chapter 7. Interestingly, it was not just those using services who questioned the importance of an offending history to this work. Julie and Lin, for example, are both peer mentors. They are also both advocates of mentoring which draws upon personal experience, yet both recognise its limitations:

> You could have gone through the same things as them, but you can never say 'I understand' because everyone goes through it totally different.
>
> (Julie, Mentor)

> I wouldn't particularly want to go into depth about what I've done in the past, because it's not about me it's about them. And I don't want the spotlight looking on me. It's not about me, it's about how I can help them...

I wouldn't want them thinking 'she's done this or that' and then asking me questions. I think it would be really inappropriate for me to disclose a lot of the past.

(Lin, Mentor and previously a Mentee)

Julie recognises that experiences of crime, even if similar, are never uniform, nor processed in the same ways. This recognition is also latent in Lin's assertion that 'it's not about me, it's about them'. Moreover, Lin considers that her own experience may act as a *barrier* to the mentoring relationship if not handled carefully. In response she strives to maintain a semi-professional 'appropriate' distance. These speakers suggest that whilst the 'ex-offender' identity offers a point of connection, a way into engaging and reassuring people in the criminal justice system, it can only take you so far.

This chapter has examined how notions of a shared 'ex-offender' identity manifest in peer mentoring settings and has highlighted several themes. First, the ex-offender identity is employed as a standpoint; both mentors and mentees make claims that personal experience of crime and desistance offer peer mentors an authenticity that professional helpers do not have. This enables a form of learning that relies upon the experiences of 'human beings in their relations with the world' (Freire, 1970: 60) and re-positions 'offenders' as 'knowers' rather than malleable projects. However, in order to achieve this standpoint many speakers employ exclusionary tactics of othering, which are aimed at undermining professional helpers by disregarding knowledge that is not based upon personal experience. These exclusions appear to reflect disillusionment with a criminal justice system in which people feel misrepresented and dehumanised. In response peer mentors position themselves as non-hierarchical, with a commitment to egalitarianism and humanity. As a result, mentors often claim that the practice is 'humanising' rather than objectifying. Peer mentoring emerges here as a 'levelling' practice. It is a place where the 'ex-offender', the marked and stigmatised outcast, is re-cast as expert. Much like the 'carnivalesque', there is a suspension of the hierarchical structure.

However, despite efforts to invert power relations, the strategy has its limits on several fronts. First, the ex-offender identity is not just utilised to connect, empower and humanise people, but also to inspire people. Peer mentoring positions ex-offenders as role models. This premise rests upon an intrinsic hierarchy between mentor and mentee because imitation explicitly acknowledges superiority (Girard, 1991: 240). Mentees are not the equals of their mentors then but are expected to become more like them. For the mentors and mentees speaking here this is not a problematic feature as most valued the offer of role models they could identify with and felt valued by their peers. There was also a perception that having people with a range of experiences in helping roles could highlight different understandings of the social world and enable more collaborative methods of communication and relationship building. The second challenge to asserting an ex-offender identity was more significant, however, this was the ready formed perceptions of intended audiences; be they the public or peers. Peer mentors must continually negotiate the power of criminal stigma in their communities and indeed amongst their own peers, presenting them with a challenging sense of inauthenticity. Moreover, both mentors and mentees acknowledged the tenuous nature of the claim that shared experience constitutes a common identity. Rather, experiences of criminality are diverse and individual. The response to this acknowledgement is not to drop the ex-offender identity, however, but to recognise it only takes you so far. The following chapters will, therefore, explore what peer mentoring offers in addition to this point of connection. Chapter 6 will begin this task by exploring some of the themes that emerge, not from shared pasts, but from individual determination. It will focus on the perceived importance of personal agency to peer mentoring.

Acknowledgements

This chapter has adapted material from the following works:

Buck, G., (2019), 'Politicisation or professionalisation? Exploring divergent aims within UK voluntary sector peer mentoring', *The Howard Journal of Crime and Justice*, **58**(3), pp. 349–365.
Buck, G., (2019), '"It's a tug of war between the person I used to be and the person I want to be": The terror, complexity, and limits of leaving crime behind', *Illness, Crisis & Loss*, **27**(2), pp. 101–118.
Buck, G., (2017), '"I wanted to feel the way they did": Mimesis as a situational dynamic of peer mentoring by ex-offenders', *Deviant Behavior*, **38**(9), pp. 1027–1041.

I am thankful to the publishers for their permission.

References

Aas, K.F., (2004), 'From narrative to database: Technological change and penal culture', *Punishment & Society*, **6**(4), pp. 379–393.
Arnds, P., (2008), 'Blasphemy and Sacrilege in the novel of magic realism: Grass, Bulkakov, and Rushdie'. In: Coleman, E.B. & Dias, M.S.F., (Eds.), *Negotiating the Sacred II: Blasphemy and Sacrilege in the Arts*. Canberra: ANU E Press, pp. 69–81.
Asencio, E.K. & Burke, P.J., (2011), 'Does incarceration change the criminal identity? A synthesis of labelling and identity theory perspectives on identity change', *Sociological Perspectives*, **54**(2), pp. 163–182.
Bakhtin, M., (1965), *Rabelais and his world* (Vol. 341). Reprint, Bloomington: Indiana University Press, 1984 edition.
Bakhtin, M., (1984), *Problems of Dostoevsky's Poetics*. Trans. Caryl Emerson. Manchester: Manchester University Press.

Ballinger, A., (2011), 'Feminist research, state power and executed Women: The case of Louise Calvert'. In: Farrall, S., Sparks, R. & Maruna, S., (Eds.), *Escape routes: Contemporary perspectives on life after punishment*. Abingdon, Oxon: Routledge.

Bernstein, B.B., (1971), *Class, codes and control*. Volume 1- *Theoretical studies towards a sociology of language*. Reprint, St Albans: Paladin, 1973 edition.

Bouson, J.B., (2000), *Quiet as it's kept: Shame, trauma, and race in the novels of Toni Morrison*. New York: SUNY Press.

Boyce, I., Hunter, G. & Hough, M., (2009), *The St Giles trust peer advice project: Summary of an evaluation report*. London: The Institute for Criminal Policy Research, School of Law, King's College. Available at: http://eprints.bbk.ac.uk/3794/ [Accessed August 2019].

Burnett, R. & Maruna, S., (2006), 'The kindness of prisoners: Strengths-based resettlement in theory and in action', *Criminology and Criminal Justice*, **6**(1), pp. 83–106.

Colley, H., (2002), 'A "rough guide" to the history of mentoring from a Marxist feminist perspective', *Journal of Education for Teaching: International Research and Pedagogy*, **28**(3), pp. 257–273.

Devilly, G.J., Sorbello, L., Eccleston, L. & Ward, T., (2005), 'Prison-based peer-education schemes', *Aggression and Violent Behavior*, **10**, pp. 219–240.

Durnescu, I., (2012), 'What matters most in probation supervision: Staff characteristics, staff skills or programme?' *Criminology and Criminal Justice*, **12**(2), pp. 193–216.

Farrall, S. (2004) 'Social capital and offender re-integration: making probation desistance focused'. In Maruna, S & Immarigeon, R (Eds.), *After Crime and Punishment: Ex-offender reintegration and desistance from crime*, Cullompton: Willan Publishing.

Feyerabend, P.K., (1993), *Against method* (3rd Edn.). London: Verso.

Freire, P., (1974), *Education for critical consciousness* (Vol. 1). Reprint, London: Bloomsbury Publishing, 2013.

Freire, P., (1970), *Pedagogy of the oppressed*. Reprint, London: Penguin, 1996.

Fuss, D., (1989), *Essentially speaking: Feminism, nature and difference*. New York: Routledge, 1990 edition.

Girard, R., (2010), 'A theory by which to work': The mimetic mechanism'. In: Girard, R., de Castro Rocha, J.C. & Antonello, P., (Eds.), *Evolution and conversion: Dialogues on the origins of culture*. London: Continuum International Publishing, pp. 56–95.

Girard, R., (1991), 'Innovation and repetition'. In: Girard, R. & Doran, R., (Eds.), (2008), *Mimesis and theory: Essays on literature and criticism, 1953–2005*. Stanford, CA and London: Stanford University Press, pp. 230–245.

Girard, R., (1977), *Violence and the sacred*. London: Continuum, 2005 edition.

Girard, R., (1962), 'Marcel Proust'. In: Girard, R. & Doran, R., (Eds.), (2008), *Mimesis and theory: Essays on literature and criticism, 1953–2005*. Stanford, CA and London: Stanford University Press, pp. 56–70.

Girard, R. & Doran, R., (2008), *Mimesis and theory: Essays on literature and criticism, 1953–2005*. Stanford, CA and London: Stanford University Press.

Goffman, E., (1963), *Stigma: Notes on the management of spoiled identity*. Middlesex: Penguin.

Goffman, E., (1961), *Asylums: Essays on the social situation of mental patients and other inmates*. Reprint, London: Penguin, 1991.

Goffman, E., (1959), *The presentation of self in everyday life*. Reprint, London: Penguin, 1990.

Grayling, C., (2012), *Justice Minister's 'Rehabilitation Revolution' speech*, 20th November 2012. Available at: www.justice.gov.uk/news/speeches/chris-grayling/speech-to-the-centre-of-social-justice [Accessed August 2019].

Holland, D., Skinner, D., Lachicotte, Jr., W. & Cain, C., (1998), *Identity and agency in cultural worlds*. Cambridge, MA; London: Harvard University Press.

hooks, b., (1994), *Teaching to transgress: Education as the practice of freedom*. New York and London: Routledge.

Hucklesby, A. & Wincup, E., (2014), 'Assistance, support and monitoring? The paradoxes of mentoring adults in the criminal justice system', *Journal of Social Policy*, **43**(02), pp. 373–390.

Hunter, G. & Kirby, A., (2011), *Evaluation summary: Working one to one with young offenders*. London: Birkbeck College.

Kavanagh, L. & Borrill, J., (2013), 'Exploring the experiences of ex-offender mentors', *Probation Journal*, **60**(4), pp. 400–414.

Maruna, S., (2001), *Making good; how ex-convicts reform and rebuild their lives*. Washington, DC: American Psychological Association.

McNeill, F., (2006), 'A desistance paradigm for offender management', *Criminology and Criminal Justice*, **6**(1), pp. 39–62.

Morales, E.E., Ambrose-Roman, S., & Perez-Maldonado, R., (2016), 'Transmitting success: Comprehensive peer mentoring for at-risk students in developmental math', *Innovative Higher Education*, **41**(2), pp. 121–135.

Morin, K.M., (2015), 'Wildspace: The cage, the supermax, and the zoo'. In: Gillespie, K. & Collard, R.C., (Eds.), *Critical animal geographies: Politics, intersections and hierarchies in a multispecies world*. Abingdon, Oxon: Routledge.

Nellis, M. & McNeill, F., (2008), Foreword. In: Weaver, A., (Ed.), *So you think you know me?* Hampshire: Waterside Press.

Newburn, T. & Shiner, M., (2006), 'Young people, mentoring and social inclusion', *Youth Justice*, **6**(1), pp. 23–41.

Pollack, S., (2004), 'Anti-oppressive social work practice with women in prison: Discursive reconstructions and alternative practice', *British Journal of Social Work*, **34**(5), pp. 693–707.

Portillo, S., Goldberg, V. & Taxman, F.S., (2017), 'Mental health peer navigators: Working with criminal justice–involved populations', *The Prison Journal*, **97**(3), pp. 318–341.

Princes Trust, (2012), *Evaluation summary: Working one to one with young offenders*. London: Princes Trust.

Robinson, G. & McNeill, F., (2008), 'Exploring the dynamics of compliance with community penalties'. *Theoretical Criminology*, **12**(4), pp. 431–449.

Sadovnik, A.R., (2008), 'Contemporary perspectives in the sociology of education'. In: Ballantine, J.H. & Spade, J.Z., (Eds.), *Schools and society: A sociological approach to education* (3rd Edn.). Chicago: Pine Forge Press, pp. 20–29.

Scraton, P., (2009), 'Protests and "Riots" in the violent institution'. In: Scraton, P. & McCulloch, J., (Eds.), *The violence of incarceration*. Chicago: Routledge.

South, J., Bagnall, A.M. & Woodall, J., (2017), 'Developing a typology for peer education and peer support delivered by prisoners', *Journal of Correctional Health Care*, **23**(2), pp. 214–229.

Spalek, B., (2008), *Communities, identities and crime*. Bristol: Policy Press.

Uggen, C. & Janikula, J., (1999), 'Volunteerism and arrest in the transition to adulthood', *Social Forces*, **78**(1), pp. 331–362.

Chapter 6

Agency, action and acknowledgement in peer mentoring

A lot of offenders have the ability to blame external things for their situation and sometimes they just need to hear that they can pilot their own life, that internal locus of control, self-efficacy. You have the ability, agency to pilot your own life, and it's not going to be easy, it's going to be difficult, people will try to make it a rocky road for you, but ultimately you determine whether that's a success or not.

(Phil, Mentor)

This chapter will explore conceptions of personal agency in mentoring relationships by looking at the intentions, activities and relational interactions of peer mentors and mentees. Agency –described by Hitlin and Elder (2007: 183) as 'attempts to exert influence to shape one's life trajectory' and Phil (above) as self-determination – is considered important in current conceptions of both desistance and peer mentoring. Laub and Sampson (2001) emphasise that 'personal agency looms large' in persistence and desistance trajectories (cited in LeBel, Burnett, Maruna & Bushway, 2008: 135). 'desisting offenders tend to express a "language of agency"' (Johnston, Brezina & Crank, 2019: 60), whereas 'pessimism and a lack of personal agency have been observed among recidivist offenders' (Rumgay, 2007: 164). Rumgay detected how 'discovery of personal agency [among female offenders] was accompanied by recognition of alternative ways of managing their lives' (2007: 205). Zdun (2011: 307) also found that 'desisters can progress quickly when agency and motivation are acknowledged by society and when receiving support'. In turn the activity of peer mentoring is often claimed to increase a sense of agency, self-worth or autonomy in both mentors and recipients (Lenkens, van Lenthe, Schenk, Magnée, Sentse, Severiens, Engbersen & Nagelhout, 2019; Shelter, 2010; Pollack, 2004). Indeed, Hucklesby and Wincup (2014: 16) argue that 'mentoring schemes need to acknowledge the agency of offenders and encourage them to build upon their capabilities and strengths in the hope that ultimately it will lead to sustainable positive outcomes'. Much of the desistance literature therefore frames agency in ideal typical ways, as a functional pre-requisite to personal behavioural change. It largely upholds 'the Western moral and political view of agents as autonomous, independent, and reflexive individuals' (Burkitt, 2016: 322), who if they can only come to see themselves as such, will foster 'positive outcomes' such as 'desistance' from crime. Freire (1970), however, as discussed in Chapter 3, imagined agency and the conditions which foster it quite differently:

> Freire believed that education, in the broadest sense was eminently political because it offered students the conditions for self-reflection, a self-managed life and critical agency. For Freire, pedagogy was central to a formative culture that makes both critical consciousness and social action possible. Pedagogy in this sense connected learning to social change; it was a project and provocation that challenged students to critically engage with the world so they could act on it.
>
> (Giroux, 2010)

Agency in these terms is not simply a pre-condition of self-discipline or socially compliant action, but it is relational and reflexive, critical questioning within groups is seen as essential to being able to act *on* the world, not just *in* the world. What Freire's work asserts is that a sense of agency may require nurturance through interactions with social others. This chapter will explore the extent to which peer mentors and their mentees see themselves as active agents and look at the ways in which peer mentoring may encourage these views. Many of the mentors and mentees speaking here do not present themselves as conscious political agents, but as accidental recruits. Their agency is only recognised when they are selected by others. In both mentor and mentee voices a sense of self-determination is often contingent upon what others determine their roles and potential to be. At other points, however, mentees actively utilise the practical activities and personal approaches of their mentors to gain a new sense of themselves. The chapter begins by looking at how people enter mentor and mentees roles; and in doing so will reveal an absence of *conscious intention* to engage with this work at the very initial stages. This is surprising given the consciously political aims highlighted in Chapter 5, aims such as asserting voices of experience and challenging professional knowledge and discrimination. The chapter then explores peer mentoring activities themselves and observe the spaces in which people act as mentors and mentees, these activities and settings provide the 'field of contest, [or] the space of authoring' in which agency takes shape (Mageo, 2002: 61). Finally, the chapter considers the role of peer mentors as givers of recognition; as creditors and cultivators of their mentees' emerging identities. This final section offers an insight into *how* peer mentoring may increase a sense of agency in mentees and in doing so it highlights how a sense of personal agency – a seemingly individual determination – can actually be formed by the reflections of social others.

How do people become peer mentors?

Whilst peer mentoring is claimed to increase a sense of agency or autonomy in both mentors and recipients, few of the respondents in this study came to the practice under their own inclination initially. Rather the process of becoming a formal peer mentor was rarely a conscious or planned one. Instead, two of the most dominant reasons offered by respondents were that it formalised their *existing activity*, or the impetus to mentor came *from elsewhere*.

Formalising existing activity

Whilst peer mentoring may well constitute a consciously political act in which mentors and mentees struggle to have their voices heard, as argued in Chapter 5, few mentors described a wish to enter a formal role; to *become* a mentor. Instead many mentors described more fluid processes whereby they *fell into* mentoring as a way of formalising work they were already doing, albeit very informally, with their friends or family. John, for example, works as a volunteer mentor attached to his local Probation Service. He found out about the role after having sought out some training at a local voluntary agency. John explained that he wanted the training to better equip him with the assistance he had been informally offering to his own friends over a number of years:

> The reason I want to get into it is because, I've lost eight friends through various substances from the age of 18... So, I'd helped a couple of friends come off their own addictions during that time period, and I don't want to see anyone else go through it... And I quite like doing it, it gives me a sense of wellbeing as well.
>
> (John, Mentor)

Similarly Katy, a volunteer mentor at a women's employment project, saw herself as already doing the work for which she is now formally recruited:

> I've also got two friends who are quite ill at the moment, mentally. One is in hospital... and I've been supporting them... I actually enjoy it. It gives me something to do with my day and it's something I enjoy doing... I do it because she's my mate and I want to do it, I like doing it.
>
> (Katy, Mentor)

Katy's sense of being a mentor is informed as much by her individual actions with friends as by the formalised space – the structured mentoring setting – she practices within. This dynamic suggests that peer mentoring is not just 'strengths-based' practice, which treats offenders as community assets to be utilised and provides opportunities for such individuals to develop pro-social self-concepts (Burnett & Maruna, 2006: 84), but that it is often more ac-curately a *strengths framing* practice – a role which showcases to mentors and those around them that they have vital skills that they already employ. This feature capitalises upon Maruna's argument that:

> [N]ot all of the roles played by participants in this sample have been deviant ones. All of the narrators [in his study] have played the role of the thief or the junkie, but they have also occasionally played the loving parent, working-class hero, loyal friend.
>
> (Maruna, 2001: 89)

Peer mentoring becomes a tool with which to build upon this dualism; to frame the socially beneficial qualities that become masked when one is la-belled an 'offender'. Phil, for example, now mentors young people involved in anti-social behaviour and adults in prison settings. He explains how it was prison staff who initially recognised his potential:

PHIL: As an ex-offender I had served on a lifer's wing and I kept in contact with a couple of offenders... and then I wrote to them on my release, whilst they were still serving... That relationship with that prison has just grown and developed over the years, and they'd asked me to come in to do some work with some of their offenders.

INTERVIEWER: The prison wanted you to volunteer based on what they'd seen you do?

PHIL: Yea, they wanted to celebrate what I'd achieved as an ex offender and kind of create that motivation for the offenders.

Phil was *invited in* as a motivational other even before he saw himself as such an influence. Before his work was formalised he merely regarded his activities as those of a friend. Similarly, Melina, is now a paid mentor at a gang reduc-tion project. She did not seek out this role, but was approached, given the helping qualities that both she and others identified within her:

> I'm just always the friend who's giving advice, listening to everyone else's problems, so everyone just said 'you'd be good like that' and I really en-joy it. So, I don't know how [I came to mentoring] actually. [Coordina-tor name] just told me she was doing the female mentoring and I thought it sounds really good.
>
> (Melina, Mentor)

Melina already saw herself as something of a mentor, a 'listener' as she put it, and took the opportunity to formalise this quality only when an external party approached her; when a frame was presented. This leads us on to a sec-ond common reason that respondents offered for becoming a mentor.

Impetus from elsewhere

Whilst the above speakers describe falling into mentoring as it matched activities they were already engaged in, Phil and Melina also describe becoming a mentor at the instigation of others. This was a common theme. Keisha, for example, who now runs her own peer mentoring project, describes her accidental introduction to the work. She explains how, on release from prison, she asked her Probation Officer what her employment options were: 'He blatantly told me: "we're not used to people coming forward like yourself". As a result, she was referred to a 'female support group'. Despite being unsure about the relevance of this referral Keisha decided to 'try it out':

> I ended up being a volunteer there, because I didn't fit the box... Going there and looking clean and not being on drugs and alcohol... They assumed I was alright, when I wasn't alright. It was at that point where I was thinking to myself: 'this is bad', but then at the same time I ended up getting voluntary work for an organisation and things started to look up. I started working with young people and one thing that I did notice is that is one of my talents.
>
> (Keisha, Mentor)

Keisha then, describes a completely accidental recruitment. In the absence of a supportive resettlement service for herself which 'fitted', Keisha was shelved into the only available service for women. By accident she discovered mentoring was something she was good at and would go on to succeed at. Similarly Brad, a volunteer mentor attached to the Probation Service, had no express wish to become a mentor, but had the opportunity presented to him and accepted given the impending lack of known structure in his life:

> I've got links with [the mentoring coordinator] from back in the day... He heard rumours that I'd sorted myself out, got in touch, we spoke. He said: how would I fancy doing it? [Mentoring], 'It sounds good, I'm looking for a new challenge'... I've exhausted all what I can do with the Army really, I got no chance of going away again, and he said 'come and do this with us, we've got a course next week'.
>
> (Brad, Mentor)

For both Keisha and Brad these unlooked-for opportunities turned into positive personal experiences. Both enjoy mentoring and see it as having opened up new avenues for them. For Cat, however, the external impetus offered something quite different:

> They chose me... A couple of months ago I was saying, I need to get out of this, it's boring me now, you know? The [inspirational group] talks.

So, I actually spoke to [coordinator name] and said 'look, I don't want to do the talks anymore. I'm getting bored, I'm sick of people hearing about my life, let's hear about somebody else's', but they say: 'it's because you're an inspiration, from what you've been through and then you've come out and done all this, really positive about stuff', even though they have seen me… living with my manic depression, up and down.

(Cat, Mentor)

Cat is a volunteer peer mentor at a women's employment project but given that she is successfully desisting after committing a very serious offence, she is often asked to speak on behalf of her service to a range of audiences. This is a task she has come to resent. Despite the fact that peer mentoring is often claimed to increase a sense of agency, self-worth or autonomy in mentors and recipients (Lenkens et al., 2019; Shelter, 2010; Pollack, 2004), Cat's experience indicates that it can also be experienced as restrictive. Cat does not describe an autonomous process here, but one in which she is selected 'they chose me', framed for the project's needs 'you're an inspiration' and coerced. She also suggests that this public presentation of her *inspirational self* is insincere given that those putting her persona on stage 'see' her 'manic depression', yet present how she has 'come out and is really positive about stuff'. This public form of peer mentoring creates a 'front stage' performance for audiences, and masks 'backstage' performances (Goffman, 1959: 112). The 'mentor' or speaker here is less part of an educational process, which encourages critical agency and poses 'problems of human beings in their relations with the world' (Freire, 1970: 60) and more a resource to be utilised by her charity. The danger of this type of peer mentoring is that it exploits, rather than enables people.

Another interesting theme, which challenged the notion that peer mentoring increases a sense of autonomy, was uncertainty of role. Having been recruited at the instigation of others, peer mentors often described a tentativeness about what their mentoring activity should be:

I didn't really understand what peer-to-peer meant until I was going through it myself.

(Lin, Mentor and previously a Mentee)

Although you've got the theory part of it, I think it's a very practical thing, it's very (huff) it's quite hard to put into words really… I just think it's quite new as well, and it's just everybody is, I think, finding their feet basically.

(Paula, Mentor)

There is a traceable *experimental* character to this practice. Mentors bring their own ideas, impressions and insecurities to create variances of practice.

This, along with the diverse and often unplanned ways that mentors come to the work is one explanation of why it is so difficult to categorise peer mentoring as a consistent, definable approach. Moreover, in terms of agency, becoming a peer mentor is often not shaped by the conscious, political intention of mentors, but rather it is an activity that people are recruited for in the context of contemporary criminal justice ideals. Mentoring offers an 'identifiable position' (Mageo, 2002: 61) into which ex-offenders often drift, rather than consciously seek out. That said, informal peer mentoring appears to be an activity that many 'ex' and active 'offenders' are already undertaking and have been informally undertaking for a number of years, albeit without formal recognition or political hype. Peer mentors are therefore selected on two apparently conflicting bases. On the one hand people are recruited in recognition of activities they have chosen to perform and on the other they are recruited externally for work of which they have little personal knowledge.

How do people become mentees?

One of the most striking features of becoming a mentee, much like becoming a mentor, was the lack of impetus from mentees themselves. Indeed, there was often a complete lack of knowledge among mentees about what peer mentoring was:

INTERVIEWER: Was it your Probation Officer who told you [about mentoring]?
EVE: Yeah, well it was [the support worker] because we'd finished by then with the Probation. She just said it was just a young girl coming, and at first I thought ahhh!! [Anxious scream], but we got on.

(Eve, Mentee)

My employment worker told me about [the mentor] and I asked her: 'What is it called? Are they volunteers?' I thought it was a job. I forget her name [the mentor], I met her five times.

(Jen, Mentee)

She [Probation Officer] said: 'you might find it helpful if you want to, but you don't have to, but I can arrange an appointment if you want?' and I said 'Yeah'. To be honest, at the time I wasn't sure what it was about, but... the more I've got speaking to them, the more they've made me realise what I'm good at, what I like... I'm glad Probation introduced me to them.

(Janet, Mentee)

I met him [the mentor] through boxing, then [the mentoring coordinator] gave me his number... My Probation Officer put me in boxing, then when he [mentor] found out I was into bikes. We used to go riding... I don't know, it was just natural.

(Will, Mentee)

Eve, Jen, Janet and Will were all involved with support workers as part of their Probation Orders and all describe being referred on to mentoring without any real familiarity with, nor introduction to, the concept. Whilst Janet and Will developed an understanding of what mentoring aimed to achieve, both Eve and Jen remained unclear at the time of interview about what the aims of mentoring were, despite both having been mentored for a number of weeks. Indeed, Jen intermittently described the work of various other services, for example, the *Women's Centre* or *Probation* when asked about mentoring, suggesting she could not easily differentiate between the various services she had been referred to. This lack of clarity was not limited to Jen alone. Karina was referred to a peer mentor attached to a gang intervention project after her teachers identified that she was at risk of exploitation from local gangs:

INTERVIEWER: How was [mentoring] explained?
KARINA (MENTEE): Just that someone's going to be coming in every week to speak to me, if I have anything to tell them...
INTERVIEWER: Why do you think school wanted you to have a mentor? Do you know?
KARINA: No... I don't know, Miss [teacher name] just told me about it, but I weren't sure, she just didn't explain it fully, she just said wait and see how it goes and it went alright.

Karina was not only unclear about why she had been referred to mentoring, but she was completely unclear about the nature of the project she was involved with. Becoming a mentee emerged here less as a conscious activity or an activity which fostered a sense of agency, and more as a vague, externally commissioned exercise. What was surprising, however, was that this lack of understanding or individual intention was not always a detrimental factor. Indeed, often respondents came to recognise their mentoring activity as beneficial, despite initial uncertainty or scepticism:

It was a bit scary cos I didn't know her at first, but then it was alright cos I got to know her... speaking about stuff, you can get it off your chest... she gives me advice, like how to avoid stuff, situations I don't need to be in... my confidence got better cos she helped me and then I just changed my attitude toward people and like respected people more.

(Karina, Mentee)

[The mentoring] was... set [by the Court] for four appointments... I didn't think it would be my thing at first, but once I'd sat down with him and got chatting to him, realised that he's alright to get along with and everything, he's helped me in a lot of ways, so it's been good.

(Paul, Mentee)

To be honest, I didn't think I needed a mentor and they [the prison chaplaincy service] said 'well it's up to you', but I went ahead anyway and it was quite shocking, because obviously I didn't know her, I was quite willing to talk to her. It was quite shocking how much I was willing to let her know. I felt comfortable.

(Georgie, Mentee)

These speakers, like most mentees that were interviewed, did not ask for a mentor themselves. In almost all cases the suggestion or will to initiate the work came from a professional, such as a Probation Officer, Chaplain, or Teacher, who themselves either didn't understand fully what it was they were referring to or didn't explain this fully to those they were referring. The ways in which mentees were entered into mentoring relationships therefore appeared to have little regard for personal agency. This is problematic given that for 'ethical and moral reasons, informed consent should be an important principle to uphold' (Hucklesby & Wincup, 2014: 13). That said, once mentees were immersed in mentoring, they often utilised the relationship in ways they found to be beneficial. Each of the speakers here, for example, found something in the process of mentoring that they valued, be it practical help, someone who listened, or a new perspective on the world. What Paul terms as 'help' will be explored later in this chapter. The notions of *listening* and gaining a *new perspective* will also be considered in their own right in chapters seven and eight. Here, however, the important point is that an absence of intention to become a mentee is not always seen as detrimental. Mentees still experienced mentoring positively, despite being vague initially about what they were consenting to.

The spaces in which peer mentoring takes place

The chapter has so far suggested that there is a lack of self-determination in how people enter mentor and mentee positions and that these roles are often entered into at the invitation of others. This section will now look more closely at *where* mentoring happens. The places in which peer mentoring happens are significant to any consideration of the practice. Indeed, it is argued that:

T[]he material environment that surrounds us is rarely neutral; it either helps the forces of chaos that make life random and disorganized or it helps to gives purpose and direction to one's life.

(Csikszentmihalyi & Rochberg-Halton, 1981: 16–17)

It is further argued that a sense of agency does not emerge in isolation, but rather:

> Agency takes shape in a field of contest, the 'space of authoring'. This space is formed, both within us and outside us, by the very multiplicity of persons who are identifiable positions in networks of social production, and of worlds of activity that are also scenes of consciousness.
>
> (Mageo, 2002: 61)

In Goffman's terms these spaces or 'settings' supply the 'scenery and stage props for the spate of human action played out before, within, or upon it' (Goffman, 1959: 32–33). These settings, therefore, both express something about what mentoring attempts to do and they frame the practice. Fiona, for example, a mentee who lacked confidence leaving her own home, described how her mentor helped her meet her health needs: 'It's good because you can go to doctors with them; say if you've got girl problems, anything: "Will you come the doctors with me?": "Course I will"' (Fiona, Mentee). Fiona's mentor therefore helped her to both navigate daunting personal boundaries and to attend an alien environment. Given the relevance of such performative spaces, it is important to document *where* it is that peer mentoring happens. The settings encountered during the research were predominantly community based, they were places aimed at *practically* meeting people's needs. Steve, a mentor at a project attached to a local Probation Office, for example, like Fiona (above) also described the importance of offering assistance in community health settings: 'Just holding their hands, getting them to doctor's appointments, getting them to see their drug counsellors' (Steve, Mentor). Mentors appear to enter non-office-based territories for practical ends. Attendance at settings related to employment was just as prominent in this regard:

> Going into the library, doing CVs to help my employment.
>
> (Paul, Mentee)

> Supporting them to the Job Centre, supporting them to the doctors.
>
> (Julie, Mentor)

> Coming here [to the Women's Centre Job Club] has helped... There's a focus on getting a job and I need that focus, they give practical help too, got applications and sent them off.
>
> (Jen, Mentee)

Supporting people into community health and employment settings is not an activity that is new to the Probation Service nor the voluntary sector. The difference here appears to be that mentors have the time to complete this work *alongside* mentees, in community rather than correctional locations, as companions rather than referrers. They are therefore able to support people in community settings and support regimes such as keeping appointments. Often mentoring takes place in multiple settings and it is dependent upon the complexity of needs presented. Don, for example, is a 'persistent offender' who was referred to mentoring by his Probation Officer. He explains how a long history of drug dependency has left him feeling ill equipped to deal with many of the demands of independent living:

> My mentor takes me shopping, makes sure my bills are paid, know what I mean? I've always got food in, he knows my electric's paid for, he makes sure I've got gas… When I came off the sick I had no money for 6–8 weeks. They got me food parcels, I don't know what I'd have done. I could have been tempted…
>
> (Don, Mentee)

On one level, these settings are sites of practical social support, a benefit which has already been highlighted regarding peer mentoring generally (South, Bagnall & Woodall, 2017; Princes Trust, 2012; Adair, 2005). However, the settings themselves communicate additional messages. Peer mentoring is often an informal and non-office-based activity, taking place in shops, cafes, gyms or outdoor sites:

> It can be anything from talking to going for a walk, just to get them away from it. Walk down the woods, might go shopping, we do days out, go on bike rides, go and walk the dog.
>
> (Ben, Mentor)

The approach is the antithesis of office-based work, which has a direct focus on the 'offender'. There was indeed a voiced ethos for such an *active,* community-based approach, in that it provides a chance to 'practice a new identity' (Cam, Mentoring Coordinator). These settings are not buildings associated with waiting to see a Probation Officer, they are not places where people are defined by their past and their associations; they are *public* places:

> It could be in a pub if you want or a coffee shop, wherever you want, wherever they're comfortable with. In the summer, get a little butty [sandwich] and go and sit in the park, do whatever you want; it's on their terms isn't it? Whereas meeting in an office, signing yourself in, being buzzed through doors to get into buildings, it's very different, isn't it?.
>
> (Joan, Mentor)

There is an acknowledgement here that 'the material objects we use are not just tools we can pick up and discard at our convenience; they constitute the framework of experience that gives order to our otherwise shapeless selves' (Csikszentmihalyi & Rochberg-Halton, 1981: 16). In other words, 'being buzzed through doors' is not an innocuous security measure, it constitutes a framework that defines the people being buzzed in as 'offenders', as 'clients' and – by implication – dangerous and excluded. As a result, there is a conscious shifting away from the settings and accoutrements that define mentees as 'offenders' or clients:

> I've offered to, instead of her coming in here, because this is also for Probation as well, we could meet in a Café and it just looks like two friends, you know? Obviously, I still have to wear my badge, but my badge is tucked in and no one needs to know. As long as I'm still wearing my badge it doesn't need to be on show, and it doesn't need to say 'I'm a Peer Facilitator', and then we're just two friends having a cup of tea.
>
> (Olivia, Mentor)

Peer mentors therefore seek to *change the space*. To borrow Goffman's terms, there is a purging of the institution's definition of identity, a rejection of the 'subtle means of maintaining social distance' (Goffman, 1961: 84). People are not 'buzzed' through closed spaces and separated by badges of authority; these dividers are consciously rejected. Such opportunities to shed the associations of criminal stigma and actively practice a new identity are likely to be useful if desistance from crime involves changes in 'self-concept' (Shover, 1983). The new self-concept offered here is that people begin to see themselves as co-community members, rather than as offenders defined by Probation offices and staff badges. This constitutes a ritual of equalisation, wherein 'risk'-based exclusions are rejected. Such an approach may also have a role to play in allowing deviant roles to be demoted as by falling back on other non-criminal identities, mentees 'are able to deemphasize the centrality of crime in the life history and suggest that they were just normal people "all along"' (Maruna, 2001: 89). Will, for example, does not conceive of his activity-based mentoring as 'sessions' at all, rather he feels *normalised*, a sense of mainstream belonging:

> I don't see 'em as workers at all… I just seen [mentor's name] then and he's got a wotsit [volunteer identity badge] round his neck. Normally I see him he's just normal round the gym, he can't be training with one… We went to Blackpool, again a boxing outing… It wasn't like a probation outing, just like lads' day out.
>
> (Will, Mentee)

The sport and leisure settings that Will joins his mentor in are not just background spaces, therefore, but they serve to dilute Will's sense of being a Probation client; they also dilute the hierarchy which can exist between helper and helped. Instead mentor and mentee become companions sharing an experience: not 'workers at all, just a lads' day out'. Furthermore, mentoring activity in these settings helps Will to keep his thoughts on the possibilities aligned with his new active identity, to 'deemphasize the centrality of crime in the life history' (Maruna, 2001: 89):

> I don't know, just need to fill time. I still get bored and I still have thoughts, but... Just keep thoughts on something else, being productive, self-achievement, boxing, other projects they have going.
>
> (Will, Mentee)

Will's narrative does not just highlight the importance of community-based activity because it helps him to shape a non-criminal sense of self, but also because it offers a physical diversion. In this sense Will's experiences of *active* mentoring constitute 'changes in routine activities' and 'different patterns of socialization' (Shapland & Bottoms, 2011: 272) which provide opportunities to 'change' habits by consciously introducing a disruptive (to the offender) routine:

> We are not suggesting that offending had become habitual, in the same way that driving a well-known route does not require conscious attention. But there might be, for example, a well-worn path to local shops to commit thefts when money was short. Given such a background, in moments of tension it is easy to revert to previous patterns of behaviour. For persistent offenders, 'achieving change' was usually therefore not straightforward, and might well have to involve significant changes in routine activities, and different patterns of socialization and friendship.
>
> (Shapland & Bottoms, 2011: 272)

This notion of needing to change routine activities, and indeed friendships, was also reinforced by other respondents in this study. Ben, for example, a mentor attached to a Probation setting explains how: 'It's just getting away from their thing, a lot of people will just sit in their little flat, in their room, go to their dealer, they've got that used to that. So, no, hang on! We'll do anything really' (Ben, Mentor). The worth of this approach was echoed by Don, a mentee at the same setting as Ben:

> Blowing money on payday on gear and stone, now my mentor takes me shopping, makes sure my bills are paid, know what I mean? ... If I've got any appointments and he can help me he'll take me there... Someone said to me 'you're a soldier [committed] aren't you? You come to any group!' It stops me using.
>
> (Don, Mentee)

Georgie, a mentee at a charity assisting people recently released from prison, described a similar benefit:

> I find it hard to break away from the routine I was used to. You have to break away from a lot of your friends, so I kind of needed a mentor cos I didn't have no mates. I used to say: I've got no-one to go out with at the weekend – she'd [mentor] say: give us a ring, don't worry.
>
> (Georgie, Mentee)

Don and Georgie highlight that desistance is often characterised, at least in the early stages, by a sense of social isolation, which mentoring aims to address. However, both also refer to the notion of 'habit', as described by Shapland and Bottoms above. There is a further theoretical parallel to be drawn between these descriptions and Pierre Bourdieu's concept of *habitus,* which is described as:

> [S]ystems of durable, transposable dispositions... 'regulated' and 'regular' without being in any way the product of obedience to rules, they can be collectively orchestrated without being the product of the organizing action of a conductor.
>
> (Bourdieu, 1980: 53)

The mentees speaking here articulate Bourdieu's ideas in more practical terms. They see a value in having their routine and time orchestrated in new ways because they recognise how established the routines that connect them to criminality are. Crucially, habitus is also an *embodied* feature: 'habitus is simultaneously collective and individual, and definitively embodied' (Jenkins, 1996: 20). People's habits relating to criminal activity may not always be *conscious* therefore, but as Ben and Don articulate, can be an almost unconscious physical performance of (in this case addiction) routines: 'blowing money on payday/ sitting round flat/ going to dealer'. If peer mentoring involves mentees being *active* in public and non–criminal spaces then, spaces complete with new *habitus*, it is potentially a powerful tool. It facilitates the embodiment of new habits and new ways of being. Indeed, one trainee peer mentor acknowledged the power of such forces directly: 'a person is created by those around them' (Mentoring Trainee). However, this same speaker also articulated that making transitions between spaces and associated habits is not easy: 'when you move away, even areas, it's a real challenge, you're insecure, trying to find out who you are, without status and influence' (Mentoring Trainee).

The active, community-based character of peer mentoring has so far been conceived of as assisting in the formation of new identities and as diverting people from criminal habits, but 'active' mentoring is also pleasurable. For Jack Katz (1988), the study of crime too often neglects 'the positive, often wonderful attractions within the lived experience of criminality'

(Katz, 1988: 3). As a result, he sought to focus on the seductive qualities of crimes, 'those aspects in the foreground of criminality that make its various forms sensible, even sensually compelling, ways of being' (Katz, 1988: 3). Drawing upon the work of Katz, Cathy Murray has more recently argued that 'the appeal of offending in terms of its thrill or excitement does not disappear once young people desist, so this is something they lose by desisting' (Murray, 2012: 32). As a result, Murray suggests, that: 'For professionals working with young desisters, it is worth considering that replacements for lost pleasures might be prioritized in post-offending programmes' (Murray, 2012: 32). The same is also true of adult desisters. By offering alternative activities, which are not mundane, but based upon leisure and belonging (as Will and Georgie seem to suggest), mentoring may go some way to compensating for such losses of pleasure or excitement. This feature was also articulated by Steve, a 'prolific offender', whose mentors concentrated on his interests and focused early support on positive leisure activities:

> I was committing ridiculous amounts of crime… I used to go out with this lad, he was an ex offender himself, clean and sorted for years and years, so I used to just go and play snooker with him… I'd go out running… They [mentors] identified that I loved running… just getting me involved in stuff that I'd never really done. I never used to go out, all my life was just chaos, and then from that day on I decided, you know what, I'm going give this a really good go. So I really put all my heart and soul into it and I really started to enjoy what I was doing. They set me up with a gym pass… I thought this might be the right time for me to really sort my life out, because I'd tried before but never done it because I'd never had any support.
>
> (Steve, Mentor and previously a Mentee)

For Steve, the combination of active enjoyment and support in his own Mentee experience is considered to be transformative. It enables him to make a different and difficult choice. However, whilst some respondents clearly perceived benefits associated with the *active* nature of peer mentoring, there are also points of tension here. One such challenge was made during a 'group analysis' session. This group took place when I was asked by a participating mentoring project to offer feedback on some of my initial research findings to a new cohort of trainee peer mentors. I used the opportunity to ask trainees to reflect on emerging findings with me, and to ask them whether they made sense in light of their own experiences. As we discussed the theme of *active community spaces*, one trainee highlighted the fact that 'offenders' are not singularly involved with criminal habits, but simultaneously perform criminal *and* socially compliant activities: 'I went to church all the time when I was offending, I was nice to my Nan, I just adapted to situations' (Trainee Peer Mentor). In line with Maruna's argument that 'not all roles played are deviant ones' the 'offender' can also be a 'loving parent, loyal friend' (Maruna, 2001: 89), this respondent's point was that desisting and persisting habits can co-exist. He was therefore sceptical that new habits *alone* could provide enough of a diversion. Whilst introducing new activities and new habits are described as helpful in many cases, this strategy on its own is limited. People can successfully play out a variety of roles and adapt to new patterns while persisting in offending.

The importance of recognition: peers as creditors and cultivators

Whilst the previous section explored the physical environments of peer mentoring, this section will focus more closely on the immediate communal environment. In doing so it will suggest that it is not enough for people to practice new identities, these identities also need to be fortified. It is therefore important for peer mentors to offer *recognition* to their mentees. Mutual recognition 'is arguably a foundational condition for humanistic relationships as each acknowledges the other as an autonomous and rational being capable of self-determination' (Morgan, 2013: 19). In a criminal justice context: 'Not only must a person accept conventional society in order to go straight, but conventional society must accept that person as well' (Maruna, 2001: 155). Like Goffman (1959, 1963) before him, Maruna acknowledges that the success of a person's identity lies not only in their performance of a role, but also in the reception this performance receives. Performing 'social conformity' is unlikely to be enough in and of itself for 'offenders' to successfully make the transition to 'ex-offenders', there also needs to be external recognition of this shift. Unfortunately for would-be 'desisters' however: 'desistance is a social possibility that takes place within a very specific set of social contexts that may or may not recognise legitimacy of transformation' (Polizzi, 2011: 150). Chapters 4 and 9, for example, both outline some vivid descriptions of scepticism towards change by offenders, and some concerns that their social inclusion would pose risks to others. Colleagues, employers and peers all communicated resistance to accepting ex-offenders as mentors. However, there is also some evidence that peer mentoring configures a different kind of audience, that it creates a space where this acceptance can occur and where the legitimacy of transformations can be recognised. This notion was alluded to in the opening section of this chapter, wherein it was suggested that mentoring can be *strengths framing* for mentors. Here, however *mentees* also describe the importance of their mentors and others recognising positive changes:

> I think it is like me wanting to change but there's someone there niggling in the back of my head saying, 'Look, just carry on doing what you're doing, you're doing well', it's nice to hear it from time to time.
>
> (Paul, Mentee)

Paul considers that his mentor both sees and recognises his potential. For Fiona, this recognition went further, as it was reported for others to see:

> The fact that I had to go back to court every month and a bit helped, because I get a report written from here [the mentoring project] saying what appointments I've attended, what achievements I've made... It's motivated me, and, you know? There were no negatives, no offending whatsoever, just to see that on paper, I've kept all my reports.
>
> (Fiona, Mentee)

These reflected and written forms of external recognition enter Fiona's 'space of authoring' (Mageo, 2002: 61) and inform her conscious awareness of the possibilities of self. They become treasured evidence of her new truth. Phil too expresses a desire for such positive recognition as he reflects upon his own experiences of being positively encouraged by prison education:

> Maybe it's a trait of offenders, but we're a bit needy, need someone to give us a pat on the back saying 'you are capable, that piece of work's good'.
>
> (Phil, Mentor)

Having been socially excluded and negatively framed by prison, Phil articulates that there needs to be positive responses to counter this truth. Mentors do not just offer mentees vital recognition of positive changes, but also cultivation or nurturing of their potential; guidance towards what that person *could* be. This is done through a persistent reinforcement of – and building upon – 'positive' features present. Brad, for example, a mentor attached to a Probation setting, vibrantly describes the advice he gave to the mother of one of his mentees when she expressed concern about her son's setbacks since release from prison: 'He might be being a dick, but you have to look beyond what you know of him, look beyond all that and see positive steps he has taken' (Brad, Mentor). Mentors also often see themselves as creating opportunities for these 'positive steps':

> It's important that the mentor also tries to find out what they [mentees] think their talents are, or hobbies, or what they think they're good at... You can pick up on things and then you can say: 'do you know what I think you'd be good at doing... and I think you'd be good doing...' you know?.
>
> (Keisha, Mentor)

This focus on personal strengths was regarded as a 'positive' approach. It was valued by mentees and represented a dominant theme in their interviews. Candice, a teenage mentee, is mentored in her high school setting having been assessed as at risk of involvement with local 'gangs'. She describes how her mentor encouraged her to:

> Think about good things about yourself, every week I had to. One week I could only do three, the next week she told me five, she said 'come back with seven, come back with ten...' Every session she came she was explaining how I'd developed my confidence and then my mates have said that. I feel more confidence in myself.
>
> (Candice, Mentee)

Janet and Gina were referred to a local women's charity following criminal convictions. They both referred to mentoring as a process of coming to see positive factors within themselves, factors that were being submerged by the overwhelming shame of their criminal actions:

> They help you to see the positive sides, whereas at the time you can't see nothing other than: 'I've been done for drink-driving and my life is crap'... The more I've got speaking to them, the more they've made me realise what I'm good at, what I like, and things like that.
>
> (Janet, Mentee)

Gina said that she came to recognise:

> You're not a bad person, that actually you're quite nice and what's happened has happened and now it's time to go forward... It wasn't like 'well you should be doing this or this or this', it was just gentle and it was only after a few weeks when I said something to [mentor] and she said 'seeeee!' And I went 'oh yeah!' It's like good psychology because it plants the seed and it grows.
>
> (Gina, Mentee)

Highlighting personal strengths is therefore regarded as 'good psychology' – it is seen to build confidence, to shift peoples' self-perceptions and to help them feel empowered. Chapter 2 outlined how there is already theoretical support for such 'strengths-based' practice, which 'focuses on the positive contribution to society that an individual can make in an attempt to re- or de-label them as a "bad person"' (Farrall & Calverley, 2006: 65). The strengths-based philosophy 'recognizes that even the most resilient individuals emerging from a shameful past need high levels of support in nurturing their pro-social inclinations, to restore their sense of belonging, mastery, independence and generosity' (Burnett & Maruna, 2006: 101). A focus on mentee strengths can therefore inform their *sense* of themselves, by helping to construct a vision of a positive new identity 'they've made me realise what I'm good at' (Janet, Mentee) and promoting engagement and motivation 'I've attended, it's motivated me, you know?' (Fiona, Mentee). This element of mentoring suggests that the practice is more than simply embodied discipline or active habit. It is also an activity which consciously positions mentors as *reflectors of personal positive factors*, as builders of potential, rather than fixers who focus upon deficits to be remedied.

Nudging the conscience

In addition to highlighting and reinforcing personal strengths, mentors were also described as *positive others* in that they acted as a second conscience. This section will explore this interesting micro-intervention, by looking at the ways in which mentors often give their mentees a discreet, gentle nudge. For example, mentors described how they often challenge mentees and offer a sounding board when opposition was likely to be needed:

> I shout at him on the phone; (laugh) 'what you doing?' I hate shouting at him… I'm his little mate on his arse all the time, mithering him.
>
> (Brad, Mentor)

> I always let them know: if they feel like they're going to re-offend, or try and use again, they can just get on the phone. If I answer it, I'm available, if I don't answer it, I'll call them back.
>
> (John, Mentor)

This was an approach that mentees often appreciated and utilised. Paul, for example, receives one-to-one mentoring following a conviction, but he also attends rehabilitation courses as part of his Probation sentence. He explains how his mentor attends these same courses to offer additional support:

> I see him [my mentor] going there as well, which is a help for me, cos I normally mess about, but when he's there he keeps me in check, I sit there and get something out of it. When I've done little things wrong, been about to go back down wrong path he has been there to say, 'look man, sort your head out. Its only little blip, carry on with it', which is good really.
>
> (Paul, Mentee)

Karina, who is mentored in a high school setting, similarly explains how thinking through decisions with her mentor helped her avoid negative consequences in her school life:

> I probably would have got sent to the Consequence Room [described as a 'time out' classroom where pupils are sent to consider the consequences

of their actions], got a detention… We done stuff about making decisions
for good reasons and bad reasons, we did worksheets on it.

(Karina, Mentee)

Mentors make overt efforts to affect their mentees' decisions here on a
micro-level and these interventions are welcomed by mentees. Even when
mentors are not directly influencing decisions, mentees often describe them
as a remembered conscience:

You sort of have their voices at a time when you need them, going in
your head… I feel like my peers are still with me on the journey… You
feel like you have other people and they understand all my mad quirks in
my head and how my head works because theirs works exactly the same,
and there is ways of dealing with it.

(Lin, Mentor and previously a Mentee)

I don't even phone sometimes I just think 'Well what would [mentor]
say?' She'd say this or that.

(Janet, Mentee)

These mentees did not just welcome their mentors' overt influence in
decision-making, but they appear to have internalised their mentors expected responses. Peer mentors' voices, whether real or remembered,
therefore, have a regulatory value. They keep people 'in check', they assist with decision-making and as a consequence, mentees say that their
mentors' voices and messages stay with them. Moreover, this regulatory
conscience is deemed to be acceptable because it comes from people who
have 'been there' themselves and have regulated themselves in this way. At
first hearing such shared discipline might be interpreted as a surrender of
agency on the part of mentees, wherein mentors are afforded the power to
decide what is right and wrong or 'good and bad'. It could be viewed, not
so much a benign nurturing of self-monitoring, as paternalistic guidance
towards what the mentor considers right. However, in explaining why, for
him, such regulation was so important, Paul challenges the pessimism of
such a concern:

In jail everything is structured for you, you're told when you go to work,
when you're getting locked up, when you have your food, when you get
to socialise or use the phone, everything's structured for you. So, coming
out of there, out of jail and not having anyone telling you what to do,
that was kind of like a free roaming thingy for me – I was just going on
a mad one! But getting out then coming here and having a mentor, when
I'm going to do them mad things [my mentor] is there like: 'Whoa, go

and do it if you want to, but this is what's going to happen'. It makes you weigh up the pros and cons in your head, obviously make a right decision instead of wrong one.

(Paul, Mentee)

For Paul, this voice of conscience helped him to gain a sense of self-control. It provided an initial buffer to the experience of being released after the complete control of prison, *which he saw as essential*, but after this initial protection was offered, it was up to him to decide which way to go next. This is not so much paternalistic control, but a tool used by Paul to help manage his perceived 'weakness of will'. This feature has been highlighted previously by Shapland and Bottoms (2011) in their concept 'diachronic self-control'. This is described as a strategy wherein:

> [O]ne engages in or deliberately does not engage in an activity so that, at another, future time, one will not face a situation of temptation, which one believes, from experience, is very likely to result in a failure to act as one truly believes one should.
>
> (Shapland & Bottoms, 2011: 274)

Shapland and Bottoms explain how these strategies are employed by people attempting to desist in order to avoid 'weaknesses' of will. Paul describes something very similar. He visits his mentor in order to be exposed to a voice of reason, a voice which dampens his temptations; temptations he sees as correlated with release from such total control. Moreover, his mentor's voice encourages him to make decisions himself whilst anchoring him with a companion in the face of this new and overwhelming self-government post prison. This voice of conscience does not work to stifle self-direction, therefore, but to *cultivate* it. A feature also highlighted by Georgie:

> When you don't talk to someone, everything's whizzing round your head: 'right start there, do this, do this'. We'd [Georgie and mentor] talk and she'd say: 'why don't you just do this', talking to someone puts it in perspective. I'm concentrating on that; deal with that later. That was a biggy [big thing] for me. Too much on my mind, I can't focus... Sometimes you just need to talk to someone and get it out.
>
> (Georgie, Mentee)

For Georgie, the combination of being listened to and having a peer collaborator, helps *her* to sort through problems she feels overwhelmed by, it helps her to gain a new perspective and to feel more in control.

This chapter has offered further support for claims that peer mentoring can increase a sense of agency or self-worth (Lenkens et al., 2019; Shelter,

2010; Pollack, 2004), albeit in ways which may not be expected. Mentors and mentees frequently speak of gaining a sense of self-direction or self-control: … 'I feel more confidence in myself' (Candice, Mentee); 'actually [I'm] quite nice and what's happened has happened and now it's time to go forward' (Gina, Mentee). But they also outline the important roles their peers play in this acquisition: 'you sort of have their voices at a time when you need them, going in your head' (Lin, Mentor and previously a Mentee); 'they've made me realise what I'm good at' (Janet, Mentee); 'Sometimes you just need to talk to someone and get it out' (Georgie, Mentee). Developing a sense of agency through peer mentoring emerges here as a dialogue, a conversation between role definers and role performers, one in which intimate levels of trust and exchange are necessary conditions. This dual aspect of mentoring, where roles are defined by one group and performed by another, is present in peer mentoring from its very origins. Peer mentors often do not *initiate* the act of supporting their peers, but their work is formalised by external parties such as professional managers and coordinators. Many mentors and mentees do not initiate the practice at all, but come to contribute and benefit once the role is made available. As a result, variances of practice emerge along with uncertainty.

Two dominant features which emerged when mentees described their growing sense of agency were not individual at all, but were made available outside of the self, that is: the *physical environment* and *social environment*. Mentees are offered opportunities to 'practice a new identity' in community-based settings, to embed new routines and to engage in activities they find pleasurable. As a result, they come to hold new perspectives of themselves and hope for the future. Mentors, in turn, reinforce these new identity performances by encouraging a positive sense of self and recognising and applauding mentee efforts. In this light, intentional self-change is not a prerequisite of desistance, but desistance emerges falteringly as a dialogue between the self, socially available spaces and socially available recognition. This is a point that will be developed further in Chapter 8. Before that, however, it will be helpful to look a little closer at the core aptitudes that mentors employ once they are engaged in the activity of mentoring, the things which mentors and mentees themselves see as core to this work.

References

Adair, D., (2005), *Peer support programs within prisons.* Tasmania: University of Tasmania School of Sociology and Social Work.

Bourdieu, P., (1980), *The logic of practice.* Reprint, California: Stanford University Press, 1990 edition.

Burkitt, I., (2016), 'Relational agency: Relational sociology, agency and interaction', *European Journal of Social Theory,* **19**(3), pp. 322–339.

Burnett, R. & Maruna, S., (2006), 'The kindness of prisoners: Strengths-based resettlement in theory and in action', *Criminology and Criminal Justice,* **6**(1), pp. 83–106.

Csikszentmihalyi, M. & Rochberg-Halton, E., (1981), *The meaning of things; domestic symbols and the self.* Cambridge: Cambridge University Press.

Farrall, S. & Calverley, A., (2006), *Understanding desistance from crime.* Berkshire: Open University Press.

Freire, P., (1970), *Pedagogy of the oppressed.* Reprint, London: Penguin, 1996.

Giroux, H.A., (2010), Lessons to be learned from Paulo Freire as education is being taken over by the mega rich. *Truth Out*, 23 November 2010. Available at: https://truthout.org/articles/lessons-to-be-learned-from-paulo-freire-as-education-is-being-taken-over-by-the-mega-rich/ [Accessed January 2020].

Goffman, E., (1963), *Stigma: Notes on the management of spoiled identity.* Middlesex: Penguin.

Goffman, E., (1961), *Asylums: Essays on the social situation of mental patients and other inmates.* Reprint, London: Penguin, 1991.

Goffman, E., (1959), *The presentation of self in everyday life.* Reprint, London: Penguin, 1990.

Hitlin, S. & Elder Jr, G.H., (2007), 'Time, self, and the curiously abstract concept of agency', *Sociological Theory*, **25**(2), pp. 170–191.

Hucklesby, A. & Wincup, E., (2014), 'Assistance, support and monitoring? The paradoxes of mentoring adults in the criminal justice system', *Journal of Social Policy*, **43**(02), pp. 373–390.

Jenkins, R., (1996), *Social identity.* London: Routledge.

Johnston, T.M., Brezina, T. & Crank, B.R., (2019), 'Agency, self-efficacy, and desistance from crime: An application of social cognitive theory', *Journal of Developmental and Life-Course Criminology*, **5**(1), pp. 60–85.

Katz, J., (1988), *Seductions of crime: Moral and sensual attractions in doing evil.* New York, USA: Basic Books.

Laub, J.H. & Sampson, R.J., (2001), 'Understanding desistance from crime'. In: Tonry, M.H. & Norris, N., (Eds), *Crime and justice: An annual review of research,* Vol. 26, Chicago: University of Chicago Press, pp. 1–69.

LeBel, T.P., Burnett, R., Maruna, S. & Bushway, S., (2008), 'The "chicken and egg" of subjective and social factors in desistance from crime', *European Journal of Criminology*, **5**(2), pp. 131–159.

Lenkens, M., van Lenthe, F.J., Schenk, L., Magnée, T., Sentse, M., Severiens, S., Engbersen, G. & Nagelhout, G.E., (2019), Experiential peer support and its effects on desistance from delinquent behavior: Protocol paper for a systematic realist literature review. *Systematic Reviews*, **8**(1), p. 119.

Mageo, J.M., (2002), *Power and the self.* Cambridge: Cambridge University Press.

Maruna, S., (2001), *Making good; how ex-convicts reform and rebuild their lives.* Washington, DC: American Psychological Association.

Morgan, S.T., (2013), 'Social pedagogy within key worker practice: Community situated support for marginalised youth', *International Journal of Social Pedagogy*, **2**(1), pp. 17–32.

Murray, C., (2012), 'Young people's perspectives: The trials and tribulations of going straight', *Criminology and Criminal Justice*, **12**(1), pp. 25–40.

Polizzi, D., (2011), 'Heidegger, restorative justice and desistance: A phenomenological perspective'. In: Hardie-Bick, J. & Lippens, R., (Eds.), *Crime, governance and existential predicaments.* Hampshire: Palgrave Macmillan.

Pollack, S., (2004), 'Anti-oppressive social work practice with women in prison: Discursive reconstructions and alternative practice', *British Journal of Social Work*, **34**(5), pp. 693–707.

Princes Trust, (2012), *Evaluation summary: Working one to one with young offenders.* London: Princes Trust.

Rumgay, J., (2007), *Ladies of lost causes: Rehabilitation, women offenders and the voluntary sector.* Abingdon, Oxon: Routledge.

Shapland, J. & Bottoms, A., (2011), 'Reflections on social values, offending and desistance among young adult recidivists', *Punishment & Society*, **13**(3), pp. 256–282.

Shelter, (2010), *In their own words - Shelter's peer education services for young people.* London: Shelter.

Shover, N., (1983), 'The later stages of ordinary property offender careers', *Social Problems*, **31**(2), pp. 208–218.

South, J., Bagnall, A.M. & Woodall, J., (2017), 'Developing a typology for peer education and peer support delivered by prisoners', *Journal of Correctional Health Care*, **23**(2), pp. 214–229.

Zdun, S., (2011), 'Immigration as a trigger to knife off from delinquency? Desistance and persistence among male adolescents from the Former Soviet Union in Germany', *Criminology and Criminal Justice*, **11**(4), pp. 307–323.

Chapter 7

The values and 'core conditions' of peer mentoring

The chapter aims to speak directly to the experience of the men and women who spoke so frankly about often harrowing personal life experiences for the benefit of this study. It aims to draw out the 'strategies for change' which *they themselves* identified. In doing so the chapter outlines what they frame as the authentic principles of peer mentoring. Chapters 1 and 4 highlighted how diverse mentoring theory and practices are. This chapter, whilst not dismissing this diversity, identifies some of the most common interpersonal approaches employed through peer mentoring, as described by those engaged with the work. The dominance of these approaches not only illustrates what is valued in this work, but also what may be missing from other forms of intervention. The first feature prominent in interview narratives was 'individualised practice'. Respondents spoke of the importance of mentees setting their own goals rather than having external ideals imposed. The first section of this chapter therefore reinforces the importance of personal agency. It examines the ways in which mentors aim to encourage self-direction in their mentees through goal setting. The second part of the chapter focuses upon what mentors and mentees articulated as the core values of this work, which include *caring*, *listening* and *setting manageable goals*. These 'core conditions' are claimed to have very specific benefits for people attempting to desist from crime. They emerge, in part, to resist the dominant interventionist discourse, but resistance to this dominance proves limited. Interventionism, as will become clear here and in Chapter 9, is never quite overturned.

Individualised practice

A significant theme of interviews across the projects was that peer mentoring is tailored to the individual. Both mentors and mentees framed this as a positive feature of the work. Mentors, for example, refer to a focus on what the mentee hopes to achieve, rather than what others assess to be in need of correction:

> I get the client to think of something that they've always wanted to do, whether it's a job or training or whatever, just getting fitter, anything like that. I try and ask them what they want.
>
> (John, Mentor)

How I work at the beginning is ask about them. What are they interested in? And then it seems to break that barrier down a little bit, because your interest is in them... I didn't say 'WE are doing this, WE are doing that' I didn't say none of that, I said 'What do you like? What are you interested in? What do you want to do?'.

(Julie, Mentor)

This ethos corresponds with the concept of 'Motivational Interviewing', which is included in some format on each of the mentoring training courses that I observed, or had described to me:

Motivational interviewing is a psychological treatment that aims to help people cut down or stop using drugs and alcohol. [The interviewer] expresses that he or she understands how the clients feel about their problem and supports the clients in making their own decisions... they discuss the clients' goals and where they are today relative to these goals.

(Smedslund, Berg, Hammerstrøm, Steiro,
Leiknes, Dahl & Karlsen, 2011: 2)

Motivational interviewing is described as an 'evidence-based' (Levensky, Forcehimes, O'Donohue & Beitz, 2007) approach to overcoming ambivalence, which builds upon the client-centred psychotherapy of Carl Rogers (Miller & Rollnick, 2013). Mentees themselves endorsed this approach, highlighting how 'owning' changes kept them engaged and allowed them to demonstrate their own potential:

She never... told me what I needed to do, she always gave me suggestions and prodded at me to get me thinking about what I needed to do. It was me who said how I would need to change and what timescales... [As a mentor, you have] got to have the skill to know when not to be pushy... let them find their own resolution and then push that forward, rather than you thinking that would work and giving them that. And maybe just find the bit – say right 'you've hit the nail on the head'.

(Georgie, Mentee)

When I first met her it was weird because she said 'what do you want to do?' So I just told her what I was doing and she was like 'whoa, you've got your head screwed on then'... It was up to us, they just wanted to know what I'd been up to and about the [college] course and other things, like how I was feeling about things.

(Eve, Mentee)

I thought at first it would be someone saying: 'right you're coming with me today, we're going to do this, we're gonna do that', but when I realised I had a choice that was a lot of it as well....

(Paul, Mentee)

These mentees describe a level of freedom to act and make individual choices, which is accompanied with the nurturance of encouragement, praise and a helping hand. What is also apparent, however, is that mentees had expected something altogether different than this level of ownership over the process, they had expected authoritarian directives, instruction and management. This is perhaps not surprising. Eve and Paul had both been subject to statutory supervision processes whose administrators (Probation Officers), whilst often utilising motivational techniques themselves, are ultimately required to *manage* offenders. Probation Officers are often trained in motivational interviewing techniques, but are ultimately required to assess risk and to plan interventions around those risks. Despite its client-centred roots then, motivational interviewing is invariably caught up in diagnostic power relations; it has become an institutionalised technique. Perhaps the popularity of the approach within peer mentoring, is not just that it allows them to *own* their own changes on a conversational level, but that the person facilitating this conversation holds less symbolic and actual power over them. The motivational discussion is not experienced – in the context of these relationships – as a disciplinary tool of expert management, but as the *focus* of the relationship. The agency of the mentee is at its (nominal) centre. This strong focus on the mentee as director of the intervention not only corresponds to motivational interviewing, but also to person-centred therapy: 'an approach to therapy that has the non-directive attitude at the centre of theory and practice' (Wilkins, 2010: xvii). Liz, a peer mentor at a project that works with young women at risk of 'gang exploitation' directly referenced person-centred counselling as one of her influences:

> The skills are the same as person-centred counselling, which I did before: empathy, active listening, un-judgemental positive regard, rapport... The good thing about mentoring is you can encourage the process... Not like counselling... Focus on the mentee, bring things to their attention: 'I notice you did this'. *See* them.
>
> (Liz, Mentor)

Liz not only highlights the similarities between person-centred practice and peer mentoring as empathy, listening, non-judgement, positive regard and rapport, but also reinforces the importance of encouragement and an active focus on personal positives. Stokes (2003), however, warns against an uncritical merging of the two philosophies. He argues that whilst mentors may recognise 'that there are benefits to be gained from being non-directive' they also often 'suggest that they are happy to intervene directly in the mentee's problems either directly by making a facilitative intervention or indirectly by directing the mentee to undertake some course of action' (Stokes, 2003: 32). This not only contradicts the non-directive ethos of person-centred counselling, but also raises the 'danger of the mentee becoming reliant on the mentor for critical insights and interventions rather than having them/making them themselves' (Stokes, 2003: 32). Despite this critique of merging non-directive and directive approaches, Liz's perception of the core skills or conditions of peer mentoring were echoed by a number of speakers in this study. These will now be explored in detail.

Core conditions

> Being an ex-offender alone doesn't qualify you – we want to be *good* mentors.
>
> (Cam, Mentoring Coordinator)

In their descriptions of good mentoring, respondents in this study voiced three clear themes which will now be explored. Much like Carl Rogers' (1980) theory that 'congruence, acceptance and empathy' are essential conditions of person-centred work (Thorne & Sanders, 2013: 36), respondents identified the *core conditions* of peer mentoring as: caring, listening and encouraging small steps. The resemblance these conditions have to Rogers' work may well reflect the pervasiveness of psychological discourse more broadly. McNeill (2006: 52), for example, identifies the 'core conditions' of effectiveness in criminal justice interventions as: 'empathy and genuineness; the establishment of a working alliance; using person-centred, collaborative and "client driven" approaches'. Brown and Ross (2010: 37) argue that the significance of these conditions 'should also ring true to those with a knowledge of mentoring'. The use of 'should' as an imperative here gives a clue as to how this discourse has entered 'lay' mentoring as a truism. The dominance of person–centred values reflects a prevailing, if only partially adopted, professional discourse. However, the repeated articulation of key approaches in this study also appears to communicate something specific to these settings. What follows will therefore suggest that it is not just the presence of *any peer* engaging on positive, or person-centred terms which is important to this work, but a peer who is able to employ a number of skills or 'conditions'.

Core condition 1: caring

In the early months of this study I attended a national conference at a prestigious venue. Speakers included academics and representatives from the government and voluntary sector. Amid the conference etiquette, formal speeches and professional discourse, a serving prisoner (granted day release to speak at the conference) stood up to explain the positive effect that an intervention had had on his life. What was remarkable, and indeed what elicited a small murmuring of uncomfortable chuckling from attendees, was the prisoner's description of his prison officer; a man whose approach he described as *loving* towards him. Much like the nervously giggling audience,

I am uncomfortable when referring to *love* or *care* in the context of an empirical criminal justice study. Particularly as:

> Research approaches that... stress the value of focusing upon emotions, the importance of drawing upon individuals' own accounts of their experiences... stand in opposition to modernist agendas, being viewed as somehow less valid and objective, and more partisan in nature, and therefore 'suspect'.
>
> (Spalek, 2008: 4)

Moreover, emotions have been seen as 'suspicious' by criminologists: 'criminology's approach to emotions has been cautious and circumspect' (Karstedt, 2011: 1). This 'distrust of emotions', Pettersen (2008) argues, is deeply rooted in:

> Western moral thinking, and can be explained on the basis of several notions: emotions are associated with the body, sexuality, nature and women, which in Western hierarchical thinking are considered inferior to reason, self-control, culture and masculinity.
>
> (Pettersen, 2008: 53)

The complex associations between care and gender will be examined further a little later in this chapter. For the moment, however, let us consider how care has been conceived of in criminal justice. The modern criminal justice system, Knight (2014) argues, shaped throughout the Enlightenment period, is 'constituted to respond to, control and punish criminal behaviour in an objective, rational and just manner. As far as possible the system aims to exclude emotion on the basis that emotions are likely to interfere with and distort the process of justice' (Knight, 2014: 2). In contrast to Knight's reading however, Karstedt (2011) argues that we have seen an end to the project of the 'rationalisation' and 'de-emotionalisation' of criminal justice since the 1990s. The 're-emotionalisation of law', she contends, is evident in 'the return of shame into criminal justice procedures, a stronger focus on victims and emotional needs... and finally highly emotionalised public discourses on crime and justice in Western democracies' (Karstedt, 2011: 3). This process is viewed as part of a broader movement or an 'emotional turn' in postmodern societies, two facets of which are the 'informalization' and 'emancipation of emotions' (Karstedt, 2011: 4). Whilst Karstedt points to a re-emergence of emotion within justice, however, rarely is the focus on 'offender' emotions, unless, that is, they are framed as 'dynamic risk factors' (Day, 2009: 119). Rarer still are calls for the nurturance or *care* of 'offenders'. Rather, where emotions are more clearly present is in 'highly emotional and mostly punitive public and political discourse' (Karstedt, 2011: 3). Despite a context which appears unfavourable to caring for people who have entered the criminal justice system, *care* is a feature that has been highlighted as important in supporting change. For example, desisters and their Probation Officers considered the following as crucial characteristics to support desistance:

> [H]aving someone that they could get on with and respect; who treated them as individuals; was *genuinely caring*; was clear about what was expected of them and trusted them when the occasion called for it.
>
> (Leibrich, 1993, 1994, cited in McNeill & Weaver, 2010: 59, emphasis added)

This corresponds with a study of youth justice by Matthews and Hubbard (2007), who argued that a supportive relationship with a caring adult mitigates the effects of high-risk environments in three key ways. First, it alters young people's self-perceptions, enabling them to believe that they are loved and valued and this gives them an increased sense of mastery. Second, it demonstrates to young people that positive relationships with adults are possible and models effective conflict resolution. Third, it acts as a protective factor for children who have experienced major trauma or stress in their lives, social support outweighs the effects of past terror and encourages healthy ways of coping. As a result of these benefits, it is argued that 'providing youth with a trusting and safe relationship with a caring adult is a viable strategy for promoting resiliency' (Matthews & Hubbard, 2007: 113–114). In an adult context, patients leaving secure Forensic Psychiatric Hospitals who received relational care and voluntary contact after treatment were much less likely to reoffend (15% of relational care recipients reoffended within two years, as opposed to 46%–47% of the control groups). It is theorised that relational care bridges the difficult period that patients face when they have left the secure setting (Schaftenaar, van Outheusden, Stams & Baart, 2018). The importance of care, which expresses 'both emotion and understanding' (Pettersen, 2008: 55) was recognised by the conference speaker with whom this section was opened, and indeed was a theme which persisted in presenting itself in this study:

> The ones that are volunteering, you know that it's not just a job for them; they do actually genuinely care.
>
> (Lin, Mentor and Previously a Mentee)

> They make you feel like you are their only priority and they're just here to help you and that makes you feel good… There is somebody out there who genuinely cares.
>
> (Janet, Mentee)

> Whenever I need to get hold of a mentor they answer the phone, even weekends… one mentor comes round on a Saturday afternoon, helped me clean and strip my bike and everything, so selfless.
>
> (Will, Mentee)

Genuine care here is seen as an expression of altruism, which is based upon understanding. These speakers consider that peer mentors are motivated by an emotional awareness of what mentees are going through rather than by personal gain. Not only is genuine care valued in this context, but emotional connections are framed as legitimate mentoring tools:

> I'd go in, I'd be crying my eyes out. She'd give me a few cuddles, I don't know if they should do that or not, but it was what I needed at the time and I was dead happy. I'd come out and feel a whole new lease of life.
>
> (Georgie, Mentee)

Georgie feels 'valued' by this act of physical affection and gains 'an increased sense of mastery', a new lease of life. *Genuine* care is also deemed to be more spontaneous than 'professional' care:

> I don't know, are they sessions? I just go boxing; we go boxing, got it this afternoon, have a hug; 'what've you been up to?' I don't know, I wouldn't call it a session (laugh).
>
> (Will, Mentee).

> Be yourself, vibrate at their level, not being an expert, allowing them, they're OK to be in that place at that moment.
>
> (Liz, Mentor)

Such descriptions of physical and felt human connections are the antithesis of structured risk assessments and of evidence-based bureaucracies, which 'thrive on impersonality and detachment' (Lippens, 2009: 84). Indeed, both Will and Liz reject associations with formal intervention: 'I wouldn't call it a session/ not being an expert', their understandings are informed as much by what men-toring *is not* as by what it is. Similarly, Georgie appears to be aware that her mentor's approach may violate professional norms: 'I don't know if they should do that or not'. Yet she nonetheless asserts her preference for a tactile, embodied approach. Peer mentoring for these speakers is a context in which they are posi-tioned as tactile fellow humans with emotions, imperfections and wishes, rather than subjects to be governed. They are personified, not objectified. Care is con-ceived of by these speakers as the opposite of judgement, expectation and oblig-atory intervention. It is described as fostering personal connection and building esteem. Carl Rogers (1980) theorised why this may be significant. For Rogers, such 'congruence' or genuineness is important for communicating acceptance of the person, complete with flaws. Reflecting upon his own 'experiences in communication', he contends such acceptance is 'growth promoting' because it allows people to *be* rather than expecting them to become another's ideal:

> "You seemed so genuinely concerned the day I fell apart, I was over-whelmed... I received the gesture as one of the first feelings of

acceptance – of me, just the dumb way I am, prickles and all – that I had ever experienced"... One of the most satisfying feelings I know – and also one of the most growth promoting experiences for the other person – comes from my appreciating this individual in the same way that I appreciate a sunset. People are just as wonderful as sunsets if I can let them *be*.

(Rogers, 1980: 21–22)

This sense of not being judged, but being openly accepted also featured strongly in the experiences and perceptions of mentees; and indeed mentors:

With counselling it can sometimes feel like you are being judged, sometimes it can be a bit patronising, I've found. Whereas with peer mentoring, with someone from a similar background who has been there and done that and been on that level, they know it, so they don't patronise. They don't try and tell you it's something else when it's not.

(Katy, Mentor)

I've been amazed that nobody has judged me, no one... Here's a person I've never met before, knows what's happened, knows what I've done, but understands why I did what I did and is telling me: 'you're not a bad person, that actually you're quite nice and what's happened has happened and now it's time to go forward'.

(Gina, Mentee)

I've got mental health problems and a lot of people don't understand and they judge you straight away, but it [mentoring] was such a nice relaxed atmosphere and there was no pressure. As well, it was all *go along with my pace*, it was very encouraging as well.

(Lin, Mentor and Previously a Mentee)

A non-judgemental approach helps these mentees to re-frame their view of themselves. They are not a diagnosis, or a bad person, but 'nice' and *normal* or on the same 'level'. However, these expressions also serve as a reminder that most criminal rehabilitation work takes place within a system of judgement. Respondents imagine professional work as distinct from volunteer caring, partly because the latter is deemed to be free of this system of judgement. Probation work and associated health improvement work is perceived through an 'us and them' divide: '*they* judge you', and through feelings of belittlement, anxiety and pressure. Peers, however, are claimed to provide a degree of separation from this; to be free of such judgements because they too have experienced them. It is important to note, of course, that these expectations do not always concur with the reality. There are many examples of professional forms of caring within criminal justice settings. Knight (2014: 66), for example, argues that many Probation practitioners operate under a 'caring credo'; this is an attitude towards service users based upon liberal and humanitarian values:

> [T]he caring credo has traditionally been exercised through the philosophical approach of 'advise, assist and befriend... [which] continues to be a significant influence in motivating current recruits to the service'.
>
> (Knight, 2014: 71)

Correspondingly there were fears that peers may not always have caring qualities:

> We might get the wrong people. They should be vetted to see how people get on with other people. An interview is never enough for me, some people probably think they're better than they actually are, so experience is more important for me... be selective in people.
>
> (John, Mentor)

Being a professional does not by default render you uncaring, just as being a peer does not automatically render you caring. Nonetheless there is a powerful belief among these speakers that judgement and understanding are incompatible. This is something that Martin Buber (1985) argued in terms of dialogue:

> "[D]ialogue," in which I open myself to the otherness of the person I meet, and "monologue," in which, even when I converse with her at length, I allow her to exist only as a content of my experience. Wherever one lets the other exist only as part of oneself, "dialogue becomes a fiction, the mysterious intercourse between two human worlds only a game, and in the rejection of the real life confronting him the essence of all reality begins to disintegrate".
>
> (Buber 1985: 24 cited in Friedman, 2005: 30)

For Buber, true dialogue and true understanding require openness to the fullness of the other's experience. This openness may be stifled by a system characterised by pre-judgement, for example, a criminal justice system which has established scientific answers to individual experiences. In this context the *offender* is less a speaker to be open to and more a *collection of risks* to be assessed, processed and managed. Katy, a mentor who had previously been mentored at the women's charity where she now works, illustrates this difference neatly. Following a conviction for selling Cannabis, Katy was mentored by Project 'Facilitate'. She was then invited to train as a mentor. During her training, she was offered an opportunity to sell drugs again by some of her old connections. As she was on the local housing waiting list she was also offered – by coincidence – the very property she had previously been selling drugs from as a possible tenancy. She refused both offers and told her mentoring supervisor about them. She explained to me, however, that she did not feel she could discuss the offers as easily with her Probation Officer for fear of risk-averse consequences:

> I told my [mentoring] supervisor about the offer [of accommodation] because it was the house it [my previous offending] was happening in… She'll have probably put it in my file and it's there, but with probation they tend to overreact on it, and my supervision probably would have got extended, and they probably would have called me in on a more frequent basis, and panicked about it, whereas [my supervisor] trusted where I was at and the fact I was honest with her stood for quite a lot.
>
> (Katy, Mentor)

Katy assumes that her words will be interpreted by her Probation Officer in terms of a judgement of risk and that her experience will then only 'exist' in these terms. The perceived responsibility of offender management services to respond to people as risks, therefore, restricts open dialogue. In contrast, peer mentoring is perceived to enable a more open dialogue. Peers separate themselves from this system of expertise, identifying themselves instead with offending and desisting experiences *and* attending to the experience of the speaker before them. They have the freedom to listen and to engage in dialogue, to open themselves and their practices to the 'otherness' of the person they meet. This makes space for a new reality, a reality wherein the mentee's voice is central; their experience and judgements afforded equal ground. The 'offender' becomes co-author; changer rather than a problem to be changed. In Freire's terms, such dialogue enables people 'to come to feel like masters of their thinking and views of the world explicitly or implicitly manifest in their own suggestions and those of their comrades' (Freire, 1970: 105). It enables mentors and mentees to feel a sense of agency in their own lives. Mentoring emerges here as a caring version of dialogue where issues of interpersonal power imbalance are not so evident. Caring and a non-judgemental disposition are seen as important qualities for a mentor to have. They foster positive human connections and potentially enable new personal perceptions, perhaps even personal 'growth'. However, Helen Colley warns against such uncritical idealism regarding care, suggesting that expectations of care in mentoring contexts may be more limiting than they initially appear:

> [W]here commitment to the client is made central to the professional role, the worker sells her personality as an integral part of her own labour power. It takes the form of emotional labour, and this emotion work brings its own costs, and does so disproportionately for women than for men, given women's lower social status.
>
> (Colley, 2001: 188)

A similar analysis is offered by Arlie Hochschild, who argues that 'the altruist is more susceptible to being used – not because her sense of self is weaker but because her "true self" is bonded more securely to the group and its welfare' (Hochschild, 2003: 196). This work also takes place within a wider social context which values 'instrumental' work more highly than 'expressive' work (Daniels, 1985). To expect mentors *to care* is not simply to expect a harmless giving of one to another then, but to expect emotional toil; a toil that is likely to demand more of female mentors than male in a society which has positioned women as: 'more caring in nature, because of their 'natural' child-bearing and child-rearing roles' (Best, 2005: 197) and emotions as inferior to reason and masculinity (Pettersen, 2008: 53). Furthermore, this toil may feel like a failure if care in and of itself does not work its desired magic.

Core condition 2: listening

One of the clearest themes emerging from the interviews in this study, indeed the most frequently voiced condition of peer mentoring was that of *listening*. The importance of listening in criminal justice settings is not in itself a new finding. Researching female lawbreakers, for example, Anne Worrall found that '"helpfulness" was defined by the women in two ways: first, material help, and second, *non-intrusive listening* and advice-giving' (Worrall, 1990: 157 emphasis added). In the context of Probation, Trish McCulloch found that 'Almost all of the participants identified "being listened to" as one of the most useful methods in addressing probationers' social problems' (McCulloch, 2005: 18). Finally, Monica Barry noted that the vast majority of her respondents 'suggested that the best approach was for supervising officers to talk and listen to their clients about the problems, fears and consequences of offending' (Barry, 2007: 416). Listening is deemed to be a useful tool, not least because:

> Offenders themselves tend to have a good understanding of what they want from practitioners and politicians to help them reintegrate into their communities... [there is a] need to listen much more to the needs and wishes of offenders.
>
> (Barry, 2007: 409)

The benefits of listening, Barry argues, include personal development, learning, and meaningful interaction (2007: 416). Being heard becomes a vehicle for self-development and shared meaning-making, it is important for self-growth. Moreover, it may be vital for the development of knowledge:

> If we are to have an informed, effective strategy and approach to deal with the problems of crime – politicians, policy makers and criminologists

must *relate, listen to* and *understand* those who are being processed by the ever widening and more punitive criminal justice system.

(Burke, 2007: 317, emphasis added)

This was an argument echoed by coordinators and volunteers in this study, who also suggest that professional practitioners have something to gain from listening. Lol, for example, works for a charity which supports care leavers (adults who spent some of their childhood in local authority care). He highlights that his motivation to become involved with mentoring was to get a 'user perspective' heard by practitioners:

> [They] don't take into account a care experience, but... twenty-five per cent plus in the prison system can say 'yes I was in care'... It's fundamental to a person's progress, throughout the rest of their life, to engage with some of those issues that have led to them feeling so fragile, so alienated, so detached from everything that can possibly support them... So this seminar [organised by Lol for criminal justice agency partners] is about trying to say these things to them, but trying to make sure we use the idea of mentoring, we use the idea of user perspective as a way to have a big impact.

(Lol, Mentoring Coordinator)

Steve, a peer mentor was similarly motivated to get a voice of experience heard:

> They're [probation staff] listening a lot more to people and I'm not bigging myself up about that, but I think they're listening a lot more to people like myself and [coordinator names]. And we're saying: 'Listen, it's doing no good! What good is it doing, him coming in here for half an hour chat with you and then he goes? Where's the support, what's that doing? It's doing nothing!' Do you know what I mean? 'You're talking about motivational techniques and they're not interested, they're just going through the rhythms'.

(Steve, Mentor)

Both Lol and Steve imply that by *doing to people* rather than *listening to people,* Probation Officers and associated professionals miss highly relevant parts of a person's experience and in fact create inauthentic transactions. The 'receivers' of these services do not engage fully, but rather they go through the expected 'rhythms', play the game, which is being shaped by the interveners' world view. Listening is also deemed to be as important within the mentoring relationship:

> Listening, good communication skills, the ability to empathise with people is key... I have met mentors that just do a lot of the talking, and forget

they're actually there to listen at the same time, so I think listening is equally as important as being able to offer, actually listening is offering.

(Phil, Mentor)

BRAD: A few of the peer mentors don't come from offending or drug using backgrounds, just people that are willing to have listening ear, and be understanding.

INTERVIEWER: Is listening a big part of your role?

BRAD: Listening is a massive part, yea. I was sat in this very room last Thursday, and a client was in for hour and half, I hardly spoke, he just spoke about problems at home, problems with his mum, his problems not having a job, all that. Just listening, for him it's somebody that will listen to his problems....

(Brad, Mentor)

For Lol and Steve, there is a value in practitioners listening to the experiences of those who have been through the system. For Phil and Brad, however, experience only takes you so far. Once the face-to-face work of mentoring is underway, it is listening – allowing space for the mentee to make their own sense of things – which is deemed to be more important. Listening in their eyes is *doing* something; it is a means and an end. When I initially identified the theme of 'listening' within this study it seemed such a blindingly obvious finding that I feared it hardly warranted discussion. As a youth justice Social Worker, I had understood *listening* to be a core requirement of the work. I therefore assumed that it would be of central importance to most criminal justice interventions, including peer mentoring. What I have since learned from respondents to this study, and indeed from critical re-assessment of some of my own past practice, is that *listening to people* is often not constant in criminal justice practice and all too often is omitted completely: 'listening does not feature as a promising factor in any of the "What Works" literature, nor is it offered as a guiding principle in the National Standards' (Barry, 2007: 419). The most recent iteration of (adult) National Standards (2015) make one reference to 'offenders' being 'listened to', yet only in relation to how far they felt unpaid work would benefit the community (p. 77). There are no explicit references to listening in the *Standards for children in the youth justice system 2019* and whilst they do recommend 'all proceedings demonstrate that children's voices are heard', this principle comes after a long list of other principles, related to criminal codes, youth detention, victims and court personnel (p. 10). Whilst listening is a tool with obvious importance therefore, its value appears to lack prominence in policy and practice:

The provision of advice and guidance is now well recognized as a useful method in helping probationers to resolve a range of problems

(McIvor and Barry, 1998; Rex, 1998) though the value of talking and, more significantly, listening to probationers is less well documented.

(McCulloch, 2005: 15)

What peer mentoring may be quietly doing in practical terms then, is asserting the importance of listening to people who are 'subject to state sanctions', something Burke (2007: 316) argues that 'insufficient attention' has been paid to. Not only do these narratives highlight that listening is important, however, but also illustrate why:

> I'd say the main [skill] was being able to listen, because nine times out of ten a lot of people who come to probation have a lot of problems that they need to get off their chest. I do feel comfortable telling them [mentors] most family problems, or problems that I have with myself and stuff like that, cos like I said, they don't criticise you, they listen. They give you good information back.
>
> (Paul, Mentee)

Georgie, who was mentored by a volunteer following her release from prison, made a similar claim:

> She was very good at listening... I just needed emotional help and I didn't know where to get it... When you can't deal with your emotions, or things that are going on, you don't realise that talking to someone can help you.
>
> (Georgie, Mentee)

And finally, Gina, who used a peer mentoring service when she committed an offence which caused her to lose her career, prioritised the importance of peers who listen. She also thought it important that mentors 'reiterate your thoughts back so that you know they have listened'. Indeed, she regarded this feature more important than a shared history:

> It was actually quite nice to be with people who knew what you'd been through... but not necessarily important, as long as they're a good listener and understand the system and understand you.
>
> (Gina, Mentee)

Listening then, is an action, an intervention in itself. It enables people to unburden themselves of problems, to begin to see themselves as capable of self-direction when conditions feel overwhelming and to feel heard. The unburdening of problems is a sub-theme that warrants further explanation here, before the third core condition of this work is outlined.

Listening as unburdening problems

Poetry can be a useful tool for representing sensitive data as it both engages readers and allows an exploration of the lived experience of the research subject (Furman, Lietz & Langer, 2006). Each of the fourteen lines here is taken from a different respondent interview. It is presented in this way to dignify the separate and individual but connected experiences of suffering that surfaced repeatedly in interviews. Each statement marks an unburdening of grief:

"Care home, YOI [Young Offender Institution], I constantly felt discarded. Nobody cared at all now. I was discarded."

"I was in pain, I had to find some help. All the time I'm feeling down."

"It hurts like a bastard, rips my heart out that I can't see my children."

"In care, abusive alcoholic family... I brought younger brothers up, got adopted and not allowed to see them... I lost five of my family in five years."

"I used to self-harm, no-one was arsed about blood trails in my bedroom... I've been hit, abused, family problems, relationship problems."

"I felt that really I wasn't worthy of anything, emotionally at rock bottom."

"I was at my lowest point, living in a hostel, I had absolutely nothing."

"I got attacked so I just never went back."

"There's a lot of damp, no heating for three days... I feel like hiding."

"I lost my Granddad, then my Nan... my Mum had had a nervous breakdown and tried to top herself... my ex [partner] raped my Mum."

"Living in a concrete coffin, the graveyard where my friends are buried."

"I put my own safety at risk; I had my face cut open."

"I feel so lonely, I feel so useless when I say that. Your life is that bad, you just want to forget... You need your drugs, you're ratting, white, feel awful, sneezing, terrible, it's awful."

"Domestic violence, self-harming, mental health issues, so much stuff that all goes together."

This stylised presentation of related interview extracts, together with a wider repeated message in the research that it was useful to talk through problems, very much reframes the experience of 'offenders'. As a listener to these narratives I was reminded that *being an offender* is often accompanied by *suffering*. This is not of course a new finding. Criminologists have consistently highlighted experiences of abuse, bereavement, family breakdown, poverty, addiction and poor mental health among offending populations. In Scotland, the entire Children's Justice System is designed around the 'links between deeds and needs', as crime is understood to be 'symptomatic of a broad spectrum of vulnerability' (McAra & McVie, 2010). What is new here however is that respondents locate their suffering within a broader context of 'recovery':

> Peer mentoring to me is helping people through recovery basically, helping them to sort out and sort of like be enabled to take on everyday life… It's actually helped me through my recovery as a concerned other, which has then helped me to help my children, so I think that's the biggest thing really.
>
> (Paula, Mentor)

> I have got problems but I really have overcome a lot since I've had a mentor… when you've lived the sort of life I have you need somebody to drill things into you or you're not going to be doing it, you need that shove to an extent, a bit of hand holding
>
> (Fiona, Mentee)

> It helps you open up and it helps you be honest with yourself, because you have a certain thought pattern, and it helps break that, it's like re-training your brain in a way and facing your fears.
>
> (Lin, Mentor and Previously a Mentee)

The mentors and mentees speaking here have very different histories, including personal drug or alcohol addiction, family members with addictions or experiences of abuse, bullying and committing violent offences. Yet despite their diverse experiences, the intertextual presentation of their descriptions of *recovery* illustrates a shared sense that personal improvement is required. Recovery here is associated with not only feeling better and feeling cared for, but also with feeling inadequate; people consider that they need re-drilling, retraining and healing. These are the very corrective processes that people are resistant to from professionals (Chapter 5), yet they appear to experience them positively from their peers. Much like the issue of 'care', however, the notion of mentoring as 'recovery' is problematic. Georgie, for example, found her mentoring experience valuable, particularly in terms of helping her to settle into life away from her established peer group when she was released from prison. As the relationship progressed, however, she felt it was lacking in terms of helping her to fully recover from her alcohol addiction:

GEORGIE: I feel it's more deeper, my stuff now…

INTERVIEWER: OK, so she [the mentor] was able to take you so far, introduce to process of talking and healing…?

GEORGIE: Yes, [but] I think I need some Counseling or something… If AA [Alcoholics Anonymous] would have been introduced to me two years ago I'd be straight now.

This point does not discount the contribution of peer mentoring in high-lighting the importance of listening approaches, but it recognises that these methods are not a panacea; they will not provide the 'answer' for every-one. Taken together, what the above narratives very clearly do however, is reposition 'offenders' and desisters. Rather than flawed individuals who must make sweeping life changes, they become people experiencing significant difficulty who can benefit from gentle support. Indeed, the changes expected in these settings are often deliberately small, rather than comprehensive, as indicated by the third and final core condition of peer mentoring: encouraging small steps.

Core condition 3: encouraging small steps

In addition to 'Caring' and 'Listening', a third important condition that mentors and mentees repeatedly referred to was the encouragement of 'Small Steps' towards change. This was initially denoted by Gina (Mentee) when she described her own mentoring as 'just gentle… it plants the seed and it grows'. Such gentle, small steps were also seen as important by mentors:

> I think that setting little goals is what gets people going.
>
> (John, Mentor)

> They've got their short-term goals, we do things like star [planning] chart, different goals where you can monitor… see how far they are in two weeks, a month's time. We can do long term/ short term goals on that.
>
> (Paula, Mentor)

> It's good to have them [personal employment] goals but it's not always as rosy as that picture being painted. So if you want to do it, you need short term goals in order to achieve that long term goal.
>
> (Phil, Mentor)

The significance of small goals is that they seem achievable and they therefore motivate people. This motivation is sustained because people begin to see the progress they are making. Whilst small steps can be overlooked within bigger bureaucratic agendas, which demand tangible 'results' such as 'real reductions in reoffending' (MoJ, 2013), peer mentors stress the importance of these smaller changes:

> To get them out of their little ways, you know? I've been like incarcerated most of my life; from the armed forces and then all the way up to prison. It's like the first time I've been in the real world and it is difficult. But because of everything I've been through and done and found out,

and the things that have blocked me, I've found ways round. I may have to take a bit longer, but I've done it and it just kind of gives them a bit of hope for the future because I was the same.

(Cat, Mentor)

Cat highlights how change, particularly from entrenched patterns of criminality or incarceration can take time, yet time is a resource which big systems no longer have. Rather 'the contacts between professional support workers and their clients are likely to be brief and episodic' (Brown and Ross, 2010: 32). However, this *time* also needs to be marked with indications of success if motivation is to be maintained:

I'm starting to get into the routine now of setting my mini goals to get the eventual thing that I want. Nine times out of ten I was just trying to get the end thing and I was just fucking myself up – sorry for swearing – messing myself up… There's the odd time where you have a little fall, but it doesn't hit you as hard as if you're about to achieve the main goal that you wanted and then you mess up, you know what I mean?.

(Paul, Mentee)

She [mentor]… used to say: 'Right, one thing at a time, let's go and deal with this'. I come back and I'll go: '[mentor name] I've had a letter back!' It'd only be one step closer but just made me feel better cos I'd got somewhere with at least something… If you're feeling vulnerable, it takes a little something to knock you over edge, commit crime, take drugs, or treat somebody how you shouldn't be treating them, and I think mentoring just takes that edge off.

(Georgie, Mentee)

For Paul and Georgie, taking small steps provides an opportunity to *demonstrate* success, however small. When success can be witnessed, it can be *felt* by mentees, it becomes a reality. In very practical terms, mentees are conditioned to have hope. Small goals constitute manageable possibilities. The achievement of these goals confirms ability and therefore instils hope. This is a feature, which was posited by McNeill and Weaver:

[H]ope and hopefulness are important factors, … Building motivation and sense of agency is likely to involve helping the individual to recognise the possibilities of a self hood and lifestyle that is more desirable than what s/he currently has; that possibility needs to be meaningful and desirable for the individual. The worker needs to work with him or her towards its formulation and realisation and to persist and maintain hope through lapses and relapses.

(McNeill & Weaver, 2010: 8)

Not only do the speakers here describe step by step motivation, which they find manageable and meaningful to them, but importantly they also begin to acknowledge that this road will not always be smooth; that lapses and relapses are a likely and acceptable feature. Indeed, both mentees and mentors explicitly described the importance of not over-reacting to slip ups. Paul and Don, for example, are mentees using a peer mentoring service attached to a Probation Service. Both regard that their mentors recognise and tolerate lapses:

> It's [change] not going to happen in a day is it? Rome wasn't built in a day. It's going to take time, there is bound to be them slip ups. But most of the time they just seem to be, like, understanding about it.
>
> (Paul, Mentee)

> If I have scored [taken drugs] they say 'don't worry, what set it off?'.
>
> (Don, Mentee)

Mentors themselves confirm that they strive for such tolerance in their work. Julie, for example, explains:

> I failed loads of times in my life. I'd say I've failed but then I've got up... People won't go straight just like that, they'll have their up and downs, but I think having a mentor will support them and show them that you're not giving up on them. And even if they do go off the rails a bit, but showing that you're not giving up on them, then sometimes they'll turn that around and think: 'well I won't do that because she's still there for me'.
>
> (Julie, Mentor)

Like Julie, Steve rationalises the need to persist with hope, even when others are tiring of lapses. Here he describes a discussion with Probation and housing staff, wherein he advocates for a mentee who has had numerous relapses during his efforts to lead a drug and crime free life:

> On the morning meeting [colleagues said]: *'He's had that many chances'* but in my mind I'm saying: I had them same chances and I kept messing up over and over... [They say]: *'We've put everything in place for him over and over'*,
>
> And I've carried on: 'I've just got that niggling feeling that just a little move like that, to a different hostel, more supportive accommodation, that could be the making of him'.
>
> (Steve, Mentor)

For the mentees speaking here, their lapses are normalised, rather than pathologised. This works with, not against a 'zig-zag' desistance process, 'whereby – as with addictions – individuals tend to desist gradually rather than suddenly' (Farrall, 2013: 21). It also creates a sense for mentees that their efforts are not futile, that their attempts to change are still on track. For the mentors, tolerance of mistakes is clearly an intentional strategy, based upon the belief that people will have 'ups and downs' but with consistent belief and support, or 'not giving up', there is always the hope of success. Uniquely, the driver for Julie and Steve's perspectives comes not from their knowledge of desistance research, but from their own experiences of change. They both describe 'failing' or 'messing up' yet both managed to desist in the end. They have an existential confidence in the possibility of change, despite repeated lapses. Moreover, both see persistent support as the thing which will eventually conquer these 'slip-ups'. This is theoretically very different to actuarial criminal justice, which regards further offending, or lapses, as risk factors or warning signs to be recorded and addressed. This element of peer mentoring creates one of the many tensions between the managerial aims of criminal justice and alternative forms of knowledge. It will be interesting to see, as time progresses, whether such tensions result in limits upon mentoring or challenges to the broader technocratic system.

Despite diverse client groups, settings and approaches, a number of core values or conditions are advocated within the work of peer mentoring. Respondents repeatedly highlight the importance of 'individualised' or mentee-centred practice, along with three core conditions: *caring; listening;* and *encouraging small steps.* These conditions are offered as antidotes to what can often be experienced as disconnected, unhearing and technocratic criminal justice practices, as highlighted here and in Chapter 5. Peer mentoring, in contrast, is claimed to be a space to release suffering, to unburden the self of grief and to become capable of new self-direction. It is seen as a safe space to do this given that mentors 'genuinely care' and are tolerant of slip-ups. The chapter therefore illuminates the interpersonal elements of mentoring, which are claimed to promote personal growth and change. Despite these ideals, however, there are a number of core tensions. First, whilst individualised practice is prized, it has roots in the approaches of motivational interviewing and person-centred counselling, practices which are invariably caught up in diagnostic power relations. Indeed, motivational interviewing in particular is a technique that has become institutionalised within Probation settings. There is therefore a strain between diagnosis, directive assistance and a non-directive ethos. Second, whilst 'genuine' care is claimed to foster personal connections and build a sense of self-worth, there is a risk that this discourse burdens peer mentors with an expectation of emotional toil without enough support or reward. Finally, whilst mentors and mentees highlight the importance of listening and encouraging small steps, it is unclear how such unquantifiable approaches will fare within an increasingly results driven technocratic justice system. These tensions are crucial to understanding peer mentoring in criminal justice settings. Indeed, what links all three findings chapters to this point are strains between established rehabilitation practices and peer-led ways of working. This chapter has highlighted the tensions which emerge when mentors attempt to replace diagnostic, technical approaches with emotional, caring and tolerant approaches; in doing so they often retain some of the features of the existing approaches and risk undermining their own practices as an inexpensive add-on to the dominant technocratic system. The following two chapters will offer further evidence of such struggles. Chapter 8 will explore mentoring as a site of 'change', including the manifold ways in which this is understood, before Chapter 9 conceives of the tensions within mentoring as practices of 'power'.

Acknowledgements

This chapter has adapted material from the following work:

Buck, G., (2018), 'The core conditions of peer mentoring', *Criminology & Criminal Justice*, **18**(2), pp. 190–206.

I am thankful to the publishers for their permission.

References

Barry, M., (2007), 'Listening and learning: The reciprocal relationship between worker and client', *Probation Journal*, **54**(4), pp. 407–422.

Best, S., (2005), *Understanding social divisions*. London: Sage.

Brown, M. & Ross, S., (2010), 'Mentoring, social capital and desistance: A study of women released from prison', *Australian & New Zealand Journal of Criminology (Australian Academic Press)*, **43**(1), pp. 31–50.

Buber, M., (1985), *Between Man and Man*. (Introduction by Maurice Friedman, trans. by Ronald Gregor Smith). Macmillan: New York.

Burke, L., (2007), 'Editorial: Is anybody listening?', *Probation Journal*, **54**(4), pp. 315–317.

Colley, H., (2001), 'Righting rewritings of the myth of Mentor: A critical perspective on career guidance mentoring', *British Journal of Guidance and Counselling*, **29**(2), pp. 177–197.

Daniels, A.K., (1985), 'Good times and good works: The place of sociability in the work of women volunteers', *Social Problems*, **32**(4), pp. 363–374.

Day, A., (2009), 'Offender emotion and self-regulation: Implications for offender rehabilitation programming', *Psychology, Crime & Law*, **15**(2–3), pp. 119–130.

Farrall, S., (2013), 'Social structural processes and the operation of the criminal justice system'. In: Dockley, A. & Loader, I., (Eds.), *The penal landscape: The howard league guide to criminal justice in England and Wales*. Abingdon, Oxon: Routledge.

Freire, P., (1970), *Pedagogy of the oppressed*. Reprint, London: Penguin, 1996.

Friedman, M., (2005), 'Martin Buber and Mikhail Bakhtin: The dialogue of voices and the word that is spoken'. In: Banathy, B. & Jenlink, P.M., (Eds.), *The dialogue as a means of collective communication*. New York: Springer US, pp. 29–39.

Furman, R., Lietz, C. & Langer, C.L., (2006), 'The research poem in international social work: Innovations in qualitative methodology', *International Journal of Qualitative Methods*, **5**(3), pp. 24–34.

Hochschild, A.R., (2003), *The managed heart: Commercialization of human feeling, with a new afterword*. London and California: University of California Press.

Karstedt, S., (2011), 'Handle with care: Emotions, crime and justice'. In: Karstedt, S., Loader, I. & Strang, H., (Eds.), *Emotions, crime and justice (Onati International Series in Law and Society)*. Oxford: Hart.

Knight, C., (2014), *Emotional literacy in criminal justice: Professional practice with offenders*. Hampshire: Palgrave MacMillan.

Leibrich, J., (1993), *Straight to the point: angles on giving up crime*. Otago, New Zealand: University of Otago press.

Leibrich, J., (1994), 'What do offenders say about going straight?', *Federal Probation*, **58**, pp. 41–46.

Levensky, E.R., Forcehimes, A., O'Donohue, W.T. & Beitz, K., (2007), 'Motivational interviewing: An evidence-based approach to counseling helps patients follow treatment recommendations', *AJN The American Journal of Nursing*, **107**(10), pp. 50–58.

Lippens, R., (2009), *A very short, fairly interesting and reasonably cheap book about studying criminology*. London: Sage.

Matthews, B. & Hubbard, D., (2007), 'The helping alliance in juvenile probation: The missing element in the "What Works" literature', *Journal of Offender Rehabilitation*, **45**(1–2), pp. 105–122.

McAra, L. & McVie, S., (2010), 'Youth crime and justice: Key messages from the Edinburgh study of youth transitions and crime', *Criminology and Criminal Justice*, **10**(2), pp. 179–209.

McCulloch, T., (2005), 'Probation, social context and desistance: Retracing the relationship', *Probation Journal*, **52**(8), pp. 8–22.

McNeill, F., (2006), 'A desistance paradigm for offender management', *Criminology and Criminal Justice*, **6**(1), pp. 39–62.

McNeill, F. & Weaver, B., (2010), *Changing lives? Desistance research and offender management, Research report 03/2010*, The Scottish Centre for Crime and Justice Research. Available at: www.sccjr.ac.uk/pubs/Changing-Lives-Desistance-Research-and-Offender-Management/255 [Accessed August 2019].

McIvor, G. & Barry, M., (1998), *Social Work and Criminal Justice: Volume 6 Probation*. Edinburgh: The Scottish Office Central Research Unit.

Miller, W.R. & Rollnick, S., (2013), Motivational interviewing: Helping people change (3rd Edn.). New York: Guilford press.

Ministry of Justice (MoJ), (2013), *Transforming Rehabilitation: A Strategy for Reform* Response to consultation, May 2013. London: Ministry of Justice.

National Standards (2015), *National Standards for the Management of Offenders: Practice Framework*. Available at: www.gov.uk/government/publications/national-standards-for-the-management-of-offenders-practice-framework [Accessed January 2020].

Pettersen, T., (2008), *Comprehending care: Problems and possibilities in the ethics of care*. Plymouth: Rowman & Littlefield.

Rex, S., (1998), *Perceptions of Probation in a Context of "Just Deserts"*. Unpublished PhD thesis. Cambridge: University of Cambridge.

Rogers, C.R., (1980), *A way of being.* Reprint, New York: Houghton Mifflin Harcourt, 1995 edition.

Schaftenaar, P., van Outheusden, I., Stams, G.J. & Baart, A., (2018), 'Relational caring and contact after treatment. An evaluation study on criminal recidivism', *International Journal of Law and Psychiatry,* **60**, pp. 45–50.

Smedslund, G., Berg, R.C., Hammerstrøm, K.T., Steiro, A., Leiknes, K.A., Dahl, H.M. & Karlsen, K., (2011), 'Motivational interviewing for substance abuse', *Cochrane Database of Systematic Reviews,* Issue 5. Art. No.: CD008063. doi: 10.1002/14651858.CD008063.pub2.

Spalek, B., (2008), *Communities, identities and crime.* Bristol: Policy Press.

Stokes, P., (2003), 'Exploring the relationship between mentoring and counselling', *British Journal of Guidance and Counselling,* **31**(1), pp. 25–38.

Thorne, B. & Sanders, P., (2013), *Carl Rogers* (3rd Edn.). London: Sage.

Wilkins, P., (2010), *Person-centred therapy: 100 key points.* Hove: Routledge.

Worrall, A., (1990), *Offending women: Female lawbreakers and the criminal justice system.* London: Routledge.

Chapter 8

The terror, complexity and limits of change

This chapter focuses on how change is made sense of within peer mentoring settings. The existing literature construes change largely in instrumental terms, such as reducing reoffending, delinquency or drug use (The Social Innovation Partnership, 2012; Frontier Economics, 2009; Clayton, 2009; Tolan, Henry, Schoeny & Bass, 2008; Jolliffe & Farrington, 2007). Transformations are imagined in individual terms and measures focus upon whether mentoring has improved the individual in ways which can be quantified. Studies of desistance have begun to challenge this narrow focus, pointing additionally to structures which require improvement (McNeill, 2012; Farrall, Sparks & Maruna, 2011). This chapter adds to existing knowledge by exploring *how* individual behaviour change happens in these relationships. In doing so it builds upon earlier theorising that personal transformation does not occur spontaneously, but can be externally inspired (Girard, 1962) and that peer associates are often required to support change (Ferguson, 1996; Freire, 1970). However, the chapter also suggests that change post criminalisation is more problematic than it may appear as people point to vivid fears, difficulties and conflicts surrounding new ways of being and the very contexts and personnel tasked with assisting these. Respondent narratives also have a broader focus than individual transformation, pointing to the need for renewed services and attitudes for desistance to appear as a realistic goal. The chapter begins by exploring how people become 'ready' to change, before examining how mentoring aims to shift individual perceptions from the past to the future. It then illustrates how personal change can often be a terrifying and difficult process, before analysing claims that peer mentoring can offer a unique antidote to this terror. Finally, the chapter outlines how mentors aim to make changes to the systems and settings they work within; in doing so they often appear to challenge some of the dominant negative discourses, which frame people with convictions.

Getting 'ready' to change

This section explores the tensions between external inspiration and individual 'readiness' to change. Chapter 5 highlighted how one of the perceived strengths of mentors with shared past experiences is that they can inspire their peers to change. This perception constructs personal change as a mediated process. In Girardian terms: 'The mimetic agent is moved by a passionate admiration of the other, who plays the role of a mediator' (Tomelleri, 2005: 245). If change is a process, this conception suggests that the process begins with *the other*: 'I wanted to feel the way they did, they weren't beaming out happiness, but they weren't sad, they was that content in their life they were offering to other people, to help them and I wanted to be able to do that' (Georgie, Mentee). However, the origin of personal change remains one of the unresolved problems within criminology. Giordano, Cernkovich and Rudolph (2002: 1000), for example, theorise that there are 'four types of intimately related cognitive transformations' which accompany desistance from crime. The first of these is not an external mediator, but 'a shift in the actor's basic openness to change' (Giordano et al., 2002: 1000). The importance of this openness, they indicate, 'has been discussed extensively in various treatment literatures, especially those dealing with addictions' (Giordano et al., 2002: 1000). Second, they develop the notion of 'hooks for change', these are external opportunities to which a person is exposed (e.g. a job or marriage), arguing that 'while a general openness to change seems necessary; by itself it is often insufficient' (Giordano et al., 2002: 1000). Whilst, like Girard (1962), they acknowledge the power of the social environment, therefore, their chronological concept of change begins with the will of the individual agent. This suggests that there is a process that happens to an individual mentee before the 'inspirational' mentor can even come to play a role. In contrast, Maguire and Raynor (2006) outline a less sequential concept of change, arguing: 'Individuals differ greatly in their readiness to contemplate and begin the process of change' and that 'readiness can be affected by a wide range of factors, including age, major life events or "transitions", physical and social circumstances and social bonds' (Maguire & Raynor, 2006: 25). Moreover, they point out that 'individuals do not move through their cycle of change in a regular, predictable fashion, nor is the process irreversible' (Maguire & Raynor, 2006: 25). Where their account meets with that of Giordano et al., is an assumption that 'a frame of mind receptive to narratives of change' (Maguire & Raynor, 2006: 25) is a necessary condition for gathering the will to alter one's life. These commentators agree that it is the agent (i.e. mentee), not a mediating other (mentor), who initiates the process of change. Worrall and Gelsthorpe (2009) however, reflecting on Eaton's (1993) work with women leaving custody, suggest that whilst respondents had all made a conscious decision to re-direct their lives 'such motivation was not something that just happened' (Worrall & Gelsthorpe, 2009: 337). They submit that 'In order to make that decision, [women] had to feel confident that change was possible. And to feel confident, they had to achieve recognition – both self-recognition and recognition from others' (Worrall & Gelsthorpe, 2009: 337). The importance of such recognition from others has been confirmed by respondents in this study (Chapter 6). In terms of change, however, Worrall and Gelsthorpe (2009) also suggest that a person's *will* to change may actually be nurtured externally.

These debates have implications for the argument that peer mentors can inspire change. Indeed, we can trace similar debates within respondent narratives. Whilst mentors and mentees often spoke of 'inspirational' role models motivating personal change (Chapter 5), there was also a strong parallel and potentially conflicting view that mentees need to be independently ready to change in order to benefit from this approach. Phil, for example, is an ex-prisoner who is now employed as a young people's mentor in the community. Phil was mentored himself by prison education staff and enthusiastically advocates the importance of setting an inspirational example. Nonetheless, he is also keen to articulate the role of individual will: 'I do believe it's down primarily to individual agency... you've got to want to do it, first and foremost where it starts from; I wanted to be crime free' (Phil, Mentor). Whilst Phil acknowledges the power of other parties in supporting change, he conceives that the process begins with the will of the mentee and therefore is not instigated by a role model. There is the possibility of course that such phraseology is formulaic; the result of messages that mentors have heard during training sessions. Three of the project coordinators, for example, reinforced the notion of being 'ready to change' and advocated prioritising services for those who are 'at this stage', fearing that accepting referrals for people who are not 'ready' to change can be detrimental to both the mentee's impression of mentoring and demotivating for volunteers. However, this belief in a resting 'readiness' in mentees was just as dominant among mentees:

> They've got to want to do it, no point you being given a mentor if you don't want the help, just flying in the wind.
>
> (Fiona, Mentee)

> If you don't want to help yourself no–one can help you can they? It's nice to have that kick up the backside, but if you're not going to do it yourself man you're not going to do it are ya?.
>
> (Paul, Mentee)

> You can draw a horse to water but can't make it drink, if you don't want to stay out of jail yourself, mentors, PO [probation officer], no–one can help you, but they are important, they are good.
>
> (Will, Mentee)

> If someone is adamant 'I am not going to change, you are not going to do anything to change me', then you're not going to change them are you?.
>
> (Ben, Mentee)

It seems important to mentors and mentees that people feel they own this decision, this desire to change; it cannot belong to the intervener or inspirer on their behalf. However, there is a problem here, which indicates an inherent tension in this work. If people must be 'ready' independently of mentoring, why have inspirational models at all? Indeed, how can people be inspired to change by an external party if the desire to change must come from within? For Girard (1977), this is not an insurmountable conflict. He reasons that whilst our desires are inspired by what we see in others, we simultaneously reject this image of ourselves as imitators because we fear our lack of originality (Girard, 1977: 155). One reading of this tension in mentoring settings then, is that mentees (who are deemed to be changing) and their mentors (who are deemed to have changed) maintain the concept of individually owned desire, in each of their narratives, because it is such a dominant cultural discourse: 'resisting social power is the stuff Western narratives are made of from history to television dramas' (Mageo, 2002: 93). It is how we believe ourselves as social beings to be, even whilst we acknowledge that inspiration can play a part. Mentees may, therefore, find inspiration to change by looking at their mentors, but to ensure they do not relinquish their own role in the change process, they insist they were 'ready' all along. However, an application of Girardian mimesis (1962) does not reduce mentees to docile followers. For Girard, all learning involves the imitation of desire. This process requires not only people to learn from, but also people who are willing to learn. Whilst motivation or readiness to change may not have taken full shape in mentees prior to mentoring, they are required to engage with the role models on offer. We can develop this reading further by listening to the words of respondents themselves. Will, a mentee, for example, argues: 'if you don't want to stay out of jail yourself, mentors, probation officers, no-one can help you'; whilst dually acknowledging: 'but they are important'. Will describes the complexity and interconnectedness of the model–protégé exchange. Mentees are not singularly inspired by an external model whilst convincing themselves that they had some individuality in that choice, nor are models irrelevant, but rather the self *and* the other play a role. This reading is closer to the conception of motivation offered by Shapland and Bottoms (2011: 272), who agree 'that the first stage in desistance is a wish to try and change one's life' yet they do not think that the formation of this wish should always be characterised as 'rational' or a 'conscious decision [but instead as] gradual, and sometimes spurred by outside events' (Shapland & Bottoms, 2011: 272). The offer or experience of peer mentoring may indeed constitute one such 'outside event', as articulated by Steve, who was mentored on release from prison:

> It wasn't just the [mentoring] system, although that was good. That was just getting me involved in stuff that I'd never really done. I never used to

go out, all my life was just chaos and then, from that on, I decided, 'you know what? I'm going give this a really good go'.

(Steve, Mentor and previously a Mentee)

Mentoring provides Steve with an invitation to try out, to become something new, but the choice to engage remains with him. In this regard, 'individual agency plays a big part' (Phil, Mentor). This dualism suggests that peer models may represent one of the factors which can enable a person's will or intention to be 'spurred' or realised. Moreover, the process is dialectic; both the agent and model play roles in ways that are not neatly sequential or conscious. Paul, for example, a mentee who had spent most of his youth and young adulthood in prison, did not feel 'ready' for change at the start of his mentoring relationship, expecting he would just 'go through the motions'. However, he came to see his mentor as a crucial model and helper, playing an important role when his own will was vacillating:

> I didn't think I was gonna get anything out of it. I just thought it would be someone talking to me for four appointments, then sending me on way. 'Cos it can be like that sometimes when you get these Court orders. But it's not like that... Most of time I would say I wanted it [to go straight], but I wasn't making the right choices, so obviously I didn't want it enough... I think it's the fact that I've had help there, but I wanted it myself as well.

(Paul, Mentee)

Readiness to change is not present in a conscious way for Paul, but rather change occurs as a stumble, a wavering advance, involving both his own will and the help of his mentor. Georgie describes a similar lack of conscious 'readiness' for mentoring at the outset:

> To be honest, I didn't think I needed a mentor, but I went ahead anyway and it was quite shocking, because I was quite willing to talk to her. It was quite shocking how much I was willing to let her know... you gotta be ready for something, something ticked in your brain to accept mentoring... Anyone that accepts a mentor gotta know they kind of want to change, but it's just doing it, even with your mentor, it's doing it.

(Georgie, Mentee)

Georgie separates the process of mentoring from her will to change and it is the process she becomes aware of before her own will, believing initially that she did not need to change. She appears to accept a 'hook for change', before she is aware of her own 'openness to change' (Giordano et al., 2002: 992–1000). Despite this sequence, however, Georgie is understandably reluctant to relinquish the influence of her own will. Indeed, despite explaining that she was inspired by her mentor and wanted 'to feel the way [her mentor] did', she retrospectively prioritised her own will as paramount: 'you gotta be ready for something'. External inspiration and internal readiness to change may work concurrently, therefore, and in ways that are understood differently at different points.

There is a complex and unpredictable interplay of social influence and self-direction at work in these relationships. Some of the inspiration that peer mentors offer may prompt the 'period of re-evaluation' (Farrall & Calverley, 2006: 9) that people like Steve often experience before coming to a decision to desist. For others, like Georgie, a subconscious decision may have been made already, but the mentoring process brings it into being and awareness. Moreover, when motivation does not seem to be present, or dips as Paul describes, external help is there. Such interaction between mentors and mentees takes us beyond Girardian mimesis. Peer mentoring does not just provide a vehicle for the mimicry of desires, but also a platform on which people can 'come to feel like masters of their thinking... explicitly or implicitly manifest in their own suggestions and those of their comrades' (Freire, 1970: 105). It also echoes Ferguson's (1996) arguments that yearnings for change can only be transformed into reality when shared with and recognised by others, who enable agents to make the 'reconstitutive leap' (Ferguson, 1996: 122). Peer mentors do not simply inspire the desire for change, nor are mentees alone with individual yearnings, but mentors can bring into reality, into action, the will of the mentee through multiple processes of inspiration, partnership and social nurturing. Whilst this section has suggested that peer mentoring may spur, support or constitute a person's will to change, respondents also placed a heavy emphasis on *sustaining* personal change. The next section will therefore focus on one of the ways in which mentoring claims to actively foster change in mentees.

Changing self-perceptions: from past to future selves

In addition to having an 'openness to change' and recognising 'hooks for change', Giordano et al. (2002: 1001) also advance the importance of actors being 'able to envision and begin to fashion an appealing and conventional "replacement self" that can supplant the marginal one that must be left behind'. Personal change, then, is not just about readiness and opportunity, but the ability to imagine a new, future self, which is often accomplished through recovery stories or 'redemption scripts' (Maruna, 2001: 87). These futures are seen as a key focus of rehabilitative work:

> Reflexive deliberations which are concerned with generating alternative future possibilities are more likely to lead to the individual exercising

transformative agency. This is because, in undertaking these reflexive deliberations, the individual wishes to distance themselves from their present context.

(King, 2013: 324)

Social Work discourse also often suggests that focusing on the past, as opposed to possible futures, may be detrimental to change processes:

[T]alking too much about the past encourages the service user to remain in a victim role... even a developing survivor identity concentrates too much on the original trauma, therefore the work should enable the service user's present to become more vivid than the past so that they can recover the ability to imagine a positive future.

(Milner, 2001: 11)

There is, of course, a large amount of assumption within this discourse. The view of a person being 'stuck in the past' assumes some kind of 'right' to diagnose a person's healing process, to 'move someone on'. However, something in the arguments of both King and Milner here resonated strongly with people in this study. Indeed, one of the more striking themes articulated by respondents was this need to focus on the present or the future as opposed to the past:

I was struggling with him, really struggling with him, to get him to do anything, to motivate him or anything like that. Now he's started looking at the future and not dwelling on his past, because that's a big thing he was doing was dwelling on his past, and he's moving on now. So that for me is a big thing for him... it's giving someone a future to look at to get away from their old habits.

(John, Mentor)

If people dwell on the past that can sometimes cause the drug or alcohol problem: 'I'm no good, I've done this' so you have to say 'right, let's put that to bed, let's move on, do this or do that'. In six months can say: 'I've done that now, that's the old me, forget that'.

(Ben, Mentor)

For these mentors 'moving forward' or going straight requires a focus not on the past but on the future. The past, including past crimes committed, are almost irrelevant:

I don't always necessarily get to know everything the person has done because it's not really a need, that's up to that person if they want to tell me, some people do, some people don't. So yes, unless there was any

massive risk then [managers would] tell you that, but yeah, I don't really
believe it's that important. Why should you judge a person on their past?.

(Ben, Mentor)

The crime is secondary really, doesn't matter. I mean I don't even ask
what people have done, they will disclose it at some point later on…
[Manager] never tells me what anyone's done, it's not my business. As
I said to [Manager]: I don't want people to know what I've done, I know
what it feels like, you don't want people to judge you.

(Joan, Mentor)

Mentors therefore consider that they move people along in a way that is
fundamentally different to a case management approach. The level of
non-judgement advocated here includes a complete rejection of the relevance
of criminal history. This represents a stark contrast to much statutory criminal justice work where risk is central, or where the focus is upon how past
actions and experiences dictate future possibilities. In many peer mentoring
settings, such historical reflections are replaced by a more future-focused,
capacity building approach. What is not clear, however, is whether this temporal reorientation, this focus on the future, transfers to mentees themselves.
Is their sense of themselves and their future potential shifted as intended?
Indications from the speakers in this study are interestingly diverse. Mentees
certainly recognise the importance of this re-focus:

He doesn't…. really dwell on the past that much, it's more the future, past
is your past man, you've done what you done, you need to get yourself
sorted now and look on.

(Paul, Mentee)

My mentor says to me 'I'm not bothered about what's happened, I'm
bothered about you' and they make you feel like you are their only pri-
ority… they're just here to help you and that makes you feel good.

(Janet, Mentee)

These mentees not only see a need to look forward but value the fact that
their mentors do too. Mentors, having dealt with their own pasts and *moved
on* direct their peers in the same forward-facing direction. However, the focus
of mentees is not always correspondingly on the future. This came to light
through a close reading of interview scripts using Gilligan's 'Listening Guide'.
The listening guide (Kiegelmann, 2009: 11), as discussed in Chapter 4, lays
out 'three steps as a way of entering and coming to know another person's
inner world, in the context of the research relationship'. This includes listening for 'I' phrases and listing them in sequence ("I want, I know, I don't
know, I think …"). In analysing scripts, I wrote 'I poems' (with a new line

for each 'I' phrase that appeared in interview) for each interviewee. I noticed to my surprise that the speaking tense differed for each party. Mentees overwhelmingly spoke in the past tense: 'I've never worked, I wanted, I thought, I started, I looked, I've done...' or sometimes the present tense: 'I put, I hand, I don't know' (from Jen, Mentee). By contrast, most of the mentor 'I' poems are spoken in a present tense majority: 'I'm able to share my experiences, I don't go in there and demand respect, I demand that we are on the same level', or sometimes future facing: 'I could, I think, I can, I should, I believe, I want' (from Hope, Mentor). This difference in grammatical tense came as a surprise given that the thematic pattern had already been identified – in the *content* of what respondents were saying – that peer mentoring is often present or future focused. Mentors rarely communicated a concern with the pasts of their mentees, particularly their criminal pasts, focusing instead on current interests and goals for the future. I therefore expected mentees to speak in terms of the future more frequently. This temporal orientation, however, did not transfer.

One explanation for this difference in self-positioning could be the fact that people were being interviewed as 'mentors' and 'mentees'. Mentors may well have felt obliged in the context of a competitive rehabilitation environment to justify their potential, whilst mentees may well have felt obliged in the face of a researcher asking about their position to justify how they got here. This difference in itself reveals how the tacit power dynamic or relational hierarchy between mentor and mentee, may not assist mentees to imagine a positive future as well as might be hoped. Rather, by positioning people as *helper* and *helped*, mentoring may reproduce feelings of power and powerlessness respectively. Maruna (2001), for example, argues that 'individuals... need to find ways of re-narrating their past lives in order to make those histories consistent with who they are in the present and want to be in the future' (cited in Farrall et al., 2011: 2). Peer mentoring offers *mentors* an opportunity to do this. It creates space for people to utilise their criminal past in ways they see as productive. The pasts of mentors can be re-narrated not only as a positive tool, but also as central to who they are and who they can become. Mentors are reminded of their criminal pasts in this context, but this occurs as they perform an influential, exemplary social role. They are therefore empowered in the present and the future. For mentees, however, this dynamic is not present. They are asked to imagine a positive future, to orient away from the past, whilst performing a social role (mentee), which simultaneously serves as a constant reminder of that past and as a reminder that outside help is required.

Change as terrifying and difficult

Whilst peer mentors may offer inspiration to change, nurture mentee's self-determination and strive to re-focus mentees toward possible future selves, there remains, nonetheless, a dominant current of struggling with change throughout mentee (and mentor) narratives. Moreover, these struggles are not simply connected to the disempowering process of being a person in need of help, but are strongly rooted in fear. Fear has been noted previously for people making such changes. Farrall and Calverley (2006: 6), for example, discuss how fear is often reported as a factor associated with desisting from crime. However, they note fear as associated with the consequences of maintaining criminality; be it the fear of experiencing serious physical harm (Hughes, 1998) or the fear of no longer coping physically and emotionally with prison life (Burnett, 2000; Shover, 1983). Similarly, Paternoster and Bushway (2009) suggest that offenders often have a 'feared self' – that is a fear of what they may become if changes are not made. The respondents in this study introduced another facet of fear in their efforts to change however – that is the fear of what changing entails, rather than the fear of staying the same:

> I've been on drugs since I were thirteen... I'm scared to death, and I've just seen someone [who has walked out of his rehabilitation placement before completion] He said: 'I couldn't stand all the rules'... I'm hoping, praying to God that I am ready.
>
> (Fiona, Mentee)

> For six weeks there was no weed and no alcohol – that's why my head come straight, not because of the jail... I know I just need to stop, no doing it in moderation, got to stop, scary.
>
> (Georgie, Mentee)

> Coming off drugs, stopping grafting, it's not easy, it frightens me. I have nothing. I've been alcoholic since I was thirteen.
>
> (Don, Mentee)

These speakers face a frightening void. The self that they strive for, which is free of substances, what Paternoster and Bushway (2009: 1103) refer to as the 'positive possible self', is also not one which they face without fear. Rather there is a tangible anxiety of leaving the known behind. In the above cases there is a fear of ending established substance addictions, addictions which they felt to be necessary to function:

> I don't know what normal is it's so un-normal to have to get up in the morning, and if I didn't take Methadone or drugs I couldn't sit here and talk to you. I'd be so poorly I couldn't talk, terrible, awful. But I've got to go through that detox, go through that pain... it is worth it.
>
> (Fiona, Mentee)

In their efforts to make a change, these mentees must not simply achieve and maintain a desire to change (which they appear to have done), or simply attain role models as motivators and examples (which they have also done), but further they must surmount the fear that surrounds their desired changes.

What is more, this fear does not imagine perils, but recognises the difficult realities of recovery and reintegration:

> The actual word 'change' used to terrify me; I used to be coming out of prison thinking 'what am I going to do?' Because I didn't have any mates, I lost them years ago. The only people I had were associates... [When] I started going running with a police officer, it was like: 'Oh My God' I'd get labelled a Grass, so I used to keep all that sort of stuff really low key... When you go to prison a Grass, [you are like] someone who harms old people or women or children, they're all classed as one person, you know? They'd get beat up.
>
> (Steve, Mentor and previously a Mentee)

Steve experiences anxiety, social isolation and the threat of physical harm. His sense of an unknown future was also articulated by Eve, a mentee at a female offender's project, albeit in a very different context. Eve received a community sentence having fraudulently claimed state benefits, something she explained she was pressured into by her abusive partner. Her partner left her after she received a community sentence, leaving her facing a different kind of unknown:

> I didn't know who I was and I had to find myself. And I was so scared because it was like: I couldn't wear certain things, I couldn't do certain things, I couldn't go to my Mum's or Dad's, because he was like: 'Where are you going? What are you doing? What time will you be back?' I couldn't go to the shop because he'd be texting me. So, I got to a point where I didn't even know who I was.
>
> (Eve, Mentee)

Eve faced the void of 'finding herself' after a life where she had felt wholly controlled, where she had lost her sense of herself. This is wrapped up with the additional pressure of having lived with the terror of domestic abuse as a norm. Whilst her circumstances are different to Steve's, her sense of an unknown future and shifting self resembles what he too described, as does the accompanying fear. Change for many of the speakers in this study is characterised by loss, be it of known pleasures, known supports, known lifestyles or even experiences of coercion. Indeed, it is not just change which is frightening, but the significant challenges that can often be associated with change. Lin, for example, had a desire to get help for alcoholism; a factor she felt led to her convictions, which she described as a result of 'drink related fights and disturbances'. However, Lin was also a single parent and she worried that revealing the extent of her alcohol use would result in her children being removed from her care:

> I'd tried getting help for my drinking a few years ago but when you first go in they have got to warn you that... if you say something that could

be endangering the kids they have to tell the appropriate services. And the way my drinking was, if I'd have been totally honest, they'd have had to get outside agencies involved, and I was scared of losing the kids. So, I kept it hidden. Thankfully everything came to a head and social services found out, so it was like a complete disaster, but it was like 'Thank God', because now I can go to the service and put all my cards on the table.

(Lin, Mentor and previously a Mentee)

These descriptions indicate that change is both physically and psychologically difficult, a process fraught with tangible dangers and frightening newness. However what Lin's account also illustrates is that some of this fear is connected to the services tasked with assisting change, she introduces a notable fear of authority.

Quelling fears of authority

Heavy-handed authority figures featured in Chapter 5 and resulted in mentors aiming to be non-authoritarian. McNeill (2013) further illustrates why interactions with authority can be so fraught for 'offenders':

[I]t is no small task to develop relationships of trust with people whose relationships with others – often especially with authority figures – have often been, at worst, abusive and traumatic and, at best, inconsistent and difficult.

(McNeill, 2013: 84)

Indeed, even when authority figures intend to be 'therapeutic', their interventions may pose dangers to the people they aim to help:

Given the realities of their lives, the inmates warned that [staff] ideals may be dangerous to them... they were expected to drop their "masks" and "badass attitudes" as signs of recovery [yet] their masks and attitudes had been key survival strategies for them, allowing them to withstand abusive family members and lovers; this armor [sic] helped them to navigate tough inner-city neighbourhoods.

(Haney, 2010: 174)

Respondents in my own study were not just fearful of the power held by authority figures, or dubious about the viability of their approaches, but they also framed such relationships as combative:

Social services put people on the defensive, that's how people feel, I'm not saying they should....

(John, Mentor)

Does she [housing officer] think I'm trying to take her job?... It could be that she's fighting for her job, cos a lot of cuts in government and sees the peer mentors a threat to her cos we do it and don't get paid for it.

(Brad, Mentor)

My old mentor got me a flat... they said stop all the shoplifting, drug use – my mentor said don't give them [the housing providers] any ammunition.

(Don, Mentee)

[Going straight], for me, is something that could be done to have no criminal record, I feel a little bit that it hangs over me like a sword.

(Gina, Mentee)

For these speakers the metaphor of a battle serves to describe how they feel positioned in relation to authority. They are not passive victims as they assume defensive strategies, yet they consider their combatants armed and poised. Fear does not just accompany the changes that people hope to make and the incumbent difficulties which attend them then, but also the very contexts and personnel tasked with assisting with these changes. On one level, this fear expresses the subcultural position of labelled offender. Becker (1963: 207) contends, for example, that 'a major element in every aspect of the drama of deviance is the imposition of definitions – of situations, acts, and people – by those powerful enough or sufficiently legitimated to be able to do so'. People with criminal convictions are acutely aware of their position within this defined hierarchy. However, the substance of these fears goes beyond labels. Lin, for example, did not *imagine* the authority of social services to remove her children from her care; Don did not invent the tenuous nature of his new social housing tenancy; and Gina is correct in assuming her criminal record is likely to restrict employment opportunities. When these 'dangers' are invested in as occasions for combat and mentees assume the position of conflict with authority, it creates a barrier to their interactions with those agencies. It is regarding this dimension of change that peer mentoring may have something unique to offer.

This chapter has so far suggested that change is difficult for mentees, not just in practical terms, but in existential terms. Mentees question their known way of being and in doing so encounter a deep sense of insecurity. In addition, they encounter agents and systems of authority, which often increase this anxiety. Where peer mentoring offers a uniquely alternative approach is through its potential to sooth such feelings of ontological insecurity. Ontological security is, at its simplest, a sense of safe familiarity, a feeling of steadiness, of being tethered to the world as we feel that we know it:

The notion of ontological security ties in closely to the... 'bracketings' presumed by the 'natural attitude' in everyday life. On the other side of what might appear to be quite trivial aspects of day-to-day action and discourse, chaos lurks. And this chaos is not just disorganization, but the loss of a sense of the very reality of things and of other persons.

(Giddens, 1991: 36)

In order to avoid this sense of chaos, this un-anchoring of a known reality: 'Individuals will routinely try to maintain a sense of ontological security, or else they would be paralysed by anxiety' (King, 2013: 323). Yet making a change from 'offender' to 'ex-offender' can provoke such feelings of losing a known reality, of plunging into chaos: 'When you move away, even areas, it's a real challenge, you're insecure, trying to find out who you are, without status and influence' (Training group participant). If such changes foster ontological insecurity however, the physical example of peer mentors can provide a reassuring comfort:

If an experience that suggests the possibility of change is perceived as something that can be easily coped with, possibly by accommodating it within the current conception of the self, then the individual is unlikely to feel a sense of ontological insecurity; the sense that one's very being is threatened.

(Hunter, 2011: 224)

Not only have peer mentors often survived the challenge ahead of their mentees, thus rendering the unknown more 'known' and demonstrating that change can be coped with, they are *peers*. To see a peer, someone you regard as closer to your own 'conception of self' making this change before you, offers a sense of security that cannot be gleaned from an external expert, a distant authoritarian:

Seeing the change helps you to not be scared of change, because a lot of people are. I was scared of change, and it's not that bad, but you don't feel like you are going it alone, because people have gone there before you and you can just… It's not like there's somebody in a suit saying 'she's said this and said that' you know? They have more of an understanding where you are psychologically if you know what I mean?.

(Lin, Mentor and previously a Mentee)

I think they see us differently because obviously I have no authority, I make that clear. I'm just another person who came here, it helped me and like I say… I've gone through the same, going through the other side. Yeah so just it's one of them, instead of being a paid person from a university or….

(Ben, Mentor)

These mentors consider that they provide a measure of comfort, which renders change manageable, because they have been in a similar position and because they strive to separate themselves from authority and officialdom. However, whilst mentors position themselves as not being coercive, there was a current of scepticism about whether peer mentors do in fact constitute less authoritarian figures. For example, at a practitioner conference about ex-service users in the criminal justice system, one conference delegate asked the important question: 'do you breach people?' referring to whether mentors are called upon to enforce community court orders. Whilst the mentor who was speaking answered that they 'don't personally' return people to court, he did acknowledge that mentors do have to 'pass on attendance feedback to Offender Managers' and admitted this can be a testing part of their role. Indeed, the mentor's Probation colleague explained: 'Steve, Cam and Adam have all got offending backgrounds, so what? They work in the same guidelines we work in' (Probation Officer). These organisational requirements indicate that whilst peer mentors may have 'gone before you' and be 'through the other side' they also now belong to a professional peer group, which locates them closely to the authority so feared. This questioning of the apparent security offered by peer mentors highlights the potentially conflicting, even oxymoronic positions of peer and mentor. In Goffman's terms: 'in making a profession of their stigma, native leaders are obliged to have dealings with representatives of other categories, and so find themselves breaking out of the closed circle of their own kind' (Goffman, 1963: 39).

Challenging the practices of the criminal justice system

Despite some resistance to peer mentors as non–authoritarian, there was a strong theme of peer mentors wanting to challenge the practices of the criminal justice system. Indeed, one of the laudatory claims for peer mentoring is that ex-offenders can uniquely contribute to the shaping or development of services (RAPT, 2013; Fletcher & Batty, 2012). The aim of much peer mentoring is not just to influence mentee lives on an individual level, therefore, but also to change the shape of services and systems. For many of the projects I studied, integrating the voice of ex-offenders was a critical motivation for engaging with the system in the first place. Adam, for example, a mentoring coordinator with lived experience, explained how:

> My experience guided how the system could be different... We [ex-offenders] complement what's already going on, we're able to add an additional perspective.
>
> (Adam, Mentoring Coordinator)

The Probation Manager who first employed Adam and who was proactive in recruiting four other people with criminal convictions into paid Probation posts, also explained that one benefit of peer mentoring was the learning that Probation could gain from their insights:

> All of our ex-offender staff changed because of their own connections, not Probation. That's not to say that Probation doesn't help, but that there are other strategies available outside professional understanding.
>
> (Probation Manager)

This section will look at the practical efforts of peer mentors to make systemic, as opposed to individual changes. Paula, a volunteer mentor, for example, highlighted that there is often a gap in provision for family members or supporters of people who are dependent upon drugs or persistently offending:

> [M]y husband used a lot of drugs, different drugs and that, basically I didn't get any help. I didn't actually know he was on a lot of drugs until quite late in, well before he died really. So, I didn't understand anything about it and I actually think that people need to understand what it's all about.
>
> (Paula, Mentor)

As a result, she decided to bridge that gap in her role as a mentor:

> We're setting up a 'concerned others' group along at Women's Centre, I think because of people that are coming in to mentoring who have got the other side of it, been a concerned other, it does help, it's all connected.
>
> (Paula, Mentor)

Paula therefore views herself as stepping into the gap. She becomes a physical agent of change because her suggestion is taken on board by the project she works for. Similarly, Lol, a mentoring coordinator, is concerned about the lack of focus on the relationship between local authority care and prison. As an ex-offender and care leaver himself this issue has particular resonance:

> Twenty-five per cent plus of those in prisons can say they've been in care, you can't just take people from the care system and say they're bad people so they end up there, there must be something happening, systemic. So, we're trying to work out, our project is about trying to work out, where those gaps exist in terms of that system.
>
> (Lol, Mentoring Coordinator)

In response Lol facilitates consultation groups with groups of criminalised care leavers in community and prison settings, to explore what improvements they would like to see to the care and justice systems and to examine how mentoring may assist with these aims. Mentoring, therefore, becomes a tool for this sub-group of 'offenders' to examine patterns that have been pertinent in their own lives, patterns which may have been missed using an individual deficit approach to rehabilitation. However, Lol did not describe the same level of success in addressing this gap as Paula did:

> When we speak to offender supervisors, we don't seem to be able to develop a relationship there... We think part of it is because they're so under the cosh, with fifty cases at the side of their desks, having to work their way through all of that, they're not giving their time to a conversation about that particular experience in care and how that all might fit in.
>
> (Lol, Mentoring Coordinator)

Lol expresses frustration that lived experiences go unheard. His 'user voice' cannot compete with the noise of a heavy caseload, which necessarily positions 'service users' as passive cases to be juggled, rather than active agents to be engaged. Despite their different short-term outcomes however, Paula and Lol's personal experiences of the criminal justice system acted as their motivation for bridging perceived gaps. These gaps may not have been noticed or have resulted in such personal conviction to affect change, without the presence of those with personal lived experiences. Keisha gives a similar example of wanting to provide a service that she felt was never provided for her. She explains that she established her own project to provide some of the information and support that she saw as lacking:

> Where the prison goes wrong is that they don't give you the right information... When I left prison, I didn't know what opportunities I had, and there was no courses that I come across in prison, and there was no-one talking about it to be truthful... So, it weren't until I come out of prison that I learnt what I could do.
>
> (Keisha, Mentor)

Keisha went on to set up her own mentoring project and, like Paula, stepped into a gap she experienced. However, Keisha went on to hit a different kind of barrier. She explained (informally and tentatively, given she was used to having her words appropriated) how her entry into mentoring was supported by a charity, which helps people leaving prison to set up businesses. The voluntary sector, therefore, supported Keisha's aim to provide a new kind of user-led advice service. However, she explained how the assisting charity later went on to use her business model as a 'success story' in their own funding bids – without consulting Keisha or obtaining permission. As a result, Keisha felt she had been used to obtain competitive justice funding, rather than as a source of knowledge and change in her own right. This experience echoes Lol's assertion in Chapter 5 that the user perspective has 'all been tokenistic' rather than 'central and as respected' (Lol, Mentoring Coordinator).

What Paula, Lol and Keisha did have in common, however, was social entrepreneurship; they each established something new (a 'concerned others' group, a user led consultation and outreach support) to address unmet needs. Entrepreneurship is not a surprising theme to uncover. Criminal justice in the UK increasingly operates as a competitive marketplace, with commercialised approaches to contracting and service delivery (Corcoran, Williams, Prince & Maguire, 2018). Entrepreneurship also provides an achievable route for criminalised people to improve life chances, as self-employment can overcome the ingrained discrimination they face in seeking employment (Smith, 2009: 169). The presence of entrepreneurship may simply reflect the social context, which encourages individuals to become justice entrepreneurs. There is a pervasiveness of market subjectivities, even by those at the edges of it. Add to this the barriers that people with criminal convictions can face in obtaining employment and entrepreneurship becomes doubly attractive. However, whilst mentors achieve varying levels of 'success' in addressing gaps, the overall shape of the services these speakers worked with largely remained unchanged.

The notion of a 'diverse market' of justice is sold on its 'flexibility to do what works' (MoJ, 2013), but what is not clear is how far it allows true flexibility to those with little economic power. Paula and Keisha, for example, meet with a seemingly 'flexible' marketplace given their ideas, which require little investment other than their own, are enacted. They are able and supported to perform actions they deemed to be missing (Group Work and Outreach). Lol, however, meets an altogether less flexible space. His aims to discover and include a peripheral voice – the voice of care leavers who are over-represented, but under consulted – does not fit with the drive to evidence 'results' or 'what works'. The changes these voices may demand are also likely to require significantly more investment than a group intervention or a volunteer outreach service. The market is therefore much less responsive. Moreover, whilst Keisha meets with flexibility initially, her lowly position as an individual entrepreneur in the wider context of better funded and better resourced charities – who are willing to appropriate her ideas – means she is soon positioned unfavourably in terms of competing for the work. What these accounts suggest is that criminalised people are not currently level players in the idealised 'market' of justice, but rather are required to accept work at the margins:

> I felt like I needed to do more, but I also knew that I had to start from the bottom and be humble.
>
> (Keisha, Mentor)

> We rely on professionals, don't tread on toes. It's a team effort, not duplicating... It depends on the personality of the Offender Manager.

Some are happy to allow us authority, others want to control the work more, know everything we're doing.

(Peer Mentoring Trainer)

These words encapsulate the need for entrepreneurs with convictions to rely upon good will and patronage. Moreover, there is concern that this situation will not change: 'how does an ex-offender get beyond where we are now? Break the glass ceiling, influence policy and training? (Phil, Mentor). The fear voiced here is that peer mentors will not move onto an equal footing but will remain deferring to policy and practices mandated by others; that they must remain as unassuming outsiders.

Changing perceptions

One of the interesting forms of change that did happen as peer mentors attempted to re-shape services, however, was that they often unwittingly came to shape people's perceptions:

My business advisor, she's a lovely woman. Before she met us she'd never been in contact with, you know, 'people like myself'... She loves us to death, and you know what? Once she got to know us and the people we were, she took us for lunch, and she goes: 'Do you know what? You and [Keisha's colleague name] have changed my whole view'. She went: 'I was so negative'. She said she used to manage this company where they used to recruit, and you know what she used to tell the people? 'Anyone with records: to the side!'.

(Keisha, Mentor)

Something similar happened at Project 'Peer'. This project is managed by two coordinators, with long criminal histories, who are well embedded within a local Probation office. They share their office with a drugs service and a building with a range of statutory Probation staff, who value their presence:

We all socialise, they're just our colleagues, on the same level as we are. They came to my wedding... The offenders see our friendship and it's really pro social, says a lot, they're not stuck in that label forever.

(Probation employee attached to Project 'Peer')

Their manager explained how such perceptions were not always dominant. She described numerous early battles in advocating for ex-offenders to be attached to the service. Colleagues in the police, prisons and Probation had reservations about the trustworthiness of ex-offender staff and the ethics of their having access to clients' personal information. This manager persisted in her commitment to these individuals, however, and the service became something of a flagship in successfully embedding peer-led practice. Not only are the two co-ordinators of the mentoring scheme ex-offenders, but two paid Probation Service Officers (PSOs) also have previous convictions and experience of services. As a Probation team they regard their work as 'desistance in action'; illustrating the positive potential of people with convictions. The manager of the team was also keen to point out that these desistance stories have added value for existing staff, who are tasked with instilling hope in criminal persisters. In her words there has been a 'change in the office, you can see hope in the workers eyes'.

The presence of 'ex-offenders' in mentoring roles may then have the potential to affect how people with convictions are perceived more broadly; to offer a lived challenge to accepted stereotypes. This is important because the dominant discourse in relation to ex-offenders is overwhelmingly negative. Reiner, Livingstone and Allen (2000: 117–118), for example, found that 'Criminals are overwhelmingly portrayed unsympathetically... in both fiction and news'. Such media representations, Garland (2000: 363) argues 'undoubtedly give shape and emotional inflection to our experience of crime, and do so in a way that is largely dictated by the structure and values of the media rather than the phenomena it represents'. Peer mentors, in contrast, offer the public a personal connection, a direct challenge to this broader discursive othering. The importance of this 'visibility' has been acknowledged elsewhere. In the field of mental health, for example, Rufus May, a clinical psychologist and former patient, has argued that: 'Mental health workers... don't see the ones like me who got away. Therefore, they have very little concept of recovery from mental health problems' (cited in Basset & Repper, 2005: 16–17). Similarly, in terms of addiction, 'visible recovery champions... can help people to believe that recovery is not only possible but desirable. I refer to both people who provide and people who receive treatment and support services' (Kidd, 2011: 174). 'Visibility' may therefore be crucial to believing in change – both for providers and users of services. This reveals another unique potential of peer mentoring. Whilst statutory Probation caseloads are full of 'offenders' and their risk scores and public news stories are laden with images of 'the criminal', rarely do we see, in either context, the ones who have desisted. Peer mentoring forges a space for desisters to become visible. Mentors come to constitute the possibility of desistance for mentees, professionals and the public alike. One commissioner of mentoring services, for example, explained the shift in attitude of her own Probation staff as peer mentors became a visible part of the service:

> There was resistance from staff, people initially wouldn't refer [to peer mentoring] and worried about sharing information, but this was four or

five years ago, now the climate has changed… We have a growing number of ex-service users now employed [in the Probation Service].

(Service Commissioner)

This speaker's motivation was clear: 'we need to practice what we preach, if we believe in change as an agency, we need to be ambassadors' (Service Commissioner). This aspect of change has obvious benefits in terms of fostering contexts conducive to desistance. Nonetheless, such shifts in perspective do not arise without personal risks and costs to those involved. Steve, for example, was a persistent and prolific offender who was mentored himself, before volunteering as a mentor then later being employed as a Probation Service Officer. He explains that this progression carried risks for his employers:

Before, it was like there's too many risks involved. Before, they [Probation] wouldn't take a risk. For them to [employ] me, I see that as a massive risk what they've done. Because going off what's in my past, they've took a massive risk and it could've gone really badly wrong.

(Steve, Mentor and previously a Mentee)

Making this transition and challenging the perceptions of colleagues also makes personal demands as Steve performs his new role:

I've got the prison officers looking at me, they recognise me, I don't say anything, I just feel uncomfortable. At first there was a lot of loopholes [Probation] had to jump through to get me in, but now I go on my own and love that side of it. Sometimes it's strange, like [in prison] walking down the main corridor… You're walking past all the prisoners and some are my old associates are like: 'fucking hell, how you doing? Used to be a nightmare him, he was a proper grafter' and I'm thinking 'ohhhhhh!' [Cringe]. I get really embarrassed by it, because obviously I am ashamed of my past.

(Steve, Mentor and previously a Mentee)

Working in the prisons previously incarcerated in serves as a reminder of a shameful past. It also brings to life an identity remembered by others, which conflicts with Steve's current conception of self. Whilst this can be helpful: 'it's an opportunity for me to revisit them dark places, just to remind myself that I never want to go back there' (Phil, Mentor), there is nonetheless an intense, lived emotionality to this work, which is not present for volunteers without such history.

The futility of working with 'big boys'

Whilst the shifts in perspective outlined above come to undermine some of the entrenched discursive othering experienced by offenders, such categorisation is not always contested. Indeed, another surprising feature of peer mentoring was how mentors often invested in their own categorisations of 'offenders':

> You get a different variety of criminals. It's like in prison, you have different sections. You get the ones that just get bullied constantly, you get the ones that I classed myself as, just the middle ground. I wasn't one of the big heads, no one ever took the mick out of me, the big heads never used to try and bully me, because I was sort of like borderline. And then you get the ones who are dead confident, and you can just tell when you're walking on the wing who's who, do you know what I mean? So you have like three sets and I think it's the same in the community as well.
>
> (Steve, Mentor and previously a Mentee)

Having established this hierarchy, Steve began to characterise those at the 'top':

> It's like one of my best ever mates, who tried for years to get me off the drugs. He's doing nine and a half years now because he was the money man. He thrived on selling drugs and the fast cars and the nice women. I think people like that will never, ever; I think it'll just be virtually impossible to sort their lives out. I know he'll never, ever sort his life out. He'll come out and within two weeks he's well respected, and because he's a money man, he makes a lot of big gangsters a lot of money. Within two weeks of getting out he can have like an M5 [sports car], he'll have a gorgeous woman on his arm, he'll have loads of money.
>
> (Steve, Mentor and previously a Mentee)

As an individual, Steve alludes to a loss of status in the old pecking order, he communicates a sense of envy and regret that he has relinquished that status and a recognition that his new status is 'no match' in the eyes of former associates. He appears to be reflecting on the respect he has given up to gain what he has; on how hard it is to be reminded of what he has lost. As a mentor, however, Steve not only establishes the character of what he terms the 'big heads', personalities who personify 'hypermasculine' (Courtenay & Sabo, 2001), capitalist values, but he also outlines what he sees as the futility of trying to intervene at this level:

STEVE: People like that shouldn't be [mentored] because when they're big boys, it's hard to explain; they don't benefit from people like us... Because they're too big, they're too past all that sort of stuff...

INTERVIEWER: You would have nothing to offer him in response to the life he's got?

STEVE: Yeah, I mean one lad was put on [mentoring] and he was a little bit, not intimidating, it's because I knew how big he was. From my past,

I knew him… and what connections he's got. I think I actually felt a little bit uncomfortable, because I didn't think I could offer him. I did try a different tack with him, I kept, I hated it that I kept repeating myself, saying: 'I'm not trying to tell you what to do, obviously, you do what you want' but you know, I kept apologizing because I didn't want him to think that I was trying to… because I knew in his head he was thinking: 'what are you doing in here? I'm too engrossed' ye know?

Steve still valorises the 'big boys' status here, elevating them not just above other criminals, but also subtly above mentors and Probation. As a result, he is intimidated, ambivalent in and discomforted by, his own position. He feels he has nothing to offer as a mentor. These beliefs inform his behaviour as he apologises for even trying to intervene. Steve's sees futility intervening with a man he deems such a socially successful criminal. This affects not only how he feels about himself in his role as a mentor, but also how he practices:

It's pointless… because he gets what he wants, you know, he's like a proper big boy, he's involved in all the guns and we shouldn't be working with people like that. He needs to be up there with the organised crime and he was, he got took off after a few weeks. So most, all the ones I've got now, no one makes me feel like that, because he made me feel uncomfortable working with him. I felt like he was, how to explain, feeling like: 'what are you doing here, what you doing?' Because everything we said to him he was like: 'yeah' (raising eyebrows sarcastically), I just thought: I'm wasting my breath here. It's nothing we can do, so there is this hierarchy that our service just can't touch them.

(Steve, Mentor and previously a Mentee)

Steve's account could be interpreted as evidence of poor matching of mentor and mentee, but it also raises other questions about assuming that shared histories will lead to constructive outcomes. Steve's reflections have real significance for how – and with whom – mentoring aims to affect change. Change here is not simply about a shift from criminal to non-criminal, about instilling a desire for such change and rendering it manageable, but rather it has regard for the social standing of the potential changer. When the mentee is of a perceived higher social standing (even in criminal terms) than the mentor, the practice is problematised. Steve does not describe here an influential, exemplary social role, which empowers him in the present and the future, but rather he describes feeling incapacitated, uncomfortable and apologetic.

The features with which Steve characterises 'big boys' are also of interest in terms of conceptualising 'change'. It is cars, 'gorgeous women', money, guns, connections and power that indicate to Steve this mentee is untouchable. The accepted value of such ideals has been highlighted in work on masculine criminal cultures. Dailey (2001: 259), for example, argues that inmate stories were typically about 'fast women, drugs and expensive cars. They always focused on the "fast life"'. What we know less about however, is the impact of such hyper masculine ideals upon volunteer mentors who have left crime behind. For Steve, whilst 'desistance' is desirable, it struggles to compete with a wealthy, masculine lifestyle, even if this is criminally supported. Steve's 'big boy', whilst criminal, simultaneously embodies the Western hegemonic ideal of manhood; he is independent, wealthy and powerful. He has means of aggression and represents virulent heterosexuality. Whilst peer mentoring may offer a replacement for some of the lost pleasures or excitements of criminality (Chapter 6), Steve is right to question whether it will compensate for the wealth and status of 'success'; success not just in criminal terms, but also in terms of the dominant patriarchal, capitalist ideology. This was a question Keisha too asked:

> I know people out there that are happy committing crime. They tell me: '*Oh I couldn't do what you do [mentoring]. Oh no love*'... They're going to Mexico every week, they're having brilliant holidays, they own their own house. Do you know what I mean? They're, like, '*Oh no*'. They're alright doing that.
>
> (Keisha, Mentor)

These narratives point to the cost of changing. They suggest that material and social success can maintain criminality as readily as they can promote conformity, a pattern which has been highlighted by Piquero and Benson (2004) regarding 'white collar offenders':

> [W]hite-collar offenders often have acquired some level of material, occupational, and social success. In other words, they have something to lose. We usually think of these trappings of success and achievement as factors that promote conformity... However, situations may arise in which these very same factors can motivate crime rather than conformity... the reasons for engaging in criminal activities may not lie with greed or financial gain but rather with the fear of losing what one has already attained.
>
> (Piquero & Benson, 2004: 160)

Having something to lose adds a significant further barrier to contemplating change therefore. Potential mentees with wealth and status may need to accept significant material losses in addition to the existential challenges outlined above. Moreover, in terms of peer mentoring, a mentee who has wealth and status can also present as a barrier to mentors even trying.

This chapter has explored how 'change' is perceived in the context of peer mentoring. Respondents spoke of change in terms of personal improvement and changes external to themselves – to the need for transformations in public perceptions and rehabilitation practices. Change for these speakers, whether individual or structural, is constructed as a site of struggle.

Peer mentors and mentees reveal struggles between feeling 'ready' to change and being externally inspired; between known habits and unknown futures; between wanting to accept help and seeing authority as dangerous. Struggles can also be traced between mentors wanting to use their experiences to reimagine and improve services and having these experiences appropriated as they are used as an add-on; a promotion; or a replica, between changing the perceptions of others and having to live and practice within dominant discursive realities. What is at play throughout all of these struggles, in addition to conceptions of change, are forms of power. The following chapter will therefore focus explicitly on some of the implicit transactions of power in peer mentoring.

Acknowledgements

This chapter has adapted material from the following works:

Buck, G., (2017), '"I wanted to feel the way they did": Mimesis as a situational dynamic of peer mentoring by ex-offenders', *Deviant Behavior*, **38**(9), pp. 1027–1041.
Buck, G., (2019), '"It's a tug of war between the person I used to be and the person I want to be": The terror, complexity, and limits of leaving crime behind', *Illness, Crisis & Loss*, **27**(2), pp. 101–118.

I am thankful to the publishers for their permission.

References

Basset, T. & Repper, J., (2005), 'Travelling hopefully', *Mental Health Today*, **5**, pp. 16–18.
Becker, H.S., (1963), *Outsiders: Studies in the sociology of deviance*. Reprint, New York: Free Press, 1966 edition.
Burnett, R., (2000), 'Understanding criminal careers through a eries of in depth interviews', *Offender Programs Report*, **4**(1), pp. 1–16.
Clayton, A.N., (2009), *Mentoring for youth involved in Juvenile justice programs: A review of the literature*. Massachusetts: University of Massachusetts. Available at: https://rhyclearinghouse.acf.hhs.gov/library/2009/mentoring-youth-involved-juvenile-justice-programs-review-literature [Accessed August 2019].
Corcoran, M.S., Williams, K., Prince, K. & Maguire, M., (2018), 'The penal voluntary sector in England and Wales: Adaptation to unsettlement and austerity', *The Political Quarterly*, **89**(2), pp. 187–196.
Courtenay, W.H. & Sabo, D., (2001), 'Preventative health strategies for men in prison'. In: Sabo, D.F., Kupers, T.A. & London, W.J., (Eds.), *Prison masculinities*. Philadelphia: Temple University Press, pp. 157–173.
Dailey, Lige Jr., (2001), 'Re-entry: Prospects for post release success'. In: Sabo, D.F., Kupers, T.A. & London, W.J., (Eds.), *Prison masculinities*. Philadelphia: Temple University Press.

Eaton, M., (1993), *Women after Prison*. Buckingham: Open University Press.

Farrall, S. & Calverley, A., (2006), *Understanding desistance from crime*. Berkshire: Open University Press.

Farrall, S., Sparks, R. & Maruna, S., (2011), *Escape routes: Contemporary perspectives on life after punishment*. Abingdon, Oxon: Routledge.

Ferguson, A., (1996). 'Can I choose who I am? And how would that empower me? Gender, race, identities and the self.' In: Garry, A. & Pearsall, M., (Eds.), *Women, knowledge and reality: Explorations in feminist philosophy* (2nd Edn.). London: Routledge.

Fletcher, D. & Batty, E., (2012), *Offender Peer Interventions: What do we know?* Sheffield Hallam University: Centre for Economic and Social Research. Available at: www.shu.ac.uk/research/cresr/sites/shu.ac.uk/files/offender-peer-interventions.pdf [Accessed January 2020].

Freire, P., (1970), *Pedagogy of the oppressed*. Reprint, London: Penguin, 1996.

Frontier Economics, (2009), *St Giles Trust's through the gates: An analysis of economic impact*. London: Pro Bono Economics.

Garland, D., (2000), 'The culture of high crime societies', *British Journal of Criminology*, **40**(3), pp. 347–375.

Giddens, A., (1991), *Modernity and self identity*. Stanford: Stanford University Press.

Giordano, P., Cernkovich, S. & Rudolph, J.L., (2002), 'Gender, crime, and desistance: Toward a theory of cognitive transformation', *American Journal of Sociology*, **107**(4), pp. 990–1064.

Girard, R., (1977), *Violence and the sacred*. London: Continuum, 2005 edition.

Girard, R., (1962), 'Marcel proust'. In: Girard, R. & Doran, R., (Eds.), (2008), *Mimesis and theory: Essays on literature and criticism, 1953–2005*. Stanford, CA; London: Stanford University Press, pp. 56–70.

Goffman, E., (1963), *Stigma: notes on the management of spoiled identity*. Middlesex: Penguin.

Haney, L.A., (2010), *Offending women: Power, punishment, and the regulation of desire*. California: University of California Press.

Hughes, M., (1998), 'Turning points in the lives of young inner-city men forging destructive criminal behaviours: A qualitative study', *Social Work Research*, **22**(3), pp. 143–151.

Hunter, B., (2011), 'Life after punishment for Nazi war criminals: reputation, careers and normative climate in post-war Germany'. In: Farrall, S., Sparks, R. & Maruna, S., (Eds.), *Escape routes: contemporary perspectives on life after punishment*. Abingdon, Oxon: Routledge.

Jolliffe, D. & Farrington, D.P., (2007), *A rapid evidence assessment of the impact of mentoring on re-offending: A summary*. London: Home Office.

Kidd, M., (2011), 'A first-hand account of service user groups in the United Kingdom: An evaluation of their purpose, effectiveness, and place within the recovery movement', *Journal of Groups in Addiction & Recovery*, **6**(1–2), pp. 164–175.

Kiegelmann, M., (2009), 'Making oneself vulnerable to discovery. Carol Gilligan in conversation with Mechthild Kiegelmann', *Forum Qualitative Sozialforschung/Forum: Qualitative Social Research*, **10**(2), pp. 1–19.

King, S., (2013), 'Transformative agency and desistance from crime', *Criminology and Criminal Justice*, **13**(3), pp. 317–335.

Mageo, J.M., (2002), *Power and the self*. Cambridge: Cambridge University Press.

Maguire, M. & Raynor, P., (2006), 'How the resettlement of prisoners promotes desistance from crime: Or does it?' *Criminology and Criminal Justice*, **6**(1), pp. 19–38.

Maruna, S., (2001), *Making good; how ex-convicts reform and rebuild their lives*. Washington, DC: American Psychological Association.

McNeill, F., (2013), 'Transforming rehabilitation: Evidence, values and ideology', *British Journal of Community Justice*, **11**(2/3), pp. 83–87.

McNeill, F., (2012), 'Counterblast: A Copernican correction for community sentences?' *The Howard Journal of Criminal Justice*, **51**(1), pp. 94–99.

Milner, J., (2001), *Women and social work: Narrative approaches*. Basingstoke: Palgrave.

Ministry of Justice (MoJ), (2013), *Transforming Rehabilitation: A Strategy for Reform* Response to consultation, May 2013. London: Ministry of Justice.

Paternoster, R. & Bushway, S., (2009), 'Desistance and the "feared self": Toward an identity theory of criminal desistance', *The Journal of Criminal Law and Criminology*, **99**(4), pp. 1103–1156.

Piquero, N.L. & Benson, M.L., (2004), 'White-collar crime and criminal careers specifying a trajectory of punctuated situational offending', *Journal of Contemporary Criminal Justice*, **20**(2), pp. 148–165.

RAPT (Rehabilitation for Addicted Prisoners Trust), (2013), *The Transformative Potential of Peer Support: Why peer mentoring rightfully has a role in the Transforming Rehabilitation agenda and can help to reduce re-offending*. Joint statement by Mike Trace, CEO of RAPT and Mark Johnson, Founder and CEO of User Voice. Available at: www.uservoice.org/news/user-voice-news-blog/2013/08/a-joint-statement-from-mark-johnson-and-rapt-about-the-transformative-potential-of-peer-support/ [Accessed January 2020].

Reiner, R., Livingstone, S. & Allen, J., (2000), 'No more happy endings? The media and popular concern about crime since the Second World War'. In: Hope, T. & Sparks, R., (Eds.), *Crime, risk, and insecurity: Law and order in everyday life and political discourse*. Abingdon, Oxon: Routledge, pp. 107–127.

Shapland, J. & Bottoms, A., (2011), 'Reflections on social values, offending and desistance among young adult recidivists', *Punishment & Society*, **13**(3), pp. 256–282.

Shover, N., (1983), 'The later stages of ordinary property offender careers', *Social Problems*, **31**(2), pp. 208–218.

Smith, R., (2009), 'Entrepreneurship: a divergent pathway out of crime'. In: Jaishankar, K., (Ed.), *International perspectives on crime and justice*, Newcastle upon Tyne: Cambridge Scholars Publishing, pp. 162–184.

The Social Innovation Partnership, (2012), *The WIRE (Women's Information and Resettlement for Ex-offenders) Evaluation Report*. London: The Social Innovation Partnership. Available at: www.stgilestrust.org.uk/misc/Support%20for%20vulnerable%20women%20leaving%20prison%20full%20report.pdf [Accessed August 2019].

Tolan, P., Henry, D., Schoeny, M. & Bass, A., (2008), 'Mentoring interventions to affect Juvenile delinquency and associated problems', *Campbell Systematic Reviews*, **4**(1), 1–112.

Tomelleri, S., (2005), 'Are we living in a society of resentment?' In: Palaver, W. & Steinmair-Posel, P., (Eds.), *Passions in economy, politics, and the media: In discussion with Christian theology*. London: Transaction Publishers.

Worrall, A. & Gelsthorpe, L., (2009), '"What works" with women offenders: The past 30 years', *The Probation Journal*, **56**(4), pp. 329–345.

Chapter 9

The hidden power dynamics of peer mentoring

This chapter examines some of the ways that power manifests within peer mentoring. Analyses of power dynamics are generally missing from functional evaluations of mentoring or can be submerged by an 'equalising' discourse. Peer mentoring is part of a movement which 'gives greater voice' to service users (Hughes, 2012) and aims to learn 'directly from (ex)offenders' experiences' (McNeill & Weaver, 2010: 10), such practice can serve as a 'counterbalance to the widespread belief that programmes are something that are "done" to offenders by specialists' (Boyce, Hunter & Hough, 2009: vi). Indeed, this book has traced similar dynamics. Chapter 5, for example, highlighted how mentors and mentees often question the authority of professionals, positioning the mentoring relationship as horizontal rather than hierarchical. Chapter 6 illustrated efforts to counter the power of criminal stigma by configuring a new audience who are willing to accept efforts to change, and Chapter 8 traced how respondents nullify feelings of disempowerment by framing their interactions with daunting authority figures in combative terms. Despite clear efforts to forge non-authoritarian relationships, ongoing practices of power do remain. Abdennur (1987: 94), for example, argued that voluntarism itself shifts the burden of guilt for social problems 'from men in power to men on the street', whilst Colley (2001: 188) reasoned that 'emotional labour… brings its own costs, and does so disproportionately for women than for men'. Furthermore, the mentor-protégé relationship, by definition, 'is one that is imbalanced in power' (Scandura, 1998: 458). Indeed, mentors' self-positioning as non-coercive, whilst subtly exhibiting an experimental authority has been a theme throughout the book. These arguments suggest that despite attempts to equalise power dynamics, mentoring participants encounter new forms of subjection, which are not always recognised.

The analysis of power presented here is inductive, resulting from relations observed in the field (Miles, Huberman & Saldaña, 2014: 238). Whilst no *a priori* grid of power is imposed, the chapter draws upon several conceptions of power, which help to make sense of respondent narratives. These include feminist standpoint theories which highlight how people make sense of their place in the world and how these accounts are credited or discredited by others. It also draws upon the work of Freire (1970) who argues that pedagogy without critical reflection can lack consensus and serve to systematically organise people, rather than develop them. Utilising themes from the data and these theoretical conceptions, the chapter will seek to make explicit some of the implicit transactions of power in mentoring settings.

The dynamics and implications of setting goals

Chapter 7 illustrated how peer mentoring is often an individualised practice, but this feature is not universal. Often, subtle influences upon individual goals can be traced. Phil, for example, himself an advocate of person-centred working, explains that there is also a need for *mentors* to be active in goal setting:

> I'd sit down with group and get them to identify [goals] and agree on them. So, they're not my goals, they're their goals, they're shared goals, and we know why we're doing them, and they're realistic.
>
> (Phil, Mentor)

There is an interesting blurring of 'mentor' and 'mentee' objectives here. The task of the mentor, as Phil presents it, is twofold; it is not just to create an environment where *shared* goals can be set, but to ensure goals are 'realistic'. This was similarly expressed by Keisha:

> A mentor needs to know what options an ex-offender has… You've got to have aims with the person, but you've got to have your personal aims that they don't know, so you know you're doing the right thing. It's not all about them, it's about you too. This is how mentors enhance and come on to higher levels; do you understand what I mean? So it's a two way thing. That's what I believe anyway.
>
> (Keisha, Mentor)

For Phil and Keisha, (mentor defined) realism avoids setting people up to fail. Both recount examples of how this could happen if what they considered the 'real' challenges of resettlement after prison, such as criminal stigma, were not envisaged. Keisha, for example, was asked by her own resettlement mentor to 'walk around the city centre and ask for jobs', a scenario she imagined with dread:

> Walking into these shops: "Hiya I'm Keisha and I'm an ex-offender. I've been released a couple of weeks. I've got a CV, but it dates back to whatever, but this is what I did in prison!".
>
> (Keisha, Mentor)

Keisha's mentor was a Probation volunteer, but not an ex-offender, as a result, Keisha felt that she missed the reality of the context ex-prisoners face. Phil also described what he saw as unrealistic expectations, this time from his own mentees:

> One offender had in his head he was going to come out and get into property management. I didn't want to deflate that goal but wanted to make it realistic for him. So, trying to let him know that, obviously, the world of buildings and houses has changed greatly over the years. And it's not that easy that you can go and get a buy-to-let.
>
> (Phil, Mentor)

> A lot of ex-offenders feel compelled to share what you've gone through, to help the next generation... We don't want to crush that desire, but we also have to be realistic: child protection. A lot of long-term offenders are in for murder, I don't want to motivate [them] and they can be crushed as soon as they get out.
>
> (Phil, Mentor)

On the one hand, Phil and Keisha are keen to ensure that mentee goals take account of personal and social realities. In this sense they agree with Farrall's (2005: 367) assertion that: 'successful desistance entails developing a sense of what the future may hold for the individual and a sense of how this future can be realised'. However, their examples also indicate that mentors can direct or shape supposedly mentee-set goals. This is less about promoting agency (Chapter 6) and more about buttressing societal limits as personal realities. The sentiments of Phil and Keisha here highlight a crucial tension in their work. Both speakers have set up their own peer mentoring businesses, having met significant barriers to employment and social acceptance as ex-prisoners. Both passionately criticise the prejudice and structural exclusions that ex-prisoners face. Yet in their practice both assist their mentees to accept these realities and work around them, to 'be realistic' and know their 'options', rather than reflecting together upon if they should exist at all, or how they can be challenged. In Freire's (1970: 60) terms they rely upon 'transferals of information' rather than 'acts of cognition'. Their mentees, in turn, become 'passive and malleable recipients of existing culture rather than active and interacting agents in construction' (Cochran-Smith & Paris, 1995: 191). That is not to say that Phil and Keisha are not active in challenging injustices they perceive in criminalisation. Indeed, both have made it their vocation to do just this. Phil is an active critical criminologist and peer mentor. Keisha is a peer mentor who campaigns for understanding and inclusion through the media and direct workshops, particularly with local businesses. However, within the *mentoring* format their work loses some of its critique and becomes a way of fitting people into a reality that they conceive of as unfair. They therefore move between spheres of politicisation (publicly) and pedagogy (in the private sphere of mentoring). Unconsciously, it seems, mentoring becomes a space where social critique is nullified.

There was also evidence of more pronounced direction from mentors, based upon pre-set ideals. Paula, who volunteers as a mentor attached to a Probation Service, for example, explains: '[mentees] do the goal chart – it's up to them what they actually want, we support them, it's their goals' (Paula, Mentor). Whilst passionately advocating person-centred work, Paula also refers to the 'goal chart' planning tool. This is an 'Outcomes Star' (Triangle Consulting, 2019a) which encourages mentees to self-assess their needs and goals on a scale of one to ten using headings such as: '*living skills and self care; mental health and wellbeing; friends and community; drugs and alcohol; positive use of time; managing strong feelings*'. Whilst it is ostensibly 'up to' mentees to set goals, therefore, they are offered a quite specific frame within which to locate their thinking, a frame which, whilst acknowledging some social factors (e.g. friends, family, accommodation), sways mentees to individualise problems in these areas and become personally responsible for addressing them should they be present. The latest edition of the 'Justice Star', for example, invites people to scale themselves from 1 to 10 in each of the above areas, the scale ranges from 'stuck', through 'accepting help; motivated and taking responsibility; and learning what works'; to 'self-reliance' (Triangle consulting, 2019b). The mentee is therefore clearly categorised in terms of the changes *they* need to make and made aware from the outset that their progress will be monitored. The subtle influence of mentors is not only present in practice tools, however, but also in the relational model itself:

> Mentors may exercise power through the assumptions they make about their protégé. Mentors may function within a framework of power relations that "assumes that one person knows what is best for the other, has superior knowledge and skills and is perceived as somewhat paternalistic in his [sic] interactions".
>
> (Brinson & Kottler, 1993: 241 cited in
> Hansman, 2002: 46)

This dynamic could be traced in the approach of John, who volunteers at a project attached to Probation, he asked one mentee who he described as 'poorly motivated':

> 'What do you want to do? Do you want me to put me arm round your shoulder or give you a kick up the arse?' and he said: *'Well I probably need a kick up the arse'*. I said: 'Well that's what we'll do... Right, well I'm telling you that we're going shopping'.
>
> (John, Mentor)

Whilst John quite probably had his mentee's wellbeing in mind, it is nonetheless *he* who presents the options available and directs the shape of the work. Indeed, John also explains how such directional attitudes are present higher up in his organisation:

> The coordinator, he's a quite good judge of character, he knows a lot of the background [of the mentee], more than I know, and he sort of... gives you an idea: 'look, what you'd probably be best doing with this one...' he knows what the mentors are capable of. He knows them, he knows us.
>
> (John, Mentor)

These subtleties indicate that peer mentoring can often be significantly more directive than the claims that are made for it. Indeed, such micro-government occurred frequently:

> One of things I like doing with clients is dog walking at a local charity, so the day before I ask him if he fancies going.
>
> (John, Mentor)

> Sometimes she asks me [what I want to do], but sometimes she has it planned, cos [her manager name] tells her what she's gotta do with somebody.
>
> (Karina, Mentee)

> He sat me down and asked me if I needed help with like searching for a job or opening a bank account and all that sort of stuff.
>
> (Paul, Mentee)

These reflections illustrate that the content of mentoring is not always 'up to' mentees, but the power to initiate activity is often 'up to' the mentor. Indeed, direction is often determined by external factors; be they a mentor's personal interests, directions of management, or the normative dictates of society (get a job, open a bank account, etc.). These latter two influences will be explored in greater detail below. For now, however, the point is that directive elements do persist despite a powerful discourse of person-centred practice. Moreover, structural goals and cultural norms exercise their own influence upon what initially appears as a binary relationship.

Routine activities

Another aspect of mentoring, which was experienced positively by most respondents, but has hidden influence in terms of personal power, is its 'active' nature. Chapter 6 outlined how active, community-based forms of peer mentoring can help to form new identities, divert people from criminal habits and compensate (in part) for losses of pleasure or excitement attached to criminality. What speakers did not problematise, however, was how the inculcation of 'good habits' can be disciplinary:

> Exercises, not signs: time-tables, compulsory movements, regular activities, solitary meditation, work in common, silence, application, respect, good habits... what one is trying to restore in this technique of corrections is not so much the juridical subject, who is caught up in the fundamental interests of the social pact, but the obedient subject, the individual subjected to habits, rules, orders, an authority which is exercised continually around him and upon him.
>
> (Foucault, 1979: 128–129)

This critique of the power inherent in routine activities suggests that *activity* as a pedagogical tool (be it boxing, shopping, drinking coffee or going to the Job Centre) is as much about obedience as it is consensus. Discipline, Foucault contends, is the effect of such habits. This reading undermines the ideal of a more negotiated interaction between mentor and mentee. Interestingly, however, peer mentors are *also* involved in disciplining mentees in order to produce a juridical subject, to restore mentees to the 'social contract' of law abiding and productive behaviour, which is another construct of power. The result of embodied activity is to restore subjects to an established normality rather than to include their situated perspective of these norms, or to support any alternative ways of being. In this light, mentoring does not encourage self-determining and diverse entities, but ideal disciplined subjects positioned through the application of bodily techniques. This is of course the antithesis of Freire's 'liberatory' notion of mentoring in which 'the oppressed must confront reality critically, simultaneously objectifying and acting upon that reality' (Freire, 1970: 34). To frame routine activity as covert discipline, however, misses the role that mentees themselves play. Few of the mentees interviewed had any objection to suggested activities; indeed, they welcomed the 'normality' of suggestions such as going for coffee, playing a sport or job seeking:

> Probation should recognise that a lot of people actually want to feel normal and want to get back into the workforce.
>
> (Gina, Mentee)

> It's hard work sorting your life out... all those stressful things that to normal people it's easy: phone up, make an appointment. But to someone with that chaotic lifestyle it's an absolute nightmare cos... I just wouldn't do it, I'd just always put it off.
>
> (Steve, Mentor and previously a Mentee)

For Gina and Steve, practical opportunities to feel 'normal' were desired, not merely imposed. Mentoring activities become conduits of normality, which these speakers welcome; they mediate a social field which people feel excluded from or ill-equipped to manage. Indeed, mentors themselves often claimed that the appeal of mentoring is belonging and normality:

> I was off doing naughty things to feed my drug habit, and I just didn't want to do it no more. I'm sick of this game, chasing money; I just want to be like everybody else.
>
> (Brad, Mentor)

These speakers do not want to be stigmatised and different, they want careers, recognition, new lives. They talk of wanting to be *normal*. This embrace of normality does not always come easily however, indeed when mentors did acknowledge such disciplinary power in their work, they were not always comfortable:

> I'm teaching them to be respectable members of the community.
>
> (Brad, Mentor)

> I get the impression some [mentors] do it… cos it's an ego thing, they want power, it's about having power over another individual and that's not the work that we [at this organisation] do, quite the opposite, I'll disempower myself in order to empower someone else.
>
> (Phil, Mentor)

> I don't think you can ever break down that hierarchy, you try to, but that hierarchy is always going to exist in that relationship because they are always going to look at you as a professional and see themselves as a service user. But it's trying to break that hierarchy as much as possible, such that that level playing field is there and if that level playing field is there then that conversation becomes so much easier.…we hope!.
>
> (Lol, Mentoring Coordinator)

Mentors, therefore, acknowledge and at times reflexively challenge their own practices of power. Whilst Brad appears comfortable with the hierarchical, pastoral character of his role and Lol acknowledges the unequal nature of this work, both Lol and Phil attempt to distance themselves from the inherent inequity. Mentoring may well involve power, but not in their hands, this is something that they actively seek to diffuse. Such 'cognitive restructuring' (Fagan, 1993: 220) fits with Sykes and Matza's (1962) notions of 'diffusion or displacement of responsibility' (cited in Fagan, 1993: 220) and is unsurprising given the non-authoritarian basis that peer mentoring nurtures. What these cognitive tussles suggest, however, is that there is a tension within peer mentoring work, given it is hierarchical and corrective, yet strives to operate on a much more egalitarian basis.

Power within organisations

Whilst respondents often strive for less authority *within* mentoring relationships, mentors did frequently recognise external powers which encroach upon their work, including *individual blockers* and a *changeable criminal justice* landscape. The concept of *individual blockers* refers to professional agents (such as prison officials, education providers or employers) who limit access to mentors on the grounds of their previous convictions and perceived riskiness. The notion of a changeable *criminal justice landscape* refers to the shifting nature of prisons and community justice; a landscape which mentors deem to be problematic for 'getting things done' with any consistency. The section begins by considering organisational power in these terms. What mentors seemed less critically aware of, however, was the pervasive power that organisations often have upon the entire structure of their work. Most of the mentors I spoke to, for example, were *selected for, trained* and *formally supervised* in their roles. Rather than seeing these measures as limiting their power, however, they framed them as positive elements supporting personal and professional development. The second part of this section will, therefore, explore the hidden power of *organisational processes* which distribute and manage mentors' knowledge within mentoring settings.

Blockers

One of the most recognised ways that organisational power manifests is through practical restrictions on peer mentoring as an activity. Peer mentors and coordinators frequently spoke of difficulties gaining access to prisoners, despite arguments that prisoner reintegration requires support before and after release from prison:

> [W]e recognise 'reintegration' as a process that starts at the point of confinement, preparing the prisoner for success after release, and continuing for some time afterwards.
>
> (Association of Chief Probation Officers, cited in Deakin & Spencer, 2011)

And that reintegration should be a key area for peer mentoring to focus on:

> There are roles for offenders acting as mentors... They can be particularly effective during transition from prison to outside world.
>
> (MoJ, 2011: 23)

The One to One model ideally involves a period of regular contact between [mentee] and Mentor prior to their release from custody to allow time to get to know one another and prepare for return to the community.

(Hunter & Kirby, 2011: 5)

Despite these arguments, many mentors complained that 'through the [prison] gate' work is a difficult basic to master, as illustrated by this exchange between a volunteer and her manager:

MENTOR: I want to go into the prisons, do an action plan, say I'll be here if you need anything, get back on your feet and get you away from the people who are going to draw you back in.

MANAGER: I wish we could, but even the staff have struggled to get into the prison. We did their security training but couldn't pin them down to a planning meeting, and that was the external partners' link person.

(Project 'Facilitate')

Prisons are therefore perceived as blocking access to the work. This perception is shared by 'Lol', a mentoring coordinator for a national charity, funded to deliver mentoring services to 'offenders' with specific welfare needs. Despite the legitimacy of his service and remit, his personal criminal history was of most interest to prison partners:

My offences are not two weeks old. My offences are many, many, many years old and principally as a young offender, by the way, and related to coming through the care system... The prison was interested in supporting us... but could not find practitioners to support the 'through the gate' mechanism... because I'm an ex offender, when they do 'Enhanced' [security] clearance for me it says 'no'. So [the Ministry of Justice...] have come up with this 'Standard Plus' which is not quite 'Basic' clearance, its nowhere near 'Enhanced', it's somewhere between the two. But what that does is allows each prison to do its own local risk assessment.

(Lol, Mentoring Coordinator)

The examples of 'blocking' described here not always direct, or even necessarily intentional, yet the reluctance of security gatekeepers to permit volunteers with previous convictions provides a tangible barrier. Moreover, whilst Lol's account indicates steps to address barriers, peer mentors are often additionally scrutinised. For example, even when granted access, there is often a staff member or volunteer without a criminal history additionally required:

We have access [in prison X] but a prison volunteer [who is not a peer] is always in the room. That has a massive impact. Last week, when I went over, she turned up late. I had forty-five minutes with the guy on my own and we did more in that forty-five minutes than we did in any of the meetings prior to that, because he just opened up.

(Lol, Coordinator)

This additional surveillance of 'ex-offender' volunteers indicates that they may struggle to overcome the 'master status' (Becker, 1963) of *deviant*, despite their current status as volunteers. In other words, they continue to be viewed in terms of a risk defined past, rather than a self-defined and publicly performed present. This dynamic is illustrated by Adam, an ex-prisoner and mentoring coordinator, as he attends a mentee's pre-release meeting in prison:

I've had it, going to [prison Y] as a paid member of probation staff... I've gone there to talk to the client getting ready to be released... I've talked about my past and what I'm doing now, and how that qualifies me to offer that support, just so he knows he can have confidence in me as well and build that relationship... By the time I had got back here [to the office] there had been a phone call from the head of [prison] security: "Next time you send an offender up here to do visits we'd like to notified beforehand" and we was saying: "He's not an offender, he's a paid member of [trust name] staff" and there was just this hoo-ha about it.

(Adam, Mentoring Coordinator)

Despite such accounts of restriction and scrutiny, there were also examples of blocks being removed: '[Prison Z] have come back and they've vetted, I went out and met with the governor last week and they're perfectly happy for us to go in three times a month' (Lol, Mentoring Coordinator). What is clear from Lol and Adam's accounts, however, is that in terms of organisational power, peer mentors are positioned in an unfavourable hierarchy. They are not multi-agency *partners* but *consigns* reliant upon benevolence of gatekeepers. Indeed, this hierarchy also exists outside of prison. Mel, for example, manages a women's peer mentoring project. She explains how her trainees were at the mercy of gatekeepers in community education settings when she attempted to organise formal accreditation for their mentoring:

Four of our women were selected and signed up for the local college's *Health and Social Care* course, but after being reassured they wouldn't have to do [a criminal history check] as they were all off site, they backtracked and all applications with a criminal record are now on hold.

(Mel, Mentoring Coordinator)

Mel's volunteers were likely misadvised at the outset of their efforts, but their experience is further evidence of how gatekeepers can raise powerful, practical blocks to (criminalised) mentors. In addition to such individual barriers, respondents often expressed concern about the power of established criminal justice agents to block peer mentoring *as a practice*:

> That kind of meaningful relationship… it sounds 'fluffy' to a lot of people, and if you're trying to sell that as a product to a prison, they'll rubbish it probably. But that's a powerful experience.
>
> (Phil, Mentor)

Phil expects that in a marketised prison context, with predominantly masculine values, mentoring will be seen as soft, feminine, 'fluffy', not a viable 'product'. This echoes Walby and Cole's (2019: 1) observation in Canadian corrections that peer mentoring is 'based on relationships, emotions, listening, compassion, and mutual aid among prisoners, all of which tends to be inhibited by the prison'. The powers at work here are a complex interaction of gender, paternalism and supposedly 'free' enterprise. These governing ideologies will be revisited. Before that, however, Phil's perception of scepticism by prison staff introduces another theme; that is, the precariousness of the criminal justice system.

A precarious criminal justice landscape

A second way in which operational power was understood by respondents was in terms of a system in continual flux. Mentors recognised that prison and community commissioners had the power to enable or terminate peer mentoring, and that this power was subject to rapidly changing trends or influences. Phil, for example, reflected how there was little structure to his volunteer mentoring when he started out in prison settings:

> It wasn't structured, it was just something the prison wanted to play with, and the member of staff that I was in contact with wanted to develop it, knew I had good intentions with what I was doing. But unfortunately, the reason it fizzled out it started getting formally delivered by *User Voice* [a charity] in the prison, it was took out of the education department and given to *G4S* [a private corporation] high up.
>
> (Phil, Mentor)

Phil, as an individual mentor, has little power in this context. His ability to practice is dependent upon the momentary inclination of prison staff 'to play' with an approach and upon the shifting structures through which such work is delivered; structures which are increasingly shaped by larger players within a competitive market. Indeed, even whilst mentoring within prisons Phil felt there was precariousness to his tenure:

> We know only too well how prison establishments think in goals, you can have a million success stories but one failure and that's enough to shut down that peer mentoring.
>
> (Phil, Mentor)

Phil perceives that ex-offender mentors are not only closely scrutinised, but likely to face harsher sanctions where 'failures' occur. This notion of 'failure' is especially important, given that outcomes-based commissioning, including 'Payment by Results' (PbR) has become an important element of public services reform on both sides of the Atlantic (Albertson & Fox, 2018: 2). PbR is a policy which aims to 'only pay providers in full for real reductions in reoffending' (MoJ, 2013). The challenges in adopting an overtly simple outcome measure of criminal justice interventions have been noted (see Albertson & Fox, 2018: 91), but the binary standard is likely to pose specific challenges for mentoring. Ben, for example, volunteers for a project attached to Probation:

> People, I've seen them after four months and they're still abstinent. There's a success in my view. And let's say if that person did go back to drinking after that, he'll know, for me he'll know, in his head he did four months and he can do it again. So that has helped him, it's got to have done. You can't take what you've learned back.
>
> (Ben, Mentor)

For Ben, success is not defined by the 'result' (i.e. abstinence), but by the experience of gaining self-belief. Even if relapse does occur, the value of mentoring has been to experience personal potential as a pedagogical process. Much like Robinson and Shapland (2008) who argue that we should not think about 'restorative justice as something which is "done to" offenders [... but] as an opportunity to facilitate a desire, or consolidate a decision, to desist' (Robinson & Shapland, 2008: 352), Ben suggests that we might re-frame peer mentoring as an opportunity to facilitate the learning of desistance – and to build confidence in this regard. This is a radically different perspective to that of PbR, which attaches principal and monetary value to the quantifiable 'result'. This also serves as a reminder that the power to determine what is deemed as 'success', remains with policymakers, few of whom have *lived* these changes. This section has so far considered the power of people and systems to block entry, accreditation, and autonomous delivery; *and* the precarious nature of the criminal justice system, which sanctions, funds and terminates practice. These features were well recognised as power dynamics by interviewees. The next part of the chapter, however, illuminates those elements of organisational power, which were taken for granted by interviewees, including processes of volunteer selection, training and supervision. These elements constitute the apparatus through which peer mentors' knowledge is shaped and managed.

Selection

During fieldwork, I was permitted to observe the interview and selection processes for prospective volunteer mentors at Project 'Peer'. Interviews were conducted by the project's two coordinators (Adam and Cam) who had histories of imprisonment and drug addiction, and their manager; a Senior Probation Officer. Adam took the lead in most of the interviews explaining to interviewees the informality of the process. Despite his statement, the interviews resembled a structured job interview. Interviewees sat opposite the panel of three and were asked a series of pre-determined questions. Afterwards, the panel discussed the merits of each candidate. It was during these discussions that the power of recruiters to select a particular type of 'offender voice' became apparent. Rather than focusing on the range of (lived) experiences that volunteers brought, the panel focused on volunteers' understanding of 'boundaries', the role and 'inter-agency working'. Where they had reservations, it was often on the grounds of candidates still being 'at the client point of view', or concerns about a candidate's ability to understand 'theories' or 'Star charts' (Triangle consulting, 2019a). In sum, they were often recruiting based on how well applicants could fit into existing knowledge streams and processes, which had been heavily influenced by the Probation Service. This is not so much creating a space for peer knowledge and understanding or claiming that standpoint 'gives access to understanding about oppression that others cannot have' (Stanley & Wise, 1993: 91), but rather it resembles a form of semi-professionalisation.

Training

Not only were volunteers often selected on the grounds of their ability to fit with institutional culture, they were also formally trained for the role:

> The best thing is… getting training. Like my NVQ Level 3 [Health and Social Care Qualification], I wouldn't have gone to college for that… No-one has ever like tried to help me like that. I mean, yeah, 'Go to college', but I'm unconfident going to college, so now a tutor comes here [to the mentoring project] to see me.
>
> (Julie, Mentor)

Like Julie, many mentors appreciated the opportunity to complete a Health and Social Care National Vocational Qualification (NVQ), which is designed to 'equip learners with the skills and knowledge needed to care for others in a broad range of health or social care settings' (City & Guilds, 2019). Courses impart ideal typical working practices such as: *effective communication; principles of safeguarding; assessment and planning; and supporting individuals to access training and employment.* Peer mentors are, therefore, given clear instruction on the type of worker to become, a becoming which requires seeing themselves as facilitators of change, seeing quasi-therapeutic methods as the conduits of change and seeing their mentees as in need of management or improvement.

The powers shaping peer mentoring, then, include established frames of professional and pedagogical knowledge, as much as previously excluded voices of experience. It is important to note, however, that such formal education offers volunteers a valuable sense of validation:

> It never even crossed my mind to come to University [which Ellie progressed to post mentoring], and then... I found [mentoring project], did an interview, did their training, and became one of their first peer mentors.
>
> (Ellie, Mentor)

Formal qualifications appear to 'empower' mentors who have previously felt disempowered. They enable people like Ellie and Julie to gain skills and pursue careers they had not thought possible and to feel valued. The trade-off, however, is that such opportunities constitute something different to a 'criminalised standpoint epistemology'; to peers forming 'solidarastic groups' to protect themselves (Pawson, 2004: 52) against a system which deconstructs the subjective experiences of crime and change. Whilst such structured training may offer individual validation and professional credibility, it also endorses normative educational and professional conformity. These programmes do not always prioritise the 'ex–offender' voice or lived experience but can rely heavily upon pedagogical frameworks borrowed from the fields of coaching, guidance and social care. They turn peer mentoring 'students' into 'containers', into 'receptacles' to be 'filled' by knowledgeable teachers (Freire, 1970: 53).

Most project-based training that I observed, and that respondents described, also prescribed specific mentoring approaches. Projects 'Peer' and 'Facilitate', for example, required volunteers to attend compulsory two- or three-day training courses, which focused upon ideal typical ethics and practices. At Project 'Peer' topics included the following: *mentoring as a teaching and guiding tool; communication and boundaries; trust building; Conflict management and confidentiality; multi-agency working, advocacy, goal setting and the need for volunteer supervision.* At Project 'Facilitate' topics included the following: *information, advice and guidance; listening skills; ways to empower and enable (including encouraging self-reliance); boundary setting; equality and coping with 'difficult situations'.* Most of this training drew upon professional norms yet worked hard to incorporate a 'user voice'. Project 'Peer', for example, heavily promoted mentees directing relationships and mentors drawing upon their own experiences:

> Have a friendly chat, see where they're [mentees] at. It's different to 'assessments'; what professionals see as important... Relate back to being an offender yourself – remember what it was like to feel rejected.
>
> (Mentoring Coordinator and Trainer)

TRAINEE: Is it appropriate to disclose our history?
TRAINER: Play it by ear, instinct plays a role.

(Peer Mentor Training)

Mentoring is about your character and sincerity. We provide the skills, but it's about you.

(Mentoring Coordinator and Trainer)

These statements were supported by role plays, in which trainees were encouraged to practice listening without 'advising', which 'is a block to listening' (Trainer) and to not 'project your issues, stick with [mentee] aims' (Trainer). However, the training also promoted well established Probation approaches. These included setting 'achievable' goals, improving skills and reporting concerns back into formal risk assessments:

Use the goal setting form. Goals must be SMART. This means specific, measurable, achievable, realistic, time bound.

(Trainer)

Social skills are key. For example, shopping, cooking skills, the life skills group…'Life skills' – helping to get them ready for work and education.

(Trainer)

Any concerns [such as mentees not attending mentoring or being involved in crime] should be fed back to the Offender Manager.

(Trainer)

Similarly, Project 'Facilitate' trainers highlighted the importance of listening mentee experiences, using 'open questions' and reflecting, yet they also advocated the need for mentors to prioritise the project's overall aims and to maintain professional boundaries. Mentors were advised to 'suspend [their] own concerns' and not speak over people, yet they were also reminded that: 'employment is our overall aim' and that there should be: 'No home visits, no child minding. Don't introduce your friends and family. No personal numbers, it is not a friendship. No personal details, if asked, keep it light. No Facebook. No gifts from clients' (Peer mentor training). Both training courses therefore aimed to *professionalise* peer mentors. Such efforts offer mentors and their agencies a sense of safety and credibility, but equally risk submerging new knowledges or approaches in established practices. The hazard in such prescribed contexts is that 'user voices' become tokenistic. Moreover, there is the danger of co-option to the very system which peer mentoring often critiques. Garland (2002) termed such incorporation a 'responsibilization strategy'. This strategy seeks to enlist the 'governmental' powers of private actors and 'spread responsibility for crime control onto agencies, organisations and individuals that operate outside the criminal justice state and to persuade them to act appropriately' (Garland, 2002: 124). Training the providers of purportedly 'peer-led' services in ways to 'act appropriately' appears to illustrate this strategy in action. Garland also argues that in the 'new culture of crime control':

> The offenders dealt with by probation, parole and the juvenile court are now less like likely to be represented in official discourse as socially deprived citizens in need of support. They are depicted instead as culpable, undeserving and somewhat dangerous individuals who must be carefully controlled for the protection of the public and the prevention of further offending.
>
> (Garland, 2002: 175)

These opposing constructions represent a conflict that has been present throughout this book. In justifications for their practice peer mentors repeatedly describe their peers as deprived citizens in need of support (see, e.g. Chapters 2, 5 and 7), yet they operate within a system which characterises 'offenders' as actual and potential risks. By adopting tools that have been developed to manage *culpable* and *dangerous offenders* therefore, these 'semi-professionalised' mentors risk compromising their own welfare philosophy. Project 'Care', in intention at least, offered a model to resist such capture. Their coordinator chose not to base volunteer training upon standardised strategies, but upon what potential mentors and mentees deemed to be priorities. To facilitate this, he hosted 'consultation groups' in prison and community settings with people who had previous convictions and a history of living in local authority care:

> The consultation process was about understanding, from the potential mentors and mentees, what would attract you to it and also in the hope that we would galvanise a number of recruits... Consultation groups are organised, the project is outlined, we talk about [local authority] care, offending, the relationship between the two, and where support would need to be if mentoring was to work.
>
> (Lol, Mentoring Coordinator)

The intention was that training was not an imposed 'banking' of known knowledge but developed in consultation. This process is closer to Freire's 'libertarian' education, which reconciles the teacher-student contradiction, 'so that both are simultaneously teachers and students' (Freire, 1970: 53). Unfortunately, this alternative training approach was not embedded before the end of the study. It would therefore be interesting to follow up on progress;

to see if planners were able to achieve their aims and to analyse if any different forms of learning resulted.

Supervision

> We do have formal supervision about once a month.
>
> (John, Mentor)

Mentors are not only carefully *selected* (according to institutional culture) and trained in *how* to mentor, but most mentors are also formally *supervised* by managers or coordinators, offering further organisational power over the mentoring relationship. In most settings this resembled Social Work supervision, wherein: 'the supervisor is in indirect contact with the client through the worker. The supervisor helps the direct service worker to help the client' (Kadushin & Harkness, 2014: 10). At all projects, volunteers met with a supervisor or coordinator every one to two months to discuss 'cases' and seek guidance. I had the opportunity of observing one of these supervision sessions between a mentor and his manager:

SUPERVISOR: What do you still think needs to be done? [With mentee being discussed]
PEER MENTOR: He definitely needs handing over [to a partner agency]. I've discussed this with him in depth.
SUPERVISOR: I'd agree, just have a conversation with him and the worker; let them know you're moving on, that [the mentoring project] is always available. Also do an Outcome Star [review tool] ASAP and this will be used to avoid duplication.

The mentor also sought advice on how his own practice could be improved:

SUPERVISOR: Take risks talking to people, get to know the paperwork, prep beforehand so you're not always relying on the mentee to come up with solution.

This exchange suggests that decision-making, which appears to take place within the mentoring relationship, may happen in supervisory spaces such as these. It is here that the work is given formal shape and informal influence, where tools are offered and tactics suggested. At Project 'Safe', supervision had a slightly different dynamic in that mentors were supervised by 'Aspirational Mentors' rather than project staff:

> [M]entors are allocated an 'Aspirational Mentor' – a local businesswoman or a woman who holds a senior post in an organisation – who they can

look up to for guidance and career advice. Some of the aspirational mentors share similar backgrounds to their mentees.

(Project 'Safe' Promotional Material)

Hope, a paid mentor at this project, described how having this aspirational figure was helpful:

> We have meetings and they'll check out how we are getting on with our mentees. If I'm unsure, I can phone her and ask for her advice or support. So, we've always got support and always have people around us that are there to help us. My mentor is a [police] Chief Constable, but we've got others who run domestic violence places or others in housing. These are all very inspirational women, and just by having them there's always different support, you know?.

(Hope, Mentor)

Melina, a paid mentor at the same project added:

> I have an Aspirational Mentor and she's great, she helps me with everything... I've not long started and she helps me with, like, helping me plan my sessions, what we need to work around, or anything.

(Melina, Mentor)

Peer mentoring in these (albeit diverse) settings is not just about drawing on personal experience and training then, but also on the advice of supervisory staff. Moreover, at Project 'Safe' these supervisory individuals' backgrounds are as varied as policing, refuge or housing management. Despite this diversity of knowledge, there is often no pre-requisite for such supervisors to undergo the kind of training that mentors themselves do. Nadia, for example, is a housing director, but volunteers as an 'Aspirational Mentor' supervising peer mentors:

INTERVIEWER: Is there any training or supervision for this role?
NADIA (ASPIRATIONAL MENTOR): Erm...no...
INTERVIEWER: Does there need to be? Or not?
NADIA: (long pause)... I think it'd be useful, because I've done other mentoring schemes whereby we had like a briefing session before... Defining what mentoring was and what our role was; sort of roles and responsibilities... I think training would be useful and it's also good that you've got that shared understanding at the beginning about what mentoring is and how it might work.

When training or formalised knowledge transfer is absent, therefore, volunteers – even highly skilled ones – can feel a sense of absence. This may be another reason, in addition to credibility, why services persist with formal training processes. What appears to *matter* in terms of supervision for Project 'Safe', however, is not a particular practice ideology, but the input of an individual who is deemed to be 'inspirational'; who provides aspiration in terms of their career status, even if this career differs in context and approach to mentoring. The job of the 'Aspirational Mentor' is not to have an intricate knowledge of mentoring, but to develop the aspirations and confidence of the mentor. This model assumes that mimetic desire (Girard, 1977) is as powerful as practical pedagogic processes. However, whilst Project 'Safe's' approach moves away slightly from directive 'managerialism', there was still an assumption that 'management knowledge [… is] the core technology' (Tsui, 2004: 8). A position which potentially undermines the peer-led ethos.

Regulatory professionals

In addition to the visible (if not problematised) structures of selection, training and supervision, there was also attempts at professional regulation from beyond the parameters of mentoring. For example, at a conference organised by a female mentoring project, aimed at raising awareness of the needs of women in the justice system, I attended a 'workshop' facilitated by two mentors with 'experience of serious youth violence'. The workshop discussion focused predominantly on young women at risk of exploitation by male gangs. At one point one of the facilitators, who was a young, black, female mentor, used the context to question the intersection of race and class in her own experiences with the police:

> Why do police have conviction rates? Crime is crime. They gave us our name as a gang, put cameras on us, we start walking like that, together as a group, cos it's well-lit and we feel safe. On the street with my urban friends I was stopped all the time, when I went to University, in the same numbers I was not stopped.
>
> (Hope, Mentor)

This was one of the few times that I heard a mentor (as opposed to a coordinator) critically question the structural influences upon her life. This may well be because, as illustrated above, the approaches of mentors are subject to much formal filtering and shaping. Coordinators in contrast are often in post as a result of their tenacity and entrepreneurship (see Chapter 8). What was particularly interesting about Hope's insights here, however, was the response they received. At the end of the workshop Hope's manager conversationally asked a Probation Officer (who had participated in the workshop) how the 'girls had done'. The Officer's response was that it was 'great' but that 'they need to rein in their personal opinions a bit'. This assumption that mentors should collude with established knowledge constituted an attempt to silence Hope's voice of experience. It also evoked the arguments of 'Angela Y. Davis (1981) and Patricia Hill Collins (2000) [who] discuss subordinating images of black women [...including] "Uppity" black women [who] do not "know their place" and expect to be treated as though they were equal to white women or to white men' (Martin & Jurik, 2006: 44). While the Officer's comment did not appear to be consciously about undermining Hope on the grounds of her race or gender, it nonetheless communicated that her personal opinions (or experiences) need external moderation; that Hope should not expect her voice to have prominence. Regardless of Hope being offered a platform, therefore as a young, black, female, peer mentor she is relegated to a denizen or 'subaltern' voice (Spivak, 1988). Her marginalised voice is dismissed as 'personal' by the dominant speaker before it is fully heard. This 'user voice' is invited to join the justice-practice conversation but is also expected to perform a marginalised status and endorse established rhetoric. Such subtle pressure conveys a similar message to the need to avoid 'failure' above. 'Ex-offenders' may play a part in the justice system, but only if they are suitably grateful and conformist; if they are 'humble' and 'don't tread on toes' (Chapter 8). For peer mentoring to move beyond paternalistic tokenism, we need to pay attention to how subordination and abjection are experienced and resisted (Tyler, 2013):

> [I]f we want to achieve the kind of 'justice' which fosters egalitarian relationships between individuals, groups and communities, then we must include informal, marginal, subaltern and subversive discourses.
>
> (Campbell, 2011: 168)

Hearing (and including) these voices, however, requires openness to challenging dominant discourses, ideologies and practices.

Macro-power: governing ideologies

What Hope's example reinforces is that power is not just manifest in a person's ability to speak, but also in the capacity of their audience to listen and define; in the capacity for those around Hope to 'define [her] as someone set apart' (Goffman, 1963: 132). Moreover, these processes of speaking and listening are made sense of through collectively held images and assumptions, by dominant value systems or 'governing ideologies'. These disciplinary powers do not solely belong to the mentoring context, but manifest here in clear ways. The following section illuminates how two such systems of thought influence peer mentoring, but often go unrecognised in critiques of the practice. These are: neoliberalism and gender socialisation. Neoliberalism is characterised by ideals of self-governance and 'responsibilisation' (Garland, 1996), whilst 'gender socialisation' begins:

> [A]lmost immediately after a child is born, when parents... interact with their child differently depending on whether it is a boy or a girl.

Parents of boys describe them as big, athletic, active, serious, angry and determined, whereas parents of girls describe them as small, pretty, delicate, well behaved, emotional and afraid.

(Renzetti, 2013: 19)

Whilst 'gender socialisation' theories are often critiqued for being 'confined to the narrow nurture theory' (Palazzani, 2012: 14), there is nonetheless 'abundant empirical evidence' (Palazzani, 2012: 14) of gender socialisation. It is also a theory that was helpful in terms of themes within this study. This section will explore the ways in which these two disciplinary influences manifest in the lives of respondents, are communicated to them and the ways in which they resist or reinforce them.

The governing power of neoliberalism

Neoliberal governmentality; government 'at a distance' (Leitner, Sheppard, Sziarto & Maringanti, 2007: 3) has had a significant influence upon the development of peer mentoring, but the literature to date is largely silent in terms of how it manifests in the micro-dynamics of practice.

Neo-liberalism encourages individuals to give their lives a specific entrepreneurial form. It responds to stronger 'demand' for individual scope for self-determination and desired autonomy by 'supplying' individuals and collectives with the possibility of actively participating in the solution of specific matters and problems which had hitherto been the domain of state agencies specifically empowered to undertake such tasks.

(Lemke, 2001: 202)

Neoliberal ideology can be traced as an influential factor in many of the findings of this study. Chapter 2, for example, linked the appeal of peer mentoring to aims to reduce state costs and fill gaps in a reducing welfare state. Chapter 5 presented mentors as exemplars of self-determination positioned to share their example and their strategies with peers. Chapters 6 and 7 outlined how mentoring invites people to account for themselves *and* nurtures them to see themselves as capable of self-direction. Finally, Chapter 8 accounted the prevalence of entrepreneurship in mentoring, of efforts to respond to a diversifying 'market' of justice'. In addition to these examples, quite specific neoliberal narratives can be traced:

Before you can get to a positive trajectory as an offender, have time to have pity and anger, to scrabble through that. Point fingers at everybody else, before you can actually reflect: hang on a minute; this is down to me.

(Phil, Mentor)

It was just my outlook on life, I felt very angry, very badly done to. I had alcohol problems. I've had drug problems in the past, but the reason I went there [to a recovery centre] was because *I* was an alcoholic.

(Lin, Mentor and previously a Mentee)

I've stopped feeling sorry for myself. I've started, it is true, when I do think positive, positive things happen. And I think it's not so much what happens, because I can't control the outside events, but it's how I deal with it. And I look at it now, that you've got to deal with everything in a positive way.

(Janet, Mentee)

These speakers each advocate the need to shift focus from the external to the internal, in doing so they endorse (and accept) neoliberal ideology. There is a strong focus on individual 'responsibilisation' (Besley & Peters, 2007: 143) and 'self-blaming' (Lyon-Callo, 2008: 154), a need to stop 'feeling sorry for [your] self', feeling 'badly done to' and pointing fingers. Individuals must be self-governing and responsible, rather than looking to external factors. What must necessarily be quashed in order for responsibilisation to take place, however, is any focus on social or structural issues. For Phil, however, some anger remained and gave him moments of doubt about replacing career criminality with mentoring work:

I'm that disenchanted with conventional living that sometimes my mind falters into criminal thinking. An example would be: I'm so bitter about the whole tax avoidance things and the injustice created as a result of the banking crisis, you know? Watching people lose their jobs, losing mortgages, family and marriage breakdowns, people committing suicide, that can be the product of say the banking crisis and yet the system is focused on criminalising people that have made bad choices.

(Phil, Mentor)

This critical perception is conceived of by Phil as a 'faltering', a personal failure, not compatible with his own personal improvement and mentoring vocation. His own *voice*, standpoint and social critique are voluntarily silenced as he responds to the weighing expectations of neoliberal individualism: '*this is down to me*'. Once a belief in personal responsibility is internalised the social and the structural become insignificant, merely things to 'point fingers at' on the road to self-realisation. In this light, the apparently benign nature of 'individualised practice' gains new significance as a governmental element, encouraging mentees to accept *personal* responsibility and 'get past' feelings of anger and injustice:

She said 'this is your life George, where do you want to take it? Take a step at a time'. You start to think: 'oh yea, I forgot this is my life'.

(Georgie, Mentee)

The attraction of a sense of agency, which may have been diminished in custodial institutions or heavily managed criminal justice interventions (Chapters 5 and 6) becomes the trade-off for critical silence:

> I [previously] felt sorry for myself, I did, and just to let that out and get it out my system. You're not walking round with this constant 'the world's against me' kind of attitude and that I think was what helped me.
>
> (Georgie, Mentee)

A sense of self-direction is accepted by Georgie at the expense of a regard for social factors which made her feel excluded. Mentees regulate their critical perspectives as they accept the ruling ideology of self-discipline. We do not know what mentoring would look like if it were informed more fully by collective politicisation, as suggested may be the potential of this work in Chapter 3, because individual responsibilisation is so strong. However, it is likely that it would include a critical focus upon, rather than a dismissal of, those factors which caused respondents to feel sorry for themselves, feel *badly done to*, feel that the *world is against them* and want to *point fingers*. Given the loaded language of these quotations, it is also likely that this focus might uncover ill-treatment, exclusion and marginalisation, for which there is currently no space. Whilst respondents rarely described collective reflections upon social disadvantage, there were traces of resistance to neo-liberal ideology, including a quiet insistence upon social and structural impacts on individual lives. Lol, for example, as highlighted previously, calls attention to the high number of care leavers in prison and questions whether this can conceivably be explained solely in terms of a problem of self-governance:

> You can't just take people from the care system and say they're bad people so they end up [in prison], there must be something happening, systemic... why's it not working? Why is it that care leavers end up in custody?.
>
> (Lol, Mentoring Coordinator)

Similarly, mentees often called attention to social factors in their lives. Eve, for example, was serving a community sentence for a fraudulent benefit claim, an offence she states was encouraged by her then partner: 'It was my ex said, "we won't go legal", and now my kids and me are paying for it' As a result she was prosecuted whilst her partner escaped consequence:

> It's not fair that we [Eve and her children] still have to suffer because it was my mistake, but he gets away scot-free, I think he should have got some of it.
>
> (Eve, Mentee)

Other mentees also insisted on circumstances that helped to account for their criminal actions. Circumstances which are often ignored or minimised by systems focused on individual improvements:

> There were circumstances that led up to what happened [the offending] and when I look at that person now I think 'Oh God', I don't recognise myself but there were triggers that caused me to do what I did. And then it was too late to stop it.
>
> (Gina, Mentee)

> What really annoys me is eighty per cent of people are in prison through drink and drugs and not once do they come to you and say: "right you committed crime through drink we need to deal with that". They don't. I went to prison for drink-driving, no-one ever mentioned to me I might be an alcoholic in prison.
>
> (Georgie, Mentee)

> I haven't faced some of the financial difficulties most offenders face, in extreme situations where it's a case of putting food in your mouth. I might have been propelled into crime like some offenders are faced with.
>
> (Phil, Mentor)

These speakers highlight triggers and underlying causes, social factors as opposed to individual flaws, and begin to resist the neo-liberal insistence upon individual responsibility. Whilst the lack of collective, critical reflection means this resistance is limited, the emergence of these voices from within a dominant discourse illustrates how peer mentoring offers a platform to reflect on issues which challenge received wisdom.

The power of gender socialisation

Neoliberalism does not exist in isolation, but endures alongside a number of neighbouring ideologies, one of which is gender normativity:

> In an environment which allocates a privileged place to the values of close regulation, self-management and "responsibilization" (Garland, 1996), women are, or are expected to be, exemplary self-governing citizens and highly self-surveilling with respect to various norms of "femininity".
>
> (Corcoran, 2006: 191)

As gender was a prominent theme in the data, this section explores its governing effects directly. It considers how peer mentoring often embraces assumptions about masculinity and femininity and in doing so becomes regulatory from a gendered viewpoint. Indeed, the assumption that peer mentoring can free itself of relations of power and control, by virtue of drawing its actors from similar communities, misses as Lynne Haney argues:

> One of the most basic of sociological insights: [that] communities also exert discipline and control over their members. And these forms of control can be just as constraining as those at work in more formal organisations.
>
> (Haney, 2010: 157)

In other words, when peer mentoring is framed as a relationship free of authority, one of the major power dynamics which is veiled is gender. It should not come as a surprise that peer mentoring is gendered, there is an established literature on gendered criminal justice practice which contextualises this claim. Following a review of women in the criminal justice system, for example, Baroness Corston (2007) concluded that:

> Women have been marginalised within a system largely designed by men for men for far too long... there needs to be a re-design of women's custody introduced in parallel with other gender specific workable disposals and sanctions.
>
> (Corston, 2007)

This 'liberal feminist' approach advanced the value of gender specific approaches for individuals and organisations, including claims they can:

> make the management of women offenders more effective... Decrease staff turnover and sexual misconduct... Improve program and service delivery... [and] Increase the gender appropriateness of services and programs.
>
> (Bloom, Owen, Covington & Raeder, 2003: vi)

Hansman (2002: 44) also points to the importance of female-focused mentoring services, arguing that women often encounter discordance in the advice offered to them by male mentors. However, Hannah-Moffat's (2010) observations, from a more 'critical feminist' perspective, question whether gender responsive ideals always translate into helpful practice:

> The well-intentioned labels 'gender sensitive' and 'women-centeredness' have been attached to a wide range of improvised and poorly adapted programs and managerial processes without substantial consideration of how gender should be operationalised.
>
> (Hannah-Moffat, 2010: 196)

As a result, specific strategies and programmes for 'female offenders' have often 'been based on essentialist conceptualisations of gender and have treated women in stereotypical ways' (Perry, 2013: 409):

> Dialogue about GR [gender responsive] principles is general and rarely questions stereotypical femininities and the implicit normative assumptions routinely made about women... GR approaches stress the differences between men and women prisoners, and in doing so constitute gender subjectivity.
>
> (Hannah-Moffat, 2010: 198)

Whilst there are complex feminist debates at play here, there is agreement that there has been a neglect of the social powers or oppressions at work in criminalised women's lives. This section will therefore explore how gender stereotypes manifest in peer mentoring settings and illustrate why the gender dimension of mentoring is important and overlooked.

Peer mentoring through gender

> With a peer it's equal, it's on the same level.
>
> (Katy, Mentor)

A focus on gender complicates the claim that peer mentoring is egalitarian. Rather, there is some evidence that it often separates male and female mentees into normative pursuits. Take, for example, the 'mentoring activities' on offer in one community setting attached to a Probation Service:

> We go boxing; I've got it this afternoon... We went to Blackpool, a boxing outing, apart from saying 'We'll meet outside probation' it wasn't like a probation outing, just like a lads' day out.
>
> (Will, Male Mentee)

> I used to help with the [women's] group, then I did a fashion show with it and one of my clients helped me do that... I've give her that confidence and it was her who wanted to do it too, because she's quite good at fashion.
>
> (Julie, female mentor)

These activities do not appear to be *just* about practising a new, non-criminal identity, but about performing idealised identities, informed by stereotypical gender norms. Male mentees are invited to 'boxing', and a 'lads' day out'; settings replete with hyper-masculine performance. Female mentees are invited to a Women's Centre group and learn about fashion; communicating traditional feminine norms of passivity, beauty and display. These activities appear to resemble a (re)disciplining of men and women to normative gendered expectations, rather than 'power-less' peer-to-peer relationships. However, whilst *my* initial response problematised this disciplinary underpinning,

I was acutely aware that I had heard little problematising from those involved. Mentors and mentees – those creating and doing these activities – did not appear to share this concern. Rather, gendered work provided a comforting familiarity, a way of bonding and building trusting relationships. Julie, for example, a peer mentor in a project attached to a Probation Service, reflects on why she chose a fashion show as a mentoring activity:

> The way she [mentee] dresses, I'd say: "Oh you're dead good at colour coordinating" etc. And I think I gave her that confidence, because I was praising her on her fashion. And she was like: "Well I'm interested in fashion" and… that maybe gave her a bit of support, confidence to think: *someone really thinks I am good at fashion, I'll get up and do it*, because… that's another thing with mentoring if they're doing good you need to praise them too, because I think everyone likes to be praised don't they? And a lot of erm, them might not have been praised by maybe their family, boyfriend etc.
>
> (Julie, Mentor)

'Fashion', in Julie's terms, is not important as a socialising or normative instrument, therefore, but it presents a familiar social script for her to work with – a script that is known in terms of expected feminine performance and which her mentee was already invested in. Rumgay (2004: 409) used the concept of scripts to describe 'socially recognized behavioural routines' of specific personal identities, such as parent, student, worker or partner. Script mastery, Rumgay argues (2004: 415), 'involves a significant investment in rehearsal across a wide range of interactions and situations [as a result] mentoring programmes might provide one mechanism for facilitating this transition process'. In Rumgay's terms, fashion may constitute a supporting 'subroutine' (2004: 410) of the 'woman' script. The difference between Rumgay's conception of mentoring as scripting and what Julie describes is which party selects the script. In Julie's example 'fashion' is not appropriated by the mentee in order to master a new, desired 'womanly' identity, but rather it is appropriated by the mentor in order to achieve some common ground, a space in which to bond. Fashion does not function as a full identity script therefore, but as a language to connect women through a known feminine subroutine. For Julie, fashion was merely employed as a *tool* to improve confidence, an available route to achieve the wider goal of relationship building.

Will, who attends a boxing group with his mentor describes a similar process: 'We go boxing, have a hug, "what've you been up to?"'. The boxing that I interpreted as hyper masculine, now emerges as a script, or more accurately, a setting, in which men invested in masculinity can attend comfortably. Once there, however, the focus is upon affection, connection and care. Boxing, like fashion, provides a known language, but its use within a frame of peer mentoring allows it to communicate new messages too. It becomes a space where men can connect and support each other emotionally without facing

the consequences of gender transgression. Where in the words of one at-
tendee, people can be taken 'out of their comfort zones', where men can draw
upon shared experiences of 'sexual abuse, being in prison... get them out in
the open, go and seek help... I impress to get everything out in the open'
(Trainee Mentor). In this light essentialist gender positions become a 'way in'.
Gendered social scripts (like the ex-offender identity itself) becomes bridges,
known ways of being on the path to new. Gendered norms, in this light, are
not (just) forms of imposed domination, therefore, but a known order which
individual subjects utilise, transgress and reproduce for particular purposes.

Resisting gender stereotypes

There were some invitations to gendered scripts, which were not read-
ily invested in however. On a warm summer morning during fieldwork,
I attended a Women's Centre in a post-industrial northern English town.
The venue was being used by peer mentors to deliver a 'Women's Group'.
Group attendees had been referred by Probation Officers or drug workers.
Organisers had specific intentions for establishing such a group. They were
aware of some of the gender-specific recommendations of the Corston report
(2007) along with strategic management plans to obtain women-only work
spaces, as the Probation building 'is not a welcoming building, particularly
for female clients' (Women's Group Coordinator). On the day I observed the
group, which took place in the shadow of decommissioned Mill buildings
and budget supermarkets; women attended a session focused on 'fashion'. It
was part of a six-week block, which included 'skin, nails and fashion' and was
described as 'women-led'. The activities I observed included matching pic-
tures of clothing and footwear (printed by peer volunteers leading the group)
as to 'what goes best' together. Group members were asked to think about
where they would wear each outfit, for example, 'an interview or a night
out?' At the end of the session there was a 'fashion show' using second-hand
clothing donations. Group members were invited to try clothes on and take
part in the show, although there was some reluctance for this and most 'models' were peer mentors. Afterwards group members could choose items of
clothing to take away. At this point mentees were most animated, and many
chose items for themselves. Throughout the session, however, the atmosphere
was distinctly less animated, many mentees crossed their arms, did not speak
and kept their eyes averted to the desks in front of them. The atmosphere was
dominated by a core group of three or four group members who sat together,
displayed defensive body language and had closed giggly chats among themselves. At one point a facilitator asked: 'If you had £50 where would you go
to buy clothes?' Some participants responded, as seemed to be expected, with
suggestions for budget retailers, including 'Primark', 'everything£5.com' and
charity shops. These suggestions were praised by facilitators: 'Yes, you can
buy more if you go to the cheaper shops'. However, there was also clear

resistance expressed, one participant, for example, shouted: 'All we need to do now is win the lottery', another complained: 'I haven't even got the internet', to which a facilitator suggested they 'go to the library, its free there'.

The practical, problem solving approach adopted by facilitators missed the social critique expressed, which was that the gendered social ideals of self-presentation being communicated do not easily reconcile with the reality of living in poverty. A reality these vocal women were presenting as more pressing. This recollects what Freire warned against: submerging voices with good advice; turning people into 'passive receptacles' (Freire, 1970: 53). In this scenario, facilitators deferred potentially oppositional or resistant perspectives (which threatened to destabilise the pedagogical objective of the event) by reducing these comments to immaterial responses. These are quintessentially dismissive devices used by facilitators assuming the teacher role. Had facilitators felt they were able to engage with these points of strain and resistance, they may have been able to *hear* their peers more fully, to create a space for voice and critical standpoint rather than positioning them as passive receivers. To do so would have been to exchange 'the role of depositor, prescriber, domesticator, for the role of student among students', thus undermining the 'power of oppression' (Freire, 1970: 56). By depositing practical advice in place of dialogue, mentors – perhaps inevitably – reinforced the dominant ideology of the wider social and justice contexts in which they are positioned. Mentees were disciplined into becoming workers and responsible consumers; they were also made subject to the broader rehabilitative project for female 'offenders', which appears to be one of 'conformity to traditional "feminine" gender norms as well as a desistance from crime' (Perry, 2013: 409). The expectation upon (group) mentees appeared to be to comply with the feminine scripts of beauty and domestic finance management and to not mention the submerged, potentially threatening realities of living with poverty and marginalisation. The mentee who is expected to emerge from such gendered mentoring is not just a desister but an *ideal* woman. This is reflective of a broader history, outlined by Malloch and McIvor (2011):

> Women who commit crimes are stigmatized on the basis that they have broken social laws; but are additionally stigmatized for breaking gendered codes of 'appropriate' behaviour for women (e.g. Smart, 1992). While women resist gender stereotypes in many ways, they are not unaffected by these expectations and the consequences of failing to conform to them.
>
> (Malloch & McIvor, 2011: 331)

Peer mentoring *through gender* may not constitute a conscious form of discipline, but it is a response to broader ideological expectations upon female offenders. Female lawbreakers are aware that they not only broke the law, but also the gender code. They are aware of a double rehabilitation project.

In this light, familiar 'scripts' such as fashion do not just constitute a functional, bonding measure, but simultaneously an ideological socialising measure. In theory then, gender sensitive groups such as the women's fashion group can offer an alternative to a system designed for men, but in practice, they can reinforce ideals of femininity, which belong to a broader patriarchal context. In this regard they constitute the kind of mentoring which aims to fit people 'into society as it exists, rather than equipping them with a critical understanding of society or any means by which they might seek to change it' (Colley, 2002: 268). This can create a message that it is not enough to go straight; you must also become a particular type of woman. Eve, a mentee at a women's employment project, describes this pressure well:

INTERVIEWER: How were you matched with your mentor?
EVE: I think it's because she was so ladylike and I'm not ladylike... I did have a lot of problems [at the job centre] because with me being in construction they didn't like the fact that a woman (tails off). Now they're a bit better, but there was a woman up the stairs and she was saying: 'Well my brother in law is out of work and he's a bricklayer'... I don't know how they matched us up, probably because they wanted me to be a bit 'girlier'.
(Eve, Female Mentee)

Eve resists the assumption that construction work is a male domain, yet in doing so feels she is seen as lacking in terms of femininity. Moreover, she feels this is the focus of her mentoring intervention – the area where she lacks. Such gendered bracketing was not only felt by female mentees however. Paul also recognised and resisted the gendered expectations of his mentoring activity:

They do an arts and crafts day for the girls who come here, so I used to sit and do that cos I enjoy doing stuff like that. But a lot of the lads wouldn't do it. So, they set up the gym for them at first and people started going, but they stopped cos they couldn't be arsed with it, so they set the boxing up now.

(Paul, Male Mentee)

Paul resists the assumption that 'arts and crafts' should be a women's activity, yet many of his peers do not share his resistance. As a result, activities which fit more closely with traditional masculine norms are introduced. Both Eve and Paul therefore resist gendered activities, yet in the absence of peer support for their resistance they both settle into compliance with mentoring which appears to support gender conformity. In the space of mentoring at least, they drop their individual acts of resistance to gender normativity. At other times, however, gender stereotypes were more consciously challenged. Project 'Safe', for example, aimed to address the 'challenges and difficulties faced by young women' including 'the representation of women within contemporary society and the social, cultural and personal pressures exerted upon women' (Project 'Safe' Evaluation Report, 2012: 4). They actively sought to minimise these challenges and cultivate alternative representations. This took the form of not only offering 'aspirational' role models, but also encouraging young women [and men] to view themselves as leaders:

> It is essential that we work towards enabling young people to move from a position of social alienation towards resilience and empowerment enabling the development of future ambassadorial and leadership roles within our communities.
>
> ('Safe' Promotional Booklet)

Peer mentoring here is informed by a critical awareness of the problems with gendered standards and this peer mentoring setting actively seeks to minimise their impact; in doing so they offer mentees small practices of re-socialisation or indeed the opportunity for *transformative agency*, whereby 'individuals' purposefully transform the structures in which they are embedded' (Tuominen & Lehtonen, 2018: 1601).

Whilst peer mentoring is often claimed to empower participants (Kavanagh & Borrill, 2013; Chapter 5 of this book), to be egalitarian and based on liberatory principles (Chapter 2) this discourse tends to mask relations of power which persist. This chapter has explored some of these relations including the power of those *inside* the mentoring relationship to set goals and arrange activities, the power of those *outside* the mentoring relationship – such as prison staff, education staff and Probation staff – to block work, sanction work and define the shape of recruitment training and delivery and finally the power of collective *social ideals* such as neoliberalism and gender. These governing ideologies can be traced through the ways in which people describe themselves and the activities which they are, or *should* be involved in. These manifestations of power are often overlooked in more favourable assessments of peer mentoring. However, whilst it is important to recognise these dynamics, it is equally important to appreciate that those subject to these powers are not power*less*. Rather the chapter has also highlighted ways in which both mentees and peer mentors push against established hierarchies and ideals. These include challenging exclusion by prisons and gaining access to those settings; developing training that includes a 'user' perspective despite the strong influence of existing pedagogical frameworks; insisting upon the social and structural factors in people's lives, which can influence their choices despite the dominance of neoliberal, responsibilising ideology and finally resisting normative masculinity and femininity, even creating environments where these expectations can be explored and challenged. Despite powerful restrictions upon the work of peer mentoring and strategies of co-option, therefore, those involved in the practice often find ways to resist powers manifest in the work. What emerges is a practice in continual tussle, which often accepts professional norms and social practices, but which also presses at the edges of received wisdom. It questions collective constructions of who 'ex-offenders' are and what responses are required. In doing so it holds a mirror to our established practices and ideals.

Acknowledgements

This chapter has adapted material from the following work:

Buck, G., (2019), 'Politicisation or professionalisation? Exploring divergent aims within UK voluntary sector peer mentoring', *The Howard Journal of Crime and Justice*, **58**(3), pp. 349–365.

I am thankful to the publishers for their permission.

References

Abdennur, A., (1987), *The conflict resolution syndrome: Volunteerism, violence, and beyond.* Ottawa: Ottawa University Press.

Albertson, K. & Fox, C., (2018), *Payment by results and social impact bonds: Outcome-based payment systems in the UK and US.* Bristol: Policy Press.

Becker, H.S., (1963), *Outsiders: Studies in the sociology of deviance.* Reprint, New York: Free Press, 1966 edition.

Besley, T. & Peters, M.A., (Eds.), (2007), *Subjectivity & truth: Foucault, education, and the culture of self.* New York: Peter Lang Publishing.

Bloom, B., Owen, B., Covington, S. & Raeder, M., (2003), *Gender responsive strategies: Research, practice and guiding principles for women offenders.* Washington: US Department of Justice: National Institute of Corrections.

Boyce, I., Hunter, G. & Hough, M., (2009), *The St Giles trust peer advice project: Summary of an evaluation report.* London: The Institute for Criminal Policy Research, School of Law, King's College. Available at: http://eprints.bbk.ac.uk/3794/ [Accessed August 2019]

Brinson, J. & Kottler, J., (1993), 'Cross-Cultural Mentoring in counselor Education: A strategy for Retaining Minority Faculty', *Counselor Education and Supervision*, **32**(4), pp. 241–253

Campbell, E., (2011), 'The cultural politics of justice: Bakhtin, stand-up comedy and post-9/11 securitization', *Theoretical Criminology*, **15**(2), pp. 159–177.

City and Guilds, (2019), *'Health and social care' qualification outline.* Available at: www.cityandguilds.com/qualifications-and-apprenticeships/health-and-social-care/care/4222-health-and-social-care#tab=information [Accessed October 2019].

Cochran-Smith, M. & Paris, C.L., (1995), 'Mentor and mentoring. Did Homer have it right?' In: J. Smythe (Ed.), *Critical discourses in teacher development.* London: Cassell.

Colley, H., (2002), 'A "rough guide" to the history of mentoring from a Marxist feminist perspective', *Journal of Education for Teaching: International Research and Pedagogy*, **28**(3), pp. 257–273.

Colley, H., (2001), 'Righting rewritings of the myth of Mentor: A critical perspective on career guidance mentoring', *British Journal of Guidance and Counselling,* **29**(2), pp. 177–197.

Collins, P.H., (2000), 'Gender, black feminism, and black political economy', *The Annals of the American Academy of Political and Social Science,* **568**(1), pp. 41–53.

Corcoran, M., (2006), *Out of order.* Devon: Willan.

Corston, B.J., (2007), *The Corston report: A report of a review of women with particular vulnerabilities in the criminal justice system.* London: Home Office.

Deakin, J. & Spencer, J., (2011), 'Who cares? Fostering networks and relationships in prison and beyond'. In: Sheehan, R., McIvor, G. & Trotter, C., (Eds.), *Working with women offenders in the community.* Cullompton: Willan.

Davis, A., (1981), 'Reflections on the Black Woman's Role in the Community of Slaves', *The Black Scholar,* **12**(6), pp. 2–15.

Fagan, J., (1993), 'The social control of spouse assault'. In: Adler, F. & Laufer, W.S., (Eds.), *New directions in criminological theory* (Vol. 4). New Jersey: Transaction Publishers.

Farrall, S., (2005), 'On the existential aspects of desistance from crime', *Symbolic Interaction,* **28**(3), pp. 367–386.

Foucault, M., (1979), *Discipline and punish: The birth of a prison.* Reprint, London: Penguin, 1991 edition.

Freire, P., (1970), *Pedagogy of the oppressed.* Reprint, London: Penguin, 1996.

Garland, D., (2002), *The culture of control: Crime and social order in contemporary society.* Oxford: Oxford University Press.

Garland, D., (1996), 'The limits of the sovereign state: Strategies of crime control in contemporary society', *British Journal of Criminology,* **36**(1), pp. 445–471.

Girard, R., (1977), *Violence and the sacred.* London: Continuum, 2005 edition.

Goffman, E., (1963), *Stigma: Notes on the management of spoiled identity.* Middlesex: Penguin.

Haney, L.A., (2010), *Offending women: Power, punishment, and the regulation of desire.* California: University of California Press.

Hannah-Moffat, K., (2010), 'Sacrosanct or flawed: Risk, accountability and gender-responsive penal politics', *Current Issues in Criminal Justice,* **22**, p. 193.

Hansman, C.A., (2002), 'Diversity and power in mentoring relationships', *Critical Perspectives on Mentoring: Trends and Issues,* no. 388. pp. 39–48.

Hughes, W., (2012), 'Promoting offender engagement and compliance in sentence planning: Practitioner and service user perspectives in Hertfordshire', *Probation Journal,* **59**(1), pp. 49–65.

Hunter, G. & Kirby, A., (2011), *Evaluation summary: Working one to one with young offenders.* London: Birkbeck College.

Kadushin, A. & Harkness, D., (2014), *Supervision in social work,* 5th edn, New York: Columbia University Press.

Kavanagh, L. & Borrill, J., (2013), 'Exploring the experiences of ex-offender mentors', *Probation Journal,* **60**(4), pp. 400–414.

Leitner, H., Sheppard, E.S., Sziarto, K. & Maringanti, A., (2007), 'Contesting urban futures: Decentering neoliberalism'. In: Leitner, H., Peck, J. & Sheppard, E.S., (Eds.), *Contesting neoliberalism: Urban frontiers.* New York: Guilford Press.

Lemke, T., (2001), presents Foucault, F.M., (1979), '"The birth of bio-politics"–Michel Foucault's lecture at the Collège de France on Neo-Liberal Governmentality', *Economy and Society,* **30**(2), p. 198.

Lyon-Callo, V., (2008), *Inequality, poverty, and neoliberal governance: Activist ethnography in the homeless sheltering industry*. Toronto: University of Toronto Press.

Malloch, M. & McIvor, G., (2011), 'Women and community sentences', *Criminology and Criminal Justice*, **11**(4), pp. 325–344.

Martin, S.E. & Jurik, N.C., (2006), *Doing justice, doing gender: Women in legal and criminal justice occupations*. London: Sage.

McNeill, F. & Weaver, B., (2010), *Changing lives? Desistance research and offender management, Research report 03/2010*, The Scottish Centre for Crime and Justice Research. Available at: www.sccjr.ac.uk/pubs/Changing-Lives-Desistance-Research-and-Offender-Management/255 [Accessed August 2019].

Miles, M.B., Huberman, A.M. & Saldaña, J., (2014), *Qualitative data analysis: A methods sourcebook*. Chicago: SAGE Publications.

Ministry of Justice (MoJ), (2011), *Making prisons work: Skills for rehabilitation review of offender learning*. London: Department for Business, Innovation and Skills. Available at: https://assets.publishing.service.gov.uk/government/uploads/system/uploads/attachment_data/file/230260/11-828-making-prisons-work-skills-for-rehabilitation.pdf [Accessed August 2019].

Ministry of Justice (MoJ), (2013), *Transforming Rehabilitation: A Strategy for Reform* Response to consultation, May 2013. London: Ministry of Justice.

Palazzani, L., (2012), *Gender in philosophy and law*. London: Springer Science & Business Media.

Pawson, R., (2004), *Mentoring relationships: An explanatory review,* Working Paper 21. Leeds: University of Leeds.

Perry, E., (2013), '"She's alpha male": Transgressive gender performances in the probation "classroom"', *Gender and Education, **25**(4), pp. 396–412.

Renzetti, C.M., (2013), *Feminist criminology*. Abingdon, Oxon: Routledge.

Robinson, G. & Shapland, J., (2008), 'Reducing recidivism a task for restorative justice?' *British Journal of Criminology*, **48**(3), pp. 337–358.

Rumgay, J., (2004), 'Scripts for safer survival: Pathways out of female crime', *The Howard Journal of Criminal Justice, **43**(4), pp. 405–419.

Scandura, T.A., (1998), 'Dysfunctional mentoring relationships and outcomes', *Journal of Management, **24**(3), pp. 449–467.

Smart, C., (Ed.), (1992), *Regulating Womanhood: Historical Essays on Marriage, Motherhood and Sexuality*. London: Routledge.

Spivak, G.C., (1988), 'Can the subaltern speak?' In: Nelson, C. & Grossberg, L., (Eds.), *Marxism and the interpretation of culture*. Urbana: University of Illinois Press, pp. 271–313.

Stanley, L. & Wise, S., (1993), *Breaking out again feminist ontology and epistemology*. London: Routledge.

Sykes, G. M. & Matza, D., (1962), 'Techniques of Neutralization: A Theory of Delinquency'. In Wolfgang, M.E., Savitz, L. & Johnston, N., (Ed.), *The sociology of crime and delinquency*. New York: Wiley.

Triangle Consulting, (2019a), *'Justice' outcomes star*. Available at: www.outcomesstar.org.uk/using-the-star/see-the-stars/justice-star/ [Accessed October 2019].

Triangle Consulting, (2019b), *Justice star scales*. Available at: www.outcomesstar.org.uk/wp-content/uploads/Justice-Star-Scales-Preview.pdf [Accessed October 2019].

Tsui, M.S., (2004), *Social work supervision: Contexts and Concepts,* London: Sage.

Tuominen, T.M. & Lehtonen, M.H., (2018), 'The emergence of transformative agency in professional work', *Organization Studies*, **39**(11), pp. 1601–1624.

Tyler, D.I., (2013), *Revolting subjects: Social abjection and resistance in neoliberal Britain,* London: Zed Books.

Walby, K. & Cole, D., (2019), "I know it's not saving a life, but I know I'm doing good…": The Peer Offender Prevention Service (POPS) at Stony Mountain Institution, Canada. *Corrections*, 1–17.

Chapter 10

Conclusion

Peer mentoring has much to offer criminal justice. This book has demonstrated some of the potentials and contradictions it brings. The approach offers people who are often excluded from the workplace a practical opportunity to prove themselves, gain new skills and in some cases move on to paid employment. As they make this transition, people with convictions often challenge stereotypes and fears held by the wider community they work with, helping in a small way to create communities more willing to support desistance efforts, although importantly, this is not always achieved and commonly peer mentors must navigate contexts and workplaces where they continue to be defined by criminality. Those involved with peer mentoring (often) critically and constructively question notions of expertise and power in correctional settings, invite and enable participants to have self-confidence and hope for the future, employ care, empathy and pragmatism and strive for personal and structural changes, which they see as needed for a more peaceable and just society. However, peer mentoring can also struggle to escape the influence – and often reproduction of – existing criminal justice approaches and broader social influences such as neoliberal ideology and gender normativity, macro-influences which must be negotiated, and can be reproduced and contested in the space of peer mentoring.

Peer mentoring and the role of the voluntary sector in [re]producing 'desistance'

One highlighted benefit is that peer mentoring can assist people to master a new redemptive self-narrative (Maruna, 2001) with the help of peers who offer blueprints for conventional, pro social roles (Rumgay, 2004) and act as an encouraging audience for new performances. Peer mentors often offer lived examples or maps to redemption where none had seemed possible (Chapter 5). These lived examples are supplemented with new interactions, social situations and behavioural routines through which people can rehearse new roles or play out revised scripts (Chapter 6). This 'active' form of mentoring in community settings constitutes a change in 'routine activities' and offers 'different patterns of socialization' (Shapland & Bottoms, 2011: 272), which are disruptive to offending routines. The emerging identities that mentees act out in these settings are buttressed by their mentors who point out emerging personal positive factors (Chapter 6), building what have been termed 'positive illusions' about mentee's essentially good self (Maruna, Porter & Carvalho, 2004: 225–226). However, the study also problematises the notion of script mastery, locating scripts within a broader context of gender socialisation. In this light, men and women often described a sense that they were 'lacking' or inhibited by gendered expectations. Peer mentors can also feel ambivalence and discomfort in their own position if the 'script' they have to promote is deemed to be of inferior status to that of more socially 'successful' offenders. Peer mentoring further connects with desistance by fostering redemptive contexts. One project, for example, regarded their work as 'desistance in action' (Project 'Peer') given they were illustrating the positive potential of people with criminal histories. Employing criminalised people as paid Probation staff not only gave individuals a practical opportunity to lead a new kind of life, but also changed the perceptions of established Probation staff 'you can see hope in the workers eyes' (Chapter 8). These shifts in perception even extended outside of criminal justice contexts. Keisha, for example, recounted how she challenged the stereotyping and excluding practices of her independent business advisor (Chapter 8). Despite these descriptions of peer mentoring as redemptive, however, there were also times when people were not redeemed. Mentors met physical barriers from colleagues in prison and education settings given their criminal histories (Chapter 9) and even objections from their own peers (Chapter 5), who at times questioned their authenticity or 'readiness' to help others. Indeed, peer mentoring work is often a constant reminder of shameful pasts (Chapter 8). These are costs that often remain obscured within more functional assessments of the practice.

Existing desistance research recognises the importance of subjective changes (e.g. motivation or self-concept) and changes in social factors (e.g. marital or employment status) in desistance from crime (LeBel, Burnett, Maruna & Bushway, 2008). This study adds a third previously unrecognised dimension to this paradigm; mimetic desire. Mimesis (Girard, 1962), or mimicking the desires of others, offers a theoretical explanation of how 'role modelling' works. Utilising Girard's inter-individual theory of mimesis, it is argued that desistance from crime may not just depend on a person's self-concept or social opportunities but can also be triggered by desire for what people see others desire. Peer mentors are significant to galvanising this process because they are often respected by mentees; and mentees repeatedly mimicked their desires. Interestingly, it was not *desistance* itself that mentees most clearly came to desire in mentoring exchanges, but to help others in ways that they had seen modelled by their mentors. This is an important finding, given that desistance often involves '"earning" one's place back in the moral community' (Burnett & Maruna, 2006: 84). However, within Girard's mimetic theory is also potential for rejection of models, given that 'the adult is generally ashamed to imitate others for fear of revealing his lack of being' (Girard, 1977: 155). Correspondingly, both mentees and potential mentees did often express concern, doubt or complete rejection of the mentors' example. This is problematic for policies which aim to offer mentoring to all as a generic good (NOMS, 2011). The mimetic conception of desistance also speaks to the unresolved criminological problem of the origins of personal change. Respondents suggest that openness or determination to change can be influenced by the presence of role models who inspire and sustain change through the offer of their lived example. Whilst there are clear parallels between peer mentoring and desistance processes, 'promoting' desistance through ideal type role models and behaviours, risks reproducing desistance as a goal, an end point. In doing so there is a danger that mentoring services replicate functional efforts to reduce (re)offending and miss the myriad additional benefits that mentoring can bring.

The wider potential of peer mentoring

There is much more to peer mentoring than its functional capacity. It does not *just* aim to promote desistance or improve the skills, opportunities and life chances of its mentors and mentees, although these objectives do feature. It is also an activity which people utilise for political and therapeutic ends. It is therefore often comprised of varying and contradictory ideals. One important contribution this book makes is that it uncovers the budding politicised elements of peer mentoring. Whilst only embryonic in many settings, and often almost completely subsumed by professionalised norms, this is a critical feature. It is also a feature that could be threatening to peer mentoring as a popular practice, given it potentially challenges the status quo; this raises the need for ethical reflection. Indeed, it was with some caution that this finding was revealed. Whilst peer mentoring has found popular and political support up to this point, this is because it is understood as a functional, desistance promoting activity: making 'good use of the old lags in stopping the new ones' (Grayling, 2012). Moreover, as these 'old lags' are usually volunteers, constituting an affordable workforce in the competitive 'market' of criminal justice. It is difficult to imagine the same level of enthusiasm for a practice which seeks to assert a voice of experience that has been submerged, critically question technocratic managerialism and financially value the contributions of people who have experienced social exclusion. However, to ignore these aims would have lacked rigor and been disingenuous. As researchers we can recognise that peer mentoring has elements of social protest, which test the boundaries and hierarchical basis of our current knowledge, or we can mask the politicisation inherent in this work and ensure that it is only understood as a functional practice, thus subsuming (subaltern) voices once again. Further research in this field should therefore shed careful light on this element of the practice by paying close attention to how far peer approaches are political, how much they offer a challenge to existing practices and how far they become subsumed by established forms of knowledge and governance. Given persistent attempts by mentors to assert a voice of experience, it would also be enlightening and fitting to utilise participatory methods in future research. Participatory action research provides 'opportunities for codeveloping processes with people rather than for people' (McIntyre, 2008: xii). Such 'alternative methodologies... [offer] a counter-discourse and challenge the status quo. They are increasingly employed to uncover state and structural violence, human suffering and inequalities of marginalised and oppressed groups' (Bhatia, 2014: 162–163). As such they fit well with a practice which critiques the marginalisation of voice and which is budding with politicisation.

Peer mentoring offers a diverse set of practices, ranging from one-to-one sessions through informal and formal group activities to very informal leisure activities. One-to-one work often employs similar approaches to Probation Services; such as individual assessment, planning, 'intervention' and review. In this sense mentoring often shows signs of becoming institutionalised or professionalised. However, it is also often accompanied by supplementary practices such as publishing academic articles, organising and contributing to conferences and raising awareness of the experience of particular groups. In these arenas mentoring staff often speak more critically, attempting to improve 'the system' from within. More than a process, a product or a critique, however, this work is about transformational and trusting relationships, it is about seeing people in different ways. Mentoring is frequently described as something separate to the (modern, managerialist) Probation approach – it overtly rejects the 'badges' of authority and being 'buzzed through' locked doors, in favour of a more egalitarian, leisure-based activity. Such levelling is valued by mentees. Group peer mentoring is also fascinatingly diverse, ranging from therapeutic self-help-type groups through formal pedagogical 'learning' environments with a clear 'leader' to more exploratory dialogue, which encourages people to reflect through discussion and consideration of contexts. This varied range of approaches was present within just the small set of local settings this study focused upon, and was influenced by client groups, the previous experience of mentors and environments. Despite this diversity, there were features common across settings that were of note. The book organised these features into five overarching themes: *identity, agency, values, change* and *power*.

Identity

Identity is central to peer mentoring, both as a resource and a focus of the work. Peer mentors often utilise the perceived authenticity of the 'ex-offender' identity to inspire change in others and assist in the narrative reconstruction (Maruna, 2001) of mentee identities. However, identity has also been uncovered as important in much broader terms than desistance alone. Peer mentors do not just utilise their 'peer' or 'ex-offender' standpoint to engage, inspire or improve their contemporaries, but also as a political tool. These standpoints elevate knowledge which is based on lived experiences above that of trained 'experts', representing a symbolic destruction of authority. In these terms, peer mentoring is claimed to offer a form of communication that is egalitarian, free of patronisation and which espouses collaborative ideals. Mentors and mentees question 'rehabilitation' practices that systematically categorise and dehumanise them, calling instead for humane approaches, which have regard for social contexts and how these can be subjectively experienced. Progress, in these terms, does not require experts employing ever more sophisticated ways of quantifying and *improving* individuals, but it requires dialogue with those individuals. It calls for more critical forms of pedagogy, which acknowledge differences and exclusions in order to build more equal relationships of knowledge exchange. The importance of these efforts at horizontal communication and mutual understanding are not always appreciated within criminology or criminal justice practice. 'Identity', in these terms, is not just another feature which requires rehabilitation, but can be utilised to deconstruct depersonalised, decontextualised and actuarial approaches to 'offender management'.

Agency

Whilst social critique and standpoint are nascent in the ways in which mentors employ identity, there are also parts of the practice which do not appear to be led by mentors and mentees. Indeed, at times this study contradicts claims that mentoring can be 'empowering' (Kavanagh & Borrill, 2013: 14). Mentors and mentees are frequently *invited in* to the practice or enter the work with little knowledge of why they are there. They are often coerced, rather than active, critical agents. Mentees are also offered externally set activities and routines along with peer mentors who act as a second conscience, subtly directing their decisions. Despite these apparently *disempowering* processes, respondents report that peer mentoring can increase a sense of agency or self-worth. Mentees are offered opportunities to practice new ways of being in community-based settings, to embed new routines and to engage in activities that they find pleasurable. As a result, a sense of agency emerges as a dialogue between peers. Mentees not only gain replacements for routines and pleasures, which may have been lost when desisting from crime, but emerging new identities are cultivated and nurtured. Mentors configure a new kind of audience, creating a space where acceptance occurs and where the legitimacy of transformations can be recognised. Importantly, collaborations provide mentees with a protective buffer after being released from the complete control of prison, allowing them to reach new perspectives of themselves and new hope for the future.

Values

In addition to political and personal aims, there were also prominent therapeutic aims espoused by those involved with mentoring services. The 'core conditions' of *caring* and *listening* were often made sense of in terms of suffering. Respondents spoke of a need to release suffering and unburden themselves of grief. Peer mentoring was understood a safe space to do this given that mentors are perceived to 'genuinely care' and are tolerant of slip-ups. The significance of *small steps* or manageable goals is that they seem achievable and therefore motivate people; people can see the progress they are making. Mentoring emerges here as a caring version of dialogue where issues of interpersonal power imbalance are not so evident. Such an approach accounts for the social contexts of people's lives, which can often be masked by a managerial focus on 'offenders' as *flawed* individuals. Indeed, by *doing to* people rather than *listening to* people, criminal justice professionals can miss highly relevant parts of a person's experience and create inauthentic transactions. Despite the perceived benefits of this reorientation, however, mentors also risked burdening themselves with high expectations of emotional toil for little or no financial reward. Their approach is also at odds with a criminal justice 'marketplace' which is increasingly 'results' driven and technocratic.

Change

Whilst peer mentoring often seeks to *inspire* personal change, respondents also point to changes external to themselves, to a need for transformations in public perceptions and criminal justice practices. Whether individual or structural; change was frequently presented as a struggle. People spoke of a tension between known habits and unknown futures, between wanting to accept help and seeing authority as dangerous. They spoke of desires to reimagine criminal justice services and of having their experiences appropriated by more powerful players. These tensions insist that we pay attention to the social and discursive contexts in which people must live out their individual desistance efforts. Personal change emerges as an often terrifying and difficult process, yet peer mentoring can offer a unique antidote to this terror, the visibility of reformed role models evidences that change is possible and provides inspiration. Success is also not defined by the 'result' of having changed, but by the experience of gaining self-belief. Even if relapses do occur, one of the values of mentoring is to experience personal potential as a pedagogical process. However, these processes are complex and dialogical – both external inspiration and internal readiness to change appear to work concurrently. There is a complex and unpredictable interplay of social influence and self-direction at work. Furthermore, there is a cost to changing. Change is described as physically dangerous, materially humbling and emotionally isolating. Mentors themselves also acquire a new professional peer group, which moves them towards the authority that is so feared and highlights the potentially oxymoronic positions of peer and mentor.

Power

What each of the above themes have in common is some form of power struggle. Whilst the mentoring literature more broadly addresses some of the inherent dynamics of power within (and without) mentoring relationships (Colley, 2001; Scandura, 1998), the limited literature on *peer mentoring* largely lacks this analysis. This may well be because the sparse research that has been done in this area, quite necessarily given the increasingly marketised setting in which projects operate, is often concerned with proving functional worth in quantitative or monetary terms. This study has examined the micro-dynamics of relationships more closely, illustrating not only what happens within mentoring and how relationships are made sense of by those involved, but also some of the unrecognised dynamics of peer practices. These include the power of peer mentors to set goals and arrange activities; the power of prison, education and Probation staff to block work, sanction work and define the shape of recruitment, training and delivery; and the power of collective social ideals such as neoliberalism and gender to shape the activities, which people are – or feel they *should* be – involved in. Whilst mentoring often aims to resist the dominant interventionist discourse, resistance to this dominance proves limited; interventionism is never quite overturned. Both mentors and mentees, at times, affirm existing power structures and ensure their continuance. However, a focus upon such manifestations of power also highlights that those subject to these powers are not power*less*. Rather mentors and mentees frequently push against established hierarchies and ideals, be it by challenging exclusion in prison settings, developing training and approaches which include a 'user' perspective, or insisting upon the centrality of social and structural factors in people's lives.

Future research

It is important to recognise that there are limitations to this study, which will be helpful for future researchers to consider. First, the findings presented here are not representative. They reflect a snapshot of *some* practices, performed by *some* actors, in *some* community settings in the North of England. Whilst they offer important insight into emergent patterns across these contexts, further research in other areas with other groups will be useful. That said, a consistent, 'generalizable' story of peer mentoring may prove unattainable, given the huge diversity of practices and the ways in which projects end or change in response to an unstable funding environment and continually transforming criminal justice context. The snapshot provided here relies on respondents selected through institutional gatekeepers. Perhaps, as a result, most interviewees presented a generally complementary picture, offering little insight into problems which commissioners and statutory providers can be fearful of, such as unethical or incompetent mentors, broken confidentiality (McKimm et al., 2007), bullying or criminal pressure (Boyce, Hunter & Hough, 2009; Devilly, Sorbello, Eccleston & Ward, 2005: 233). It would be interesting to seek out more perspectives which did not rely upon gatekeepers, or indeed seek perspectives from those who *opted out* of peer mentoring to see if a different picture emerges. These findings are also drawn from fieldwork undertaken with *active* mentors and mentees and therefore shed no light on whether benefits persist when people move on, a limitation noted by Jolliffe and Farrington (2007). Finally, as the analysis here focuses on themes *unifying* peer mentoring, it does not drill down into differences between groups and settings, e.g. how mentoring by students differs from mentoring by ex-prisoners, or how mentoring in the community differs from mentoring delivered in prison. Given these confines, it would be helpful for future studies to add nuance to this emerging field by including larger samples, other geographical locations, comparisons across populations and settings, or longitudinal work to look at perspectives and experiences post mentoring.

One of the follow-on pieces of work from this study will be a dialogue of essays, co-produced with peer mentoring entrepreneurs and pioneers, to explore *their* ideas and concerns for policy and practice moving forward. One such piece of work is in print (Buck, Lawrence & Ragonese, 2017) and another is in progress (Buck, Harriott, Ryan, Ryan & Tomczak, forthcoming). These ongoing dialogues are vital, given that our current understandings of peer mentoring – and participatory approaches more broadly – are too narrow and that workers with lived experiences have much to teach us. Those engaged in peer-led work are not *just* concerned with reducing (re)offending, offering supplementary criminal justice services or even promoting desistance, but also with listening to and offering a platform to submerged voices, with offering a practice based upon care and tolerance and with promoting broader social changes. A key contribution of this book has been to draw attention to the multi-faceted depth and richness of peer mentoring and to highlight how radical pedagogical approaches – including dialogue with dis-empowered parties – reflectively used, have the power to enhance learning on all sides.

References

Bhatia, M., (2014), 'Researching "bogus" asylum seekers, "illegal" migrants and "crimmigrants"'. In: Lumsden, K. & Winter, A., (Eds.), *Reflexivity in criminological research: Experiences with the powerful and the powerless*. Hampshire: Palgrave Macmillan.

Boyce, I., Hunter, G. & Hough, M., (2009), *The St Giles trust peer advice project: Summary of an evaluation report*. London: The Institute for Criminal Policy Research, School of Law, King's College. Available at: http://eprints.bbk.ac.uk/3794/ [Accessed August 2019].

Buck, G., Harriott, P., Ryan, K., Ryan, N. & Tomczak, P., (forthcoming), 'All our justice: People with convictions and "participatory" criminal justice'. In McLaughlin, H., Duffy, J., Beresford, P., Casey, H. & Cameron, C., (Eds.), *The Routledge handbook of service user involvement in human services research and education*. Abingdon, Oxon: Routledge.

Buck, G., Lawrence, A. & Ragonese, E., (2017), 'Exploring peer mentoring as a form of innovative practice with young people at risk of child sexual exploitation', *British Journal of Social Work*, **47**(6), pp. 1745–1763.

Burnett, R. & Maruna, S., (2006), 'The kindness of prisoners: strengths-based resettlement in theory and in action', *Criminology and Criminal Justice*, **6**(1), pp. 83–106.

Colley, H., (2001), 'Righting rewritings of the myth of Mentor: A critical perspective on career guidance mentoring', *British Journal of Guidance and Counselling*, **29**(2), pp. 177–197.

Devilly, G.J., Sorbello, L., Eccleston, L. & Ward, T., (2005), 'Prison-based peer-education schemes', *Aggression and Violent Behavior*, **10**, pp. 219–240.

Girard, R., (1977), *Violence and the sacred*. London: Continuum, 2005 edition.

Girard, R., (1962), 'Marcel Proust'. In: Girard, R. & Doran, R., (Eds.), (2008), *Mimesis and theory: Essays on literature and criticism, 1953–2005*. Stanford, CA and London: Stanford University Press, pp. 56–70.

Grayling, C., (2012), *Justice Minister's 'rehabilitation revolution' speech*, 20th November 2012. Available at: www.justice.gov.uk/news/speeches/chris-grayling/speech-to-the-centre-of-social-justice [Accessed August 2019].

Jolliffe, D. & Farrington, D.P., (2007), *A rapid evidence assessment of the impact of mentoring on re-offending: A summary*. London: Home Office.

Kavanagh, L. & Borrill, J., (2013), 'Exploring the experiences of ex-offender mentors', *Probation Journal*, **60**(4), pp. 400–414.

LeBel, T.P., Burnett, R., Maruna, S. & Bushway, S., (2008), 'The "chicken and egg" of subjective and social factors in desistance from crime', *European Journal of Criminology*, **5**(2), pp. 131–159.

Maruna, S., (2001), *Making good; how ex-convicts reform and rebuild their lives*. Washington, DC: American Psychological Association.

Maruna, S., Porter, L. & Carvalho, I., (2004), 'The liverpool desistance study and probation practice: Opening the dialogue', *Probation Journal*, **51**(3), pp. 221–232.

McIntyre, A., (2008), *Participatory action research* (Series 52). London: Sage Publications.

McKimm, J., Jollie, C. & Hatter, M., (2007), *Mentoring theory and practice*. London: Imperial College School of Medicine. Available at: www.faculty.londondeanery.ac.uk/e-learning/explore-further/e-learning/feedback/files/Mentoring_Theory_and_Practice.pdf [Accessed August 2019].

National Offender Management Service (NOMS), (2011), *Mentoring in NOMS*. London: National Offender Management Service. Available at: https://essl.leeds.ac.uk/download/downloads/id/489/mentoring_in_noms.pdf [Accessed August 2019].

Rumgay, J., (2004), 'Scripts for safer survival: Pathways out of female crime', *The Howard Journal of Criminal Justice*, **43**(4), pp. 405–419.

Scandura, T.A., (1998), 'Dysfunctional mentoring relationships and outcomes', *Journal of Management*, **24**(3), pp. 449–467.

Shapland, J. & Bottoms, A., (2011), 'Reflections on social values, offending and desistance among young adult recidivists', *Punishment & Society*, **13**(3), pp. 256–282.

Index